# RETURNS FROM EDUCATION TO EMPLOYED WOMEN IN INDIA

*Books by the same Author*

Status of Nurses in India
Status of Banjara Women in India

# Returns from Education to Employed Women in India

## (A STUDY OF BANGALORE CITY)

**N. Shantha Mohan**

Uppal Publishing House

NEW DELHI-110002

UPPAL PUBLISHING HOUSE
3, Ansari Road, Daryaganj, New Delhi-110002

Indian Council of Social Science Research gave financial support towards the publication of this work. However, the responsibility for the contents of the book-facts, opinions, conclusion, etc. is entirely that of the authors and not of the Indian Council of Social Science Research, New Delhi.
ICSSR. Consultant ; Dr. Brahm Prakash.


First Edition 1989
ISBN 81-85024-63-4

Printed in India
Pnblished by B.S. Uppal for Uppal Publishing House, New Delhi-110002 and printed at Parashar Printers, through Parashar Composing Agency, Delhi-110053

*To the fond memory of*
*my mother*
*Shakunthala Narayan*

# PREFACE

During the past few decades, education has been considered as a viable investment accounting for a major portion of both the national and individual income. With the concept of human capital being accepted, there has been a greater emphasis on the profitability of investment in education. Educational institutions have been growing at a rapid speed, resulting in the so-called 'Education-Explosion'. One possible explanation being that education is a profitable personal investment yielding both monetary and non-monetary benefits. These benefits catalyse and augument further the demand for education, which in turn directs the entire educational development.

While the profitability of education is unquestionably accepted, evidence regarding the level and type of education from which maximum profit is accrued, especially with that concerned with women is totally lacking. While they appear to choose different levels and types of education as if they were making a rational investment response to certain monetary returns, the evidence was to the contrary. This study attempts to find out the monetary returns to women investing in various levels and types of education. Further, it extends to include the non-monetary returns from their education in terms of their attitudes and behaviour towards the institutions of education, employment, marriage and family, religion, politics and social life. These returns are expected to highlight the levels and types of education that are most viable to women both monetarily and non-monetarily.

Several people have been instrumental in the successful completion of this study.

With all sincerity and regard, I wish to record may deep indebtedness to Dr. A.S. Seetharamu, Professor of Education, Institute for Social and Economic Change, Bangalore, for not only initiating this study but by being an able guide and supervisor through his inimitable professional interaction, interpretation and guidance.

I must especially acknowledge the expert advice and suggestions given at the stage of planning this investigation and developing the tool by Dr. (Mrs.) Promilla Kapur, Dr. (Mrs.) Kala Rani, Dr. (Mrs.) Neera Desai and Mrs. Vina Mazumdar.

I am greatly indebted to the Heads of the Public and Private Establishments in Bangalore City, who extended the kind cooperation by permitting me to interview the women employee during working hours.

My profound gratitude to each of the women respondents who patiently furnished information during the course of the interview which extended over an hour. But for their unstinted cooperation, this work would not have materialised.

My sincere thanks to Ms. N.S. Chanchal, who was a constant companion during my fieldwork spread over a period of five months. Mr. V. Srinivasa and Mr. V. Padmanabha have helped to a large extent in coding and tabulating the data. I take this opportunity to thank them profusely.

My particular gratitude to Mr. Srikanth from the Indian Institute of Science, who whenever I sought, has given advice on statistical techniques. I thank the Administration Officer of the Bangalore Institute of Computer Application, for getting the data computerised and thus giving the study its present structural model.

I should also record my gratitude to all the members of the staff of the Institute library and Mr. J.R. Ramamurthy at

Bangalore University Library for the timely bibliographical services.

I owe in large measure to my father, Mr. T.S. Narayanaswamy, fond gratitude not only for his unfailing moral encouragement at every stage but also for the efficient typing of the manuscript.

I am thankful to the ICSSR, New Delhi, for the timely financial assistance granted to me for publication. I am also thankful to Dr. Brahm Prakash, NIEPA, New Delhi, who has meticulously read through the entire thesis and given me the benefit of his valuable suggestions, thus giving the book its present form.

I am specially thankful to Mr. B.S. Uppal of Uppal Publishing House, New Delhi for undertaking the publication of this book.

Last but not the least, my sincere thanks to my husband, Mr. G. Mohan, for all the encouragement and help he has rendered in the execution of this study.

Bangalore
15-8-89

**Dr. N. Shantha Mohan**

## CONTENTS

## LIST OF TABLES

| Tables | | Pages |
|---|---|---|
| 5.A.9 | Undiscounted Unregressed and Regressed net Earning Advantage by Levels of Education (in Rs. 1000's) | 160 |
| 5.A.10 | Ratios of Earnings at the Zero, Five and Six per cent Discount Ratios | 162 |
| 5.A.11 | Private Enternal Rates of Return to Levels of Education in percentage points | 168 |
| 5.A.12 | Economic and Non-Economic Returns from Education | 234 |

# CHAPTER 1

# Introduction

> "The most valuable of all capital is
> that invested in human beings."
>
> —**Alfred Marshall**

Recognition of the potential of human resources for economic growth and development is embodied in the concept of human capital which acknowledges that inputs of physical capital, and labour time only partially account for increments in total output. Empirical studies of the sources of economic growth indicate increase in output at a higher rate than can be explained by an increase in only the standard physical inputs of capital and labour. A large part of the increase in total output remains to be attributed to some "unexplained residual factor" in the economy. The studies of several advanced countries, the "residual factor" accounts for as much as 50 to 85 per cent of the increase in the total output.[1] This residual is what

1. S. Fabricant : "Basic Facts on Productivity", National Bureau of Economic Research, New York, 1959 ; R. Solow : "Technical Change and Aggregate Production Function", Review of Economics & Statistics, Aug. 1957, pp. 312-320 ; E.F. Denison : "The Sources of Economic Growth in the United States and the Alternatives Before US", Committee for Economic Development, Supplementary Paper, No. 13, 1962, Ch. 7.

Abramovitz calls a "measure of our ignorance" of the determinants of a rise in productivity—the complex of little understood forces which cause output per unit of utilized resources to rise.[2] A prominent element among the many "unidentified factors" which comprise the residual is the improvement in the quality of inputs. Although some of this progress may be incorporated in physical capital, the improvements in intangible human qualities are more significant. Human factors have also come into focus to explain divergences between the developed and underdeveloped countries. Improvement in human resources has been recognised as both an objective and instrument of economic development. As such, during the last two decades, much attention has been devoted to developing theoretical and methodological concepts necessary to understand and measure the possible influence of human resources on national and individual incomes. Thus, policy makers and administrators have been reminded increasingly of the need to invest in human capital by academicians and social scientists. The many forms of such investments include schooling, on-the-job training, medical care, etc. According to Schultz,[3] a typical list of activities that would improve human capabilities are :

1. Health facilities and services, broadly conceived to include all expenditures that affect the life expectancy, strength and stamina, and the vigour and vitality of people ;
2. On-the-job training, including apprenticeship organised by firms ;
3. Formally organised education at the elementary, secondary and higher levels ;

2. Moses Abramovitz : "Resources and Output Trends in the United States Since 1870", American Economic Review (Papers & Proceedings), May 1956, pp. 11-14 ; T. Balogh & P.P. Streeten : "The Coefficient of Ignorance", Bulletin of the Oxford Institute of Economics & Statistics, May 1963, pp. 99-107.
3. T.W. Schultz : "Investment in Human Capital", American Economic Review, March 1961, p. 9.

4. Study programmes for adults that are not organised by firms, including extension programmes notably in agriculture ; and

5. Migration of individuals and families to adjust to changing job opportunities.

Of the many forms of investments education seemed the most viable, explaining a major portion of both the national and individual income. The relationship between educational attainment and income are reflected by the studies carried out by Houthakker,[4] Gary S. Becker,[5] H.P. Miller,[6] Ahluwalia M.S.,[7] Psacharopoules and Marvin A.,[8] Psacharopoules,[9] and C.R. Wine Garden.[10] The positive relationship between inequal distribution of income and unequal education emphasizes the role of education as investment in "Human Capital".

Among those who have looked upon human-beings as capital and education as an investment, Adam Smith is the oldest. He compares the investment on education with capital investment in his "Wealth of Nations". "A man educated at the expense of much labour and time to any of those employments which require extra-ordinary dexterity and skill may be compared to one of those expensive machines. The work which

4 H.S. Houthakker : "Education and Income", Review of Economics and Statistics, Feb. 1959, pp. 24-28.

5. Gary S. Becker : "Under-investment in College Education", American Economic Review, Proceedings, May 1960, pp. 346-354.

6. H.P. Miller : "Annual & Lifetime Income in Relation to Education", American Economic Review, Dec. 1960, pp. 962-986.

7. Ahluwalia M.S. : "Income Distribution & Development : Some Stylized Facts", American Economic Review 66, 1976, pp. 128-135.

8. Pscharopoules G. & Marvin A. : "Schooling & Income Distribution", Review of Economic & Statistics 58, 1976, pp. 332-337.

9. Pscharopoules G. : "Unequal Access to Education and Income Distribution", Do Economist 123, 1977, pp. 383-392.

10. C.R. Wine Garden : "Schooling and Income Distribution", Evidence from International Data", Economica, 1979, Vol. 46 (181).

he learns to perform, it must be expected, over and above the usual wages of common labour, will replace to him the whole expense of his education, with atleast the ordinary profits of an equally valuable capital."[11] Alfred Marshall also takes account of the connection between education and earnings of labour when analysing the forces governing wages. While Marshall pursued the same line of thought as Adam Smith, he also stressed both the imperfection of the investment analogy between human and physical capital and the various sociological complications which arise when analysing investment in education. He held that while human beings are incontestably capital from an abstract and mathematical point of view, it would be out of touch with the market place to treat them as capital in practical analysis. The failure to treat human resources as a form of capital, as a product of investment, has resulted in the retention of the classical notion of labour as a capacity to do manual work requiring little knowledge and skill, a capacity with which labourers are endowed about equally. Investment in human-beings has accordingly seldom been incorporated in the formal core of analyses, though many have seen its relevance at one point or another. It was only in the late 1950s that intensive economic analysis of education as an investment in human capital was stimulated, much of it being contributed by T.W. Schultz. Besides Schultz, complementary work have been done by Gary S. Becker, Jacob Mineer, Edward P. Denison, Denial C. Rogers, T. Les Haneen, Mark Blaug, B.A. Weisbrod and others, which throw light on the subject of human capital and education as an investment.

An economic analysis of any investment has to consider the benefits to be derived from it and the costs of attaining those benefits. The benefits of investing in education can accrue both to the individual (i.e. private returns) and to the society (i.e. social returns). The private returns aspect considers the relation between costs incurred by individuals in obtaining a

11. Adam Smith : "The Wealth of Nations", New York : Modern Library, 1937, p. 101.

particular level of education and the income benefits they as individuals derive from that education. This is relevant for the individual trying to make private calculations of the income benefits that will accrue to him by investing in a particular level of education and also to compare the benefits for different levels of education in order to choose the level that is most viable. It is also relevant to a country's decision as to what fraction of the costs of education should be borne by the individuals themselves. Thus, the purpose of the private returns calculations is to explain and predict the demand for education by individuals.

The social returns aspect considers the relation between costs and income benefits accruing to the society as a whole. This is relevant to the question whether society is investing the right share of its resources in education. Social returns calculations usually serve a normative purpose i.e., they provide a criterion by which public policy towards public expenditure on education may be judged.

**Costs and Benefits from Education**

The costs of earnings benefits from education viewed as an investment will be discussed from the private and social points of view.

**Private Costs and Benefits from Education**

The private returns calculus relies on the comparison of the costs to individuals of an increment of education with the returns or extra-earnings gained by individuals as a result of investing in that level of education.

The costs of education to the individual can be divided into two types : the direct and the indirect costs. The direct costs include expenditure on fees, books and stationery, transport, etc. The indirect costs consist of the income foregone by individuals in order to obtain education. It is also referred to as the opportunity cost of education i.e., if individuals secured employment instead of pursuing education, they would have profitted by earning an income and not spending on education. The opportunity lost in earning an income is a real cost to them. Thus, the opportunity of the time put in by students (income foregon) is a clear case of 'resource loss' in education. If earnings foregone were ignored, studies of life-time earnings differential associated with levels of schooling would indicate an exceedingly high rate of return. Then earnings foregone were included in the estimates of costs, estimates of the rate of return were found to be cut by about 60 per cent[12]. This is because the earnings mature students forego while attending school are likely to exceed all of the other costs incurred by them. According to H N. Pandit[13] the income foregone formed about 75 per cent of the total private costs of education in India.

Income foregone also provides an unified explanation of three other behaviours. They are :

1. Why many talented children from low-income families dropout of schools within the compulsory school going age of 14 years, even though tuition is free or scholarships are available to cover tuition ;

2. Why many children from rural families attend school less regularly than those from urban families ; and

3. Why there is a high dropout rate in primary schools in low-income countries.

In all these three situations, earnings foregone appears to be significant because children are called upon to do work and thus contribute to the meagre family income.

The estimation of benefits involves a series of statistical

12. Theodore W. Schultz : "The Economic Value of Education", Columbia University Press, New York, 1963, p. 5.

13. H. N. Pandit : "Cost-Analysis of Education in India—Private and Social Participation", Indian Educational Review, Vol. 7, No. 2, July 1972, NCERT, p. 119.

operations which is summarised as follows :

What is needed is an estimate of the economic benefits resulting from a given increment of education or a level of education. These benefits will consist of the extra earnings which will result from having obtained that education. For the calculation of private returns the lifetime earnings should be estimated not of all direct taxes, since the monetary gain to the individual is measured by his disposable income.

**Social Costs and Returns from Education**

As society comprises of individuals, all of the private costs and benefits from education can also be considered as social costs and benefits. However, in addition, there are costs and benefits which are realised by society as an unit. The major items of social costs are :

1. Institutional costs which consists of both capital and current costs ; and

2. Private costs which consists of non-tuition costs and income foregone. In estimating the social returns, the gross value of the incremental earnings is used, because this represents the total given to the community from his education i.e., taxes should not be deducted from the earnings in calculating the lifetime earnings of the individual.

For a more valid measurement of the economic benefits from increments in education from the private and social points of view, adjustments to both the costs and earnings data should be made. Adjustments to the costs data include those for receipt of scholarships, fee-concessions, wastage and stagnation. Adjustments in respect to the estimation of earnings data include probability of survival, unemployment and growth of the economy. With the help of these adjustments a stream of expenditures and income returns spread over the life of an individual while he was studying and latter while working can be drawn. The estimated lifetime earning benefits from the different levels of education may not be entirely a function of education as education, earnings, endowed ability, individual motivation, family-background, experience, sex and age are all inter-correlated and no one has yet succeeded in satisfactorily isolating and attributing a definite portion of the observed differentials in earnings to education alone. However, attempts have been made to adjust the earnings for the influence of variables other than education on earnings. The two methods of accounting for other variables are by using an alpha-coefficient ($\alpha$) to attribute atleast a part of the earnings differential to factors other than education. This approach is adopted by E. F. Denison[14], Becker[15], Maglen and Layard[16], Selby Smith[17] and others. The other method for standardising the earnings for the influence of other variables is the application of the multiple regression analysis. Hanoch[18], Carnoy[19], Schultz[20], Morgan et al[21], Daniel C. Rogers[22], and others used this approach.

14. E. F. Denison : 1962, op. cit.
15. Gary S. Becker : "Human Capital", National Bureau of Economic Research, New York, 1964.
16. Maglen L. & Layard R. : "How Profitable is Engineering Education ?", Higher Education Review, II (2), 1970.
17. Selby Smith C. : "Costs and Benefits is Further Education : Some Evidence from a Pilot Study", Economic Journal, Sept. 1970.
18. Hanoch G. : "An Economic Analysis of Earnings and Schooling", Journal of Human Resources, II (3), 1967.
19. Carncy M. : "Rates of Return to Schooling in Latin America", Journal of Human Resources, II (Summer, 1967).
20. Schultz T. W. : "Returns to Education in Bogota, Columbia", The Rand Corporation Memorandum RM-5645, RC/AID, Sept. 1968.
21. Morgan et. al. : "Income and Welfare in the United States", New York, 1962, pp. 387-427.
22. Daniel C. Rogers : "Private Rates of Return to Education in the United States : A Case Study", Yale Economic Essays, Vol. 9 No 1, Spring 1969.

**Methods of Evaluating Relation between Costs and Benefits**

The two methods most generally employed to compare the costs and benefits of alternative investments are :

1. The net discounted present value method ; and
2. The internal rate of return method[23].

**The Net Discounted Present Value Method**

Discounting the costs and benefits of an investment is necessary to reflect the effect of time perferences on the value of future income. Present value puts two streams of earnings on an equal footing, thereby objectively determining the one that is more valuable. However, the present values are extremely sensitive to the discount rate used, with the rate chosen becoming more crucial the longer the life of the investment. Furthermore, the appropriate discount rate is to some degree subjectively determined because of the differences in individual time perferences and risk assessment. Since there is no identifiable market rate of interest to make use of, discount rates are more or less arbitarily chosen in studies of education[24]. The present values of costs and benefits can be compared as either ratios or as differences.

**The Internal Rate of Return Method**

It is defined as that discount rate which equates the present value of the stream of costs to the present value of the stream of benefits. In practice, the internal rate of return is found by calculating the present values of the costs and benefits at different discount rates, plotting these values and interpolating

23. For extensive discussions of these two methods of comparing investments see Ezra Soloman (ed), "The Management of Corporate Capital", New York : Free Press, 1959
24. Rates of 0, 3, $3\frac{1}{2}$, 4, 5, 6, 8 and 10 per cent have been used by researchers.

or extrapolating to find the discount rate at which they are equal[25].

Though both these techniques offer alternative ways of calculating returns to education, conceptually the net discounted present value criterion is considered the better method[26]. However, in practice, the internal rate of return method has been used more widely in calculating returns to education. Either of these methods or both can be used in studies of the returns from education.

Most economic analyses of the returns from education have been focussed on the contribution of education to earnings capacity. While this is valuable, it is only part of the picture, as earnings are an incomplete measure of the productivity of education. Apart from the economic benefits that accrue to individuals and the society at large from education, there are innumerable non-economic benefits from education which are not included in the estimation of the rates of return. The non-economic benefits are variously known as the external benefits, indirect benefits, social benefits, etc. According to Musgrave R. A.[27], "Perhaps the most important aspect of the external benefits of education lies in the change in the social and cultural climate, incident to the widening of horizons, which education entails. As has been pointed out many times, such a change is an essential condition of success for many developing nations." For a society to be socially and culturally sensitive, education should bring about necessary changes in the 'mental makeup' of its populace. "A community in which there is a rapid communication of ideas due to common habits of understanding and high potential mobility, due to wide-

25. W. Lee Hansen : "Total and Private Rates of Return to Investment in Schooling", Journal of Political Economy, 71, April 1963, pp. 128-140.

26 Baumol W.J. : Economic Theory and Operations Analysis", New Jersey, Englewood Cliffs, 1965, p. 433.

27. Musgrave Richard A. : "Notes on Educational Investment in Developing Nations", In OECD Study Group in the Economics of Education, Paris, 1966, pp. 31-39.

spread training of general intelligence, is likely to be more productive absolutely and more capable of development than a community otherwise similarly situated, in which such standards do not prevail[28]. Nalle Gounden has attempted to distinguish between the non-economic benefits that accrue to the individuals and to the society. He mentioned the greater individual employment choices, protection against the vicissitudes of technical change and psychological benefits as examples of the non-monetary returns to the individuals and the improved housing and employment as examples of the social non-monetary returns[29]. Harberger also pointed out that education produced non-monetary returns which were not yet capable of quantification, but none-the-less, influence decisions about resource allocation[30]. Even Vaizey, a critic of the rate-of-return approach, having rejected all existing methods of measuring the direct economic returns from education, nevertheless affirmed that, "expenditure on education pays", by virtue of the fact, "that indirect benefits of education are so great that its direct benefits are not necessarily the most important"[31]. As such, the non-monetary benefits from education and their role in the development process have been increasingly recognised. While it is unquestionably accepted that the non-economic benefits are important, the question arises as to how the estimates of returns should be adjusted to take account of them. By omitting their inclusion in the estimation of returns, it is assumed that people are motivated

28 Lord Robbins : "The Theory of Economic Development" in "The History of Economic Thought", Macmillan, New York, 1968, pp. 76-77.

29. H.N Pandit : "Measurement of the Economic Value of Education : An International Comparison", Teacher Today, Mar. 1977.

30. Harberger A.C. : Investment in Man Vs. Investment in Machine : The Case of India", in "Education & Economic Development", C.A. Anderson & N.B. Sowman, Chicago, Aldine Publishing Co , 1966.

31. Vaisey : Economics of Education", Faber & Faber, 1962, pp. 46 & 150.

solely by consideration of the economic gains of additional schooling. Thus, attempts have been made to incorporate them in the estmation of returns. The standard method is to make an estimation of the magnitude of these benefits and adjust the returns upwards which is highly arbitrary. The other method is to present a descriptive analysis of these benefits alongside the estimates of the economic returns from education. Due to the inherent difficulty in quantifying these benefits as they are both enormous and divergent, they have been omitted in many studies relating to the returns from education. Exponents who have omitted their quantification are of the opinion that though the exclusion of the estimates of the non-monetary benefits in the rate-of-return calculations involve a certain bias, certainly, it is not significant enough to effect the positive correlation between education and monetary benefits. Others opine that the non-monetary returns of education should be included in the estimation of returns atleast in a non-quantifiable way so that they are kept in mind while taking investment decisions. The inclusion of the non-economic benefits in evaluating the returns from education holds special practical significance for the developing and under-developed countries. Thus, the economic and non-economic benefits from investment in education must be considered in order to help take policy decisions about the amount to be invested in education and within the educational system itself the level of education that is most viable.

The available evidence on the non-monetary benefits from different levels of education are not supporting each other. While most of the studies in developed countries indicate diminishing social returns with additional years of education those of developing countries indicate an increase with education upto the secondary level and then a decline for higher education. The Indian situation is, however, non-conclusive. It is observed that the highest returns are for primary education, followed by a decline for secondary education and again an increase to higher education. In this connection, the findings of an interesting study conducted by A. S. Seetharamu[31a, 32] on rural responsiveness to development programmes from educational stimuli, revealed that lower primary education returned higher response to development than higher primary education. However, higher secondary education provided increasing returns.

Thus, while there is evidence on the value of education in terms of both economic and non-economic benefits, there is incomplete evidence about the relative returns from different levels of education.

**Purpose of the Study**

A widespread phenomenon in less developed countries has been the rapid growth of schools and institutions of higher learning resulting in the so-called "education explosion"[33]. One possible explanation for the educational explosion is that education is a profitable personal investment, both in terms of the monetary and non-monetary benefits that accrue to individuals. These expected private benefits from education, are translated into demands, which in turn directs the entire educational development, especially in developing and under-developed countries.

A vast body of social survey data indicate that parents and students are principally motivated by vocational considerations in making educational choices. They appear to choose more

31a. A. S. Seetharamu : "A Study of Responsiveness to Development Programmes from Educational Stimuli in Rural Areas", Institute for Social and Economic Change, Bangalore, Oct. 1977.

32. Hansen W. L. : "Patterns of Rates of Return to Investment in Education : Some International Comparisons", in Conference on Policies for Educational Growth, Paris, DECO/Memo DAS/EID/ 70, 3, 1970.

33. G.Z.F. Bereday & Joseph A. Lanwergs : "The Education Explosion", London, Evans Brothers Ltd., 1965. Also see "The World Year Book of Education" which has devoted its entire 1965 volume to consideration of the many aspects of the education-explosion.

education and different types of education as if they were making a rational investment response to certain monetary returns[34]. But, are these decisions taken by individuals to invest in education on rational economic grounds ? The available evidence is to the contrary. Their investments in levels of education which do not fetch the maximum returns could be a possible explanation for the high un-employment and under-employment rates in developing countries[35].

Labour force studies conducted have shown a substantial relationship between education and employment Higher the level of education, greater the chance of employability. Thus, it is unquestionably accepted by planners, society and individuals that education is a highly profitable investment, but evidence regarding the level or type of education from which maximum profit can be derived is far from clear. Exclusive information on returns from investment in women's education is totally lacking. This is because, women who are considered as only secondarily involved in potential labour, have been largely ignored. In recent years, however, planners have become increasingly aware of the role of women in national development. Policies aimed at integrating them in the process of development were framed not only because simple justice demanded it, but also because excluding them meant under-utilizing a high potential resource which can eventually have an adverse effect on the economic growth of a nation. Women represent about half the population endowed with a productive petential which is at the moment largely untapped. Cognizant of this fact, the Government has taken stringent measures by way of incentives to encourage them to receive education and participate in the work force. The development of a country cannot be realised if half of its population lag behind. It has been observed that the proportion of literate and

34. Mark Blaug : "An Introduction to the Economics of Education", Penguin Books, 1970.

35. M. Blaug : Ibid.

employed women is higher in the advanced countries than in the developing and under-developed countries.

Table 1.1 offers a comparison of the percentages of literate and employed women in advanced and under-developed countries.

TABLE No. 1.1

**Percentages of Literate and Working Women in a Few Countries**

| Countries | Percentage of Literate Women[a] | Percentage of Working Women[b] | Year |
|---|---|---|---|
| U.S.A. | 97.1 | 53.1 | 1975 |
| Sweden | | 67.6 | 1975 |
| Belgium | 96.6 | 43.9 | 1975 |
| France | 96.2 | 56.5 | 1975 |
| Hungary | 94.6 | 40.3[c] | 1974 |
| India | 18.7 | 7.0 | 1973 |
| Algeria | 1.8 | 1.83* | 1974 |

a. Source : Encyclopaedia of Social Science Research.

b. OECD, "Equal Oportunities for Women", Paris, 1979, p.17.

c. Year Book of Labour Statistics, 1974, International Labour Office, Geneva, 1974.

* Note : Economically active population figures do not include about 12,00,000 females mainly occupied in agriculture.

Viewed in this international perspective, the proportion of literate women in India is much lower than those of USA, Sweden, Belgium, France and Hungary, while the rates in countries like Algeria and India are quite low. This variability may be due to problems of comparability of data, particularly with respect to agricultural work and to contradictory definitions and methods used in identifying the economically active segment of the population. But even when female participation in the non-agricultural sector is considered, which is a better defined and restricted segment where labour force concepts have a more precise meaning and measurement there are still pronounced differences in the female employment rates, as is observed from Table No. 1.2.

TABLE No. 1.2

**Female Participation in Non-agricultural Economic Activities in a Few Countries**

| Countries | Activity Rate | |
|---|---|---|
| | Male | Female |
| United Kingdom | 78.6 | 40.4 |
| Germany | 78.4 | 35.1 |
| Switzerland | 74.9 | 34.3 |
| United States | 71.5 | 32.0 |
| France | 62.8 | 29.3 |
| Japan | 62.6 | 28.8 |
| Chile | 56.1 | 21.8 |
| Greece | 41.9 | 12.2 |
| Morocco | 36.4 | 4.5 |
| Syria | 35 0 | 3.2 |
| India | 31.9 | 8.8 |
| Pakistan | 26.4 | 2.3 |
| Sudan | 14.6 | 1.6 |

Source : Nadia Haggag Youssef : "Women and Work in Developing Societies", Population Monograph Series, No. 15, University of California Berkeley, 1974, p. 10.

According to a study conducted by the researcher in Bangalore City, there are 7.72 lakh women and they form 46.7 per cent of the total population. The literacy among these women is 51.0 per cent. As such one out of every two women in the city is a literate. Though one out of every two women is a literate, only one out of every three literate women is employed[36].

What could account for these differentials ? What could be the factors that determine the extent to which women participate in the non-agricultural labour force ? It could be their differential achievement in the educational sphere, which is translated into work participation which further depends on the openings in the labour market. Indiscriminate investment in education will only result in diminishing returns. In order to make a rational decision as to the level of education in which investment is most viable, they should have information regarding levels which fetch the maximum returns. Such information will also have policy implications for the Government as to what fraction of the costs of education should be borne by the individuals themselves.

In a developing country like India, there is not only a large domain of unexplicited womenpower resources but also an enormous wastage of these resources in the form of underemployed and unemployed womenpower. However, owing to the changed socio-economic structure and the opportunities of education and employment, more women are receiving education of all kinds and getting into a variety of jobs and professions. Thus, over years, there has been a steady increase in the literacy and employment rates of women. Even so, in 1971 only 18.7 per cent of women were literate as against 39.5 per cent of that of men and only 7 per cent were employed as

36. Shantha, N. : "A Study of the Profile of Employed Women in the Public Sector in Bangalore City", Pre-Ph.D. Project Report (un-published), Institute for Social & Economic Change, Bangalore, 1976.

against 27.8 per cent of men.[37] According to the 1971 census, of the total female labour force, the bulk of the women workers (80 per cent) were employed in agriculture, the remaining in industry (7 per cent), mining and quarrying (7 per cent), Services (3 per cent) and plantations (3 per cent). In this context, it may be noted that of the total female labour force, 65.9 per cent are illiterates. Thus, only one out of every three literate women is employed. It is further observed that among literate women who form 18.7 per cent of the population, a great number of them are educated only upto the matriculation level. The low participation of women in the work force may be due to their ignorance of the economic returns that might accrue to them through employment or because of their indiscriminate investment in education which retains them as either under-employed or unemployed.

Those who did not venture investing in education, it may be due to the lack of knowledge about the benefits from education.

The non-economic benefits from education to women have also their value which cannot be undermined. As Alfred Marshall has said "General ability depends largely on the surroundings of childhood and youth. In this, the first and the foremost powerful influence is that of the mother. Next comes the influence of the father......".[38] Apart from being economically productive, women are users of basic services, bearers and socialisers of children and keepers of the home. As such, their own attitudes and behaviour have a direct bearing on members of the family, especially that of their children. These attitudes and behaviour of women are a function of education. Further, a study on women bears special relevance

37. Source : Annual Employment Review", 1972-73, Published by the Directorate of Employment & Training, Government of Karnataka, Bangalore.
38. Alfred Marshall : "Principles of Economics", 8th edn., 1946, p 207.

during the decade, 1976-1985, as the United Nations has resolved to focus and intensify efforts in relation to women's development. This is also referred to as the 'Women's Development Decade'.

In the context of the foregoing discussion, a study of private economic and non-economic benefits from investment in various levels of education to employed women was felt both relevant and necessary. The title of the study runs as follows :

"A Study of Returns from Education to Employed Women in Bangalore City."

**Objectives of the Study**

The main focus of the study is to evaluate the returns that accrue to working women with different levels of education.

The study is set with the following objectives :

1. To make a comparative study of the economic returns to private investment in various levels and types of education with reference to education and employment of women.

2. To make a comparative study of the non-economic returns from education to employed women in terms of attitudes and behaviour.

The study has also set for itself the following objectives of specificity :

1. To evaluate and compare the private costs of different levels of education to women.

2. To compare the lifetime earnings associated with the various levels of education.

3. To evaluate the net present value of lifetime earnings of women with various levels of education in relation to the cost of acquiring that education.

4. To compare the rates of return from investment in the various levels of education.

5. To examine and compare the attitudinal and behavioural returns from education towards the institutions of education, employment, marriage and family, religion, politics and social life.

6. To highlight the levels of education that are most viable for women from the investment point of view.

**Organisation of the Study**

This study proposes to evaluate the returns to investment from education to employed women in Bangalore City. While most researches on returns confine themselves to only economic returns, a point of departure of this study is that it attempts to study even the non-economic returns from education i.e., the attitudinal and behavioural returns. The organisation of the study is as follows :

In the foregoing chapter a systematic exploration of this problem has been made in an attempt to measure, compare and evaluate the returns from education.

In the following chapter, work to date on the returns from education has been reviewed with a view to develop a framework of reference for the present study.

Chapter 3 discusses the Operational Definitions of the key words in the study, the Universe and Sample choosen, tools used for collecting information, method of data collection, statistical techniques used for analysing the data and finally the limitations of the current study.

Chapter 4 presents the profile of the sample of the study. The data relating to the general characteristics are presented in the context of their employment sector.

Chapter 5 analyses and interprets the data relating to the economic and non-economic returns that accrue to working women with different levels of education. This chapter is divided into two sections. Section 1 discusses costs of different levels of education from the private point of view. Further, it demonstrates the magnitude and importance of including foregone earnings among the cost components. Section 2 analyses the returns from education. This section is further divided into sub-sections A and B. Sub-section A discusses the economic returns from education in the form of lifetime earnings, net present values of earnings and internal rates of return to various levels of education. The levels that are most viable for women and the private demand for education are discussed in detail. Sub-section B discusses the attitudinal and behavioural returns from various levels of education. This Sub-section is further divided into six divisions. They are attitudes and behaviour of women towards the institutions of : (1) education, (2) employment, (3) Marriage and family, (4) politics, (5) religion, and (6) social life. It also attempts to examine the consistency between the attitudes and behaviour of women with different levels of education.

Chapter 6 summarises the findings of the study and attempts to derive a few policy suggestions.

CHAPTER 2

# Review of Related Literature

Interest in the profitability measure of investment has been growing during the last two and a half decades. The reason for this is that education is now being considered as an area of investment and as such preferences among alternative forms and levels can be made depending upon the benefit and cost ratios. This reason, however, does not suggest that economic criterion is the only one which should be used to justify educational expenditures. There are non-economic benefits also from education.

An economic analysis of any investment has to consider the benefits to be derived from it in relation to the costs. It is suffice to observe that monetary returns from education can be calculated on the basis of the investments to levels of education and earnings obtained in jobs leading from the various levels over a life-time.

Since the present study is confined to only the private returns from education, literature which throws some light on the methodological and analytical viewpoints are reviewed and discussed. The review is done with the purpose of clarifying the components of cost and benefits to be enumerated, their measurement, the multiplicity of computational adjustments to be made, the methods of accounting for variables other than education that have an influence on earnings, the evaluation methods, returns to education in both foreign countries and India and finally to highlight the gaps in the literature reviewed and to develop a methodological and analytical frame-work for the present study.

**Components of Costs and Benefits**

In assessing the economic value of education, Schultz[1] delineates different types of costs that should be taken into account. He defines total factor costs of schooling as the costs paid by the student and his family, and costs paid by others like community, state, government, voluntary organisations, etc. The costs paid by the student and his family is called private costs and that by others, the social costs.

Becker[2] also classifies costs as private and social, and subdivides each of these into direct and indirect costs. By direct private costs he means costs of tuition, books and supplies and additional living expenditure incurred by students. By indirect private costs he means income foregone by students.[3]

Pandit[4] classifies the cost of education as Institutional, Student and Opportunity Costs. He defines Institutional Costs as having the following components : (1) Capital Cost, (2) Equipment Cost, and (3) Non-divisible Recurring Costs. He defines student costs as including tuition and fees, cost of books, equipment and stationery purchased by the students,

1. Theodore W. Schultz : "The Economic Value of Education", New York, Columbia University Press, 1963, p. 20.
2. Gary S. Becker : "Human Capital", New York, Columbia University Press, 1964.
5. For a detailed conceptual discussion of each of these types of costs, refer to Gary S. Becker : "Investment in Human Beings", the Journal of Political Economy LXX (Part 2), Supplement, Oct. 1962.
4. H.N. Pandit : "Cost Analysis of Education in India—Private and Social Participation", Indian Educational Review, Vol. 7(2), July 1972, NCERT.

additional living expenditure and transportation charges. He defines opportunity cost as income foregone by students. Vaizey,[5] however, is of the view that opportunity costs of students should not be included in the measurement of costs in education.

**Components of Benefits**

Weisbrod[6] and Sharma[7] classify the benefits of education under two categories as internal and external benefits.

Weisbrod sub-divides internal benefits into five categories as follows :

1. Financial return accompanying additional education ;
2. Financial option return i.e., the value of the option to obtain further education and the rewards accompanying it ;
3. The non-monetary opportunity operations involving the broadened individual employment choices which education permits ;
4. Hedging option ; and
5. Non-market benefits like the preparation of his own income-tax return by an educated person.

Sharma classifies the internal benefits as monetary and non-monetary benefits. Monetary benefits are the salary, allowances, fringe-benefits and other earnings. Non-monetary benefits are

5. Vaizey J. : "The Economics of Education", London, Faber and Faber, 1962, p. 43.
6. Burton A. Weisbrod : "External Benefits of Public Education", Princeton Industrial Relations Centre, New Jersey, 1984, p. 20.
7. R.C. Sharma : "Benefit-Cost Analysis of Educational Projects : A Review of Researches", in H.N. Pandit (ed) "Measurement of Cost Productivity and Efficiency of Education", NCERT, 1969, pp. 395-396.

those which lead to increased satisfaction, options, guidance to children, etc.

**Measurement of Private Costs and Benefits**

Schultz[8] breaks up the Private Resource Costs as follows : (1) Direct Costs, (2) Opportunity Costs, and (3) Incidental School Related Costs as incurred by the individuals.

**Private Direct Costs**

Becker[9] estimated the private direct costs of education from statistics published by the U.S. Office Health, Education and Welfare by subtracting from the gross tuition and fees, contributions made by the Federal Government on account of the tuition and fees of veterans. He then made correction for the tuition and fees paid for extension courses and public services, because enrolment figures include such students. He also made correction for part-time students by assuming two part-timers equivalent to one full-timer. A third correction applied was based on the retaionale that the tuition paid by students would be lower than the tuition received by colleges because of scholarships from colleges and other sources. He found that scholarships were 20.7 per cent of the tuition. After making these adjustments, tuition payment was 242 per student in the year 1958. He calculated the costs on books, supplies, travel, etc., by assuming that these expenditures bore the same relationship to tuition and fees as they did in 1952-53. He set the high school tuition as zero. He estimated the other direct costs of high school students by assuming that the ratio of "these costs to expenditures per student by high schools equalled one half the observed ratio for college students". He, however, accepts, "The use of one half is quite arbitrary

8. Theodore W. Schultz : "Capital Formation by Education", Journal of Political Economy, LXVIII, Dec. 1960, pp 571-583.
9. Gary S. Becker : "Human Capital", National Bureau of Economic Research, New York, 1964, p. 174.

and perhaps a somewhat different ratio would be more justifiable"[10].

Rogers[11] estimated the direct costs to the individual by the type of school he attended. While the costs of the public school students' education are met by society, the private school student must pay fees. He apppoximated the direct private costs of higher education by arriving at National averages by dividing the total income of colleges from tuition and fees by the total number of college students.

**Private Indirect Costs**

These are constituted by the earnings foregone by students. In estimating earnings foregone, Schultz[12] assumed that students forego 40 weeks of earnings. Using the median earning per week of males and females at different age levels, he obtained weighted average of earnings at each educational level. The estimates of earnings foregone by high school and college students were $ 583 and $ 1369 respectively. These were equivalent to 11 and 25 weeks of earnings of workers in manufacturing sector. He suggests that these earnings should be corrected for unemployment. According to Rudolph Blitz[13], the estimates drawn by Schultz have a downward bias, especially for younger age-groups. To test his contention, Blitz reviewed five studies all of which yielded an estimate of foregone income, atleast 50 per cent higher than Schultz's figures.

Becker[14] estimated foregone earnings in a slightly different

10. Gary S. Becker : "Human Capital", National Bureau of Economic Research, New York, 1964, p 174
11. Daniel C. Rogers : "Private Rates of Return to Education in the United States : A Case Study", Yale, Economic Essays, Vol. 9, No. 1, Spring 1969.
12. Schultz : 1960, op. cit. pp. 571-583.
13. Rudolph C. Blitz : "A Calculation of Income Foregone by Students", supplement to Nation's Educational Outlay in Selma Mushkin (ed). "Economics of Higher Education", Washington DCUS Dept. of Health, Education and Welfare.
14. Gary S. Becker : 1964, op. cit. pp. 171 and 172.

way. He argued that full-time students spend three-fourth of their available working time in school and could, therefore, work in the remaining one-fourth time. He thus concludes that college students "earn about one-quarter of the amount earned by high school graduates of the same age" and that high school students earn one-quarter of the estimated earnings of elementary school graduates of the age 14 to 17.

Pandit[15] estimated the income foregone by students by multiplying together the following three factors : (1) Number of students in a given level of education above the age of 14 years ; (2) Education specific working force participation rates, and (3) Wage rates of workers of comparable age and ability.

**Measurement of Private Benefits**

Attempts made so far at measuring monetary private benefits, with a few exceptions, have utilised cross-sectional data in a chosen year, to estimate the life-time earnings of individuals with different levels of education. In other words, these attempts assumed that the income earned by different age-groups in a year could be used to measure the income of a cohort as it aged and retired from the work-force. They assumed that cross-sectional data could be converted into longitudinal data. The reasons for following the cross-sectional approach, instead of tracing an individual's income, have been given, convincingly, by Miller[16] "Cross-sectional data have the advantage that they are free from the influence of variants such as periods of industrial depression, or usual activities with changes in opportunities for employment, in wage rates and in cost of living".

Cross-sectional data obtained from census reports have been used to prepare age-income profiles, to arrive at the estimates

15. H. N. Pandit : 1972, op cit. pp. 142-147.
16. Herman P. Miller : "Income in Relation to Education", American Economic Review, L(5), Dec. 1960 p. 979.

of life-time earnings, and to draw conclusions in regard to education-income relationships.

Miller's[17] estimates of life-time earnings were based on wages and salaries (1939), on earnings (1948) and total income (1949, 1956 and 1958). These estimates were not discounted and adjusted for economic growth. He, however, advocated such suggestions subsequently. He suggested that the present value of the life-time income should be calculated by the formula :

$$V18 = \sum_{n=18}^{45} \frac{Y_n. W_n .P_n(1+x)}{(1+r)n-18} + \sum_{n=46}^{75} \frac{Y_n. W_n. P_n(1+y)}{(1+r)n+18}$$

where V is the present value of life-time income, the working life-span is from 18 to 75 years, $Y_n$ is the average income of a person in the education group whose life-time earnings are being estimated, $W_n$ is the proportion of persons with income $Y_n$, $P_n$ is probability of survival, r is the discount rate and X and Y are the gains in income associated with economic growth.

Houthakker[18] in his study points out that census data present median incomes which are not the type of average to be used for studying income since income-distributions are positively skewed. He, therefore, suggests the use of mean. He adjusts these mean incomes for mortality and then obtains their present values at different discount rates.

Becker[19] used the midpoints of all closed income-classes to calculate means for different education-age groups. With these representative income-points, he arrived at income estimates which he adjusted for mortality, growth, taxation unemployment and under and over-reporting of incomes.

17. Herman P. Miller : "Life-time Income and Economic Growth" American Economic Review, LV Sept. 1965 pp. 634-644.
18. H. S. Houthakker : "Education and Income", Review of Economics and Statistics, XLI, Feb. 1959, pp. 24-28.
19. Gary S. Becker : 1984, op. cit p. 154.

Rogers[20] estimated the life-time earnings of 364 American males based on longitudinal data about their earnings. Information regarding earnings were collected through questionnaires for the years 1950, 1955, 1960 and 1965 along with the capital value of owned business, occupation, length of military service and years of schooling. Additional sources of data employed were the census records. The estimates of total life-time earnings for each individual were derived in four parts : (1) an estimate of earnings during periods of education or military service ; (2) a retrodictive estimation based on the 1950 earnings of each individual as compared to 1960 earnings of all production workers with corrections for national unemployment and the influence of age on earnings ; (3) an interpolation between the 1950, 1955, 1960 and 1965 earnings figures ; and (4) a projection based on the assumptions that each man would remain at the same percentile of the earnings distribution for his occupation at each age until retirement and that the economy would grow at 3½ per cent per annum until 1985.

Rate of return studies to investment in education conventionally mearure solely the benefits by consideration of the earnings streams. This is not because the other benefits which flow from education are ignored but rather due to the theoretical and practical difficulties of handling the consumption, pychic or non-monetary benefits. In the absence of quantitative information of their magnitude the alternative ways in which they can be included are : (1) an arbitrary estimate of their size may be made and added on to the direct errnings stream ; (2) a proportion of the costs can be laid aside ; and (3) the statement can be made that the rates of return based on earnings alone are underestimated, and refer only to the investment component of education[21]. However, Blaug[22] who is of a

20. Daniel C. Rogers : 1969, op. cit. p. 98.

21. Schultz : 1963 op. cit.

22 Blaug M. : "An Introduction to the Economics of Education", London : Allen Lane, The Penguin Press, 1970, pp. 16 to 22.

totally different view argues that education is always both an investment and a consumption.

Quantification of the external or indirect benefits of education to the individual is again difficult as the list of such benefits is both enormous and divergent. A fuller presentation of the external benefits are covered in depth with various implicit and explicit assumptions to their size, by Blaug[23], Vaizey[24] and Sharma[25].

In general, there are two ways to view the external benefits of education :

1. They can be named and presented alongside the rates of return calculated using earnings data, with the statement that the economic effects of education as measured do not provide a complete basis for decision making although they do present a reasonable picture of the direct benefits ; and

2. An arbitrary estimate may be made of the magnitude of the external benefits, but such an estimate necessarily involves highly subjective weighing.

Of the above two methods, the former appears to be more appropriate because a descriptive analysis of the external benefits will lend itself to a better understanding and insight than just arbitrarily estimating its value.

**Benefits and Costs Relationship**

Two methods are generally employed to compare costs and benefits of alternative investments. They are the net present value method or additional life-time method as used by Miller[26] and Houthakker[27] and internal rates of return as used by

23. Blaug M. : "An Introduction to the Economics of Education", London : Allen Lane, The Penguin Press, 1970, pp. 16 to 22, ch. 4.
24. Vaizey J. : 1962, op. cit.
25. R. C. Sharma, in H. N. Pandit (ed), op. cit. p. 402.
26. Herman P. Miller : 1960, op. cit. p. 979.
27. H. S. Houthakker : 1959, op. cit. pp. 24-28.

Becker[28] and Hansen[29]. Work to date on the economic returns to education falls into two main categories, namely, tabulation studies and case studies. Tabulation studies undertaken include those of Glick and Miller[30], Houthakker[31], Hansen[32] Bridgman[33] and Becker[34]. Each of them attempted to estimate the increment in earnings associated with an increment in education. They used census data of average income for males with a given education and age to estimate life-time income for those with that education. However, these tabulation studies have certain undesirable characteristics. Firstly, they deal with income rather than earnings. Since individuals with more family wealth and hence more non-earned income have on an average more education, use of income overestimates the increment in earnings associated with an educational increment. Secondly, these studies were not able to control for other variables which might expect to have an effect on earnings, such as social class, ability, etc. Finally, life-time earnings are based on income data for one year. The results of the analysis are, therefore, determined by the particular economic conditions of that year and consequently any predictions or generalizations based on these studies are subject to great error. These studies use group data which do not lend themselves to multivariate analysis.

Case studies, on the other hand, provide data which are specific to individuals so that multivariate analysis can be

28. Becker : 1964, op. cit.
29. W. L. Hansen : "Total and Private Rates of Return to Investment in Schooling", Journal of Political Economy, April 1963, pp. 128-141.
30. Paul Glick and Herman P. Miller : "Education Level and Political Income", American Sociological Review, 21, 1956, pp. 307-312.
31. Houthakker H. S. : 1959, op. cit.
32. Hansen : 1963, op. cit.
33. D. S. Bridgman : "Problems in Estimating the Monetary Value of College Education", Review of Economics and Statistics, 42, Aug. 1980, op. cit.
34. Gary S. Becker ; 1964, op. cit.

conducted. They are, however, cross-sectional and not longitudinal. They include studies by Wolfle and Smith[35], Morgan and David[36], Adams[37], Hirsch and Segelhorst[38] and Shane Hunt[39]. A problem common to several of these is that variables such as occupation, self-employment and supervisory responsibility are introduced into the analysis as independent variables. Especially when people with different amounts of education are being studied, these variables tend to distort the measured effect of education since occupation and the other characteristics mentioned are to a great degree results of the education process. They may not have completely independent effects on earnings, and therefore, should not be included as independent variables. Furthermore, all of the case studies, like the tabulation studies, have the shortcoming of drawing on data which cover only one year.

Rogers[40], however, used longitudinal data and omitted variables which are to a greater degree results of the education process.

Earnings differentials were not totally dependent on the level of education received. Atleast part of the earnings differential was attributed to factors like ability, social class, sex, motivation, family background, race, etc. Two months

35. Dael Wolfle and Joseph Smith : "The Occupational Value of Education for Superior High School Graduates", Journal of Higher Education, 27, April 1956, pp. 201-212.
36. James Morgan and Martin David : Education and Income", Quarterly Journal of Economics, 77, Aug. 1963, pp. 423-437.
37. F. Gerard Adams : "The Size of Individual Incomes : Socio-Economic Variables and Chance Variation", Review of Economics and Statistics, 40, Nov. 1958, pp. 390-398.
38. Werner Hirsch and Elbert Segelhorst : "Incremental Income Benefits of Public Edducation", Review of Economics and Statistics 47, Nov, 1965, pp. 392-399.
39. Shane Hunt : "Income Determinants for College Graduates and the Return to Educational Investment", Yale Economic Essays, 3, Fall 1963, pp. 305-357.
40. Daniel C. Rogers ; 1969, op. cit. pp. 88-129.

have been used to deal with factors "other than education" in the rate of return analysis. The first one has been to apply an adjustment factor to the earnings—what Blaug[41] calls the "alpha coefficient" ($\alpha$). Early studies in the United States led to the earnings differential being adjusted downwards by 40 per cent, the remaining 60 per cent reflecting differences in earnings due to differences in education[42], and consequently an $\alpha$ coefficient of 0.6 had been used in a great number of studies.

The second and better method for dealing with earning-related variables other than education is the process of earnings standardisation through regression analysis. When data on earnings and other characteristics of individuals are known, it is possible to estimate the "earnings function" by multiple regression, accounting for the variance of earnings in terms of education, age, social class, father's occupation, region, etc. Once these earning functions have been estimated all other variables are set at their means and expected age-earnings profiles are constructed. In this way, the difference in earnings between any two schooling levels is 'standardised' for factors other than education[43]. This procedure can be applied only in cases where large number of individual observations are available.

The other adjustments that are usually incorporated are those for unemployment, taxes, mortality, wastage and growth.

41. Mark Blaug : "The Rate of Return on Investment in Education in Great Britian", The Manchester School, Sept. 1965.
42. Gary S. Becker : 1964, op. cit. Also refer Denison E.F. "Measuring the Contribution of Education to Economic Growth" in "The Residual Factor and Economic Growth" OECD, 1964.
43 For illustration of this approach see : Carnoy M. ; "Rates of Return to Schooling in Latin America". Journal of Human Resources ; II (Summer) 1967 ; M. Blaug : "The Rate of Return on Investment in Education in Thailand", Journal of Development Studies, Vol. 12(2), Jan. 1977 ; Hans Heinrich & Martin Carnoy ; "Cost-Benefit Analysis in Education : A Case Study of Kenya", International Bank for Reconstruction and Development, 1972.

It is appropriate in this context to mention that the decision for investment in education is not necessarily governed only by the "rate-of-return" criterion, part of this investment may be in the nature of "consumption" expenditure, governed more by considerations of social good rather than economic returns.[44]

**Private Returns to Education : Studies Conducted Abroad :**

A review of the studies conducted on the private economic returns from education can be grouped on the basis of the sources of data, sample size, sex, method of computation of return and the types of adjustments made therein.

While there are scores of studies measuring the returns from education for countries in all five continents,[45] only such studies as those of methodological interest are discussed. Further, as studies have been already discussed in the appropriate context of methodolody, measurement of costs, benefits and cost-benefit relationship, only studies based on the adjustments made are reviewed here alongwith an outline of the conclusions drawn.

Studies conducted by Hansen,[46] Hines et al,[47] Cary S. Fields[48]

44. M.M. Mehta : "Contribution of Human Resources to Economic Growth" in "Readings in Development and Planning", Vol. 1., United Nations Asian & Pacific Development Institute, Bangkok, June 1980, p. 123.
45. For a review of the rate of return studies around the world in detail, see : G. Psacharopoulos & K. Hinchliffe : "Returns from Education: An International Comparison". Elsevier Scientific Publishing Co., Amsterdam, 1973, Ch. 3.
46. W.L. Hansen : 1963, op. cit.
47. Hines F. Tweeten L. and Redfern M : ' Social & Private Rates of Return to Investment in Schooling by Race—Sex Groups and regions", Journal of Human Resources, V (3), 1970.
48. Gary S. Fields : "Private Returns to Investment in Higher Levels of Education in Kenya", University of Michigan, Discussion Paper 19, March 1972.

Clark and Fongs,[49] and Hinchliffe[50] have incorporated either all or a few of the usual adjustments that are made to the data such as taxes, unemployment, wastage, growth and mortality. The most interesting of these studies is the one carried out by Hines et al[51] which demonstrates that the final rates of return figures are almost similar for the adjusted and unadjusted data, as many of the adjustments act in opposite directions and hence cancel out.

The drawback of the above studies is that they have not accounted for the influence of variables other than education on the earnings. Studies by Becker,[52] Blaug,[53] Maglon and Layard,[54] Selby Smith,[55] Nalla Gounden[56] and Blaug et al[57] have used the $\alpha$ coefficient to attribute atleast part of the earnings differential to factors like age, ability, social class, sex origin, region, motivation, etc. In all these studies the co-efficient varies between 0.5 and 0.8. The most commonly used coefficient by several researchers was 0.6.

Carnoy[58] carried out a study in Maxico on a cross-sectional sample of 4,000 male wage earners in 1963. The most important finding of his study was that standardisation for factors other

49. Clark D.H. & Fong P.E. : "Returns to Schooling and Training in Singapore", Malayan Economic Review, Oct. 1970.
50. Hinchliffe K. : "The Rate of Return to Education in Ghana", Economic Bulletin of Ghana, June 1971.
51. Hines et al : 1970, op. cit.
52. Becker G.S. : 1964, op. cit.
53. Blaug M. : 1965, op. cit.
54. Maglon L. & Layard R. : "How Profitable is Engineering Education ?" Higher Education Review, II (2), 1970.
55. Selby Smith C. : "Costs and Benefits in Further Education : Some evidence from a Pilot Study", Economic Journal, Sept. 1970.
56. Nalla Gounden A.M. : Investment in Education in India", Journal of Human Resources, (Summer) 1967.
57. Blaug M., Layard P.R.G. and Woodhall M. : "The Causes of Graduate Unemployment in India", London ; Allen Lane, The Penguin Press, 1969.
58. Carnoy M. ; 1965, op. cit.

than education reduced the returns by 15 per cent for lower educational levels and by only 2 or 3 percentage points for the higher levels, thus suggesting that a single value of $\alpha$ should not be used for all educational levels but rather a range of values which increases up the educational ladder, i.e., lower the educational levels compared, lower that part of the earnings which is strictly due to education.

To account for the varied influence of variables other than education on the earnings differential of individuals with different levels of education, regression analysis as the process of earnings standardisation was preferred to $\alpha$ coefficient by a few researchers. A brief review of the independent variables included in the earnings functions in some of the regression studies follows.

Hanoch's[59] study in the United States is based on a .001 sample of the 1960 census, which reported earnings and other characteristics of more than 57,000 males in 1959. He estimated the earnings functions which included as large as 23 explanatory variables. The sample was divided into 24 groups defined by race, religion and age. Earnings functions within each group were estimated. Beyond schooling and age, the explanatory variables referred to the type of residence, origin of the individual, mobility, marital status, size of the family and number of children. By means of multiple regressions, expected age-earnings profiles by years of schooling were estimated. No other adjustments were made. The findings for White/North sub-group were as follows :

The private rate of return for elementary school over 0-4 years of schooling was above 100 per cent, 4 years of high school yielded a rate of 16.1 per cent, and the extra 4 years of college yielded 9.6 per cent. The rate of 17 versus 16 years of schooling was equal to 7 per cent.

59. Hanoch C. : "An Economic Analysis of Earnings and Schooling", Journal of Human Resources, II (3), 1967.

In a study conducted by Morgan and others[60] in American Households, multivariate analysis was used for isolating the pure effect of education on earnings by allowing for all the various factors that influence personal income such as age, formal education, on-the-job training, sex, race, intelligence, need-achievement, parents' education, family size, father's occupation, religion, geographic region, city size, occupational choice, occupational mobility, mortality, unemployment and hours of work. Despite the tendency towards over-adjustment (as the authors themselves point out), education emerged as the single most powerful determinant of family income. Factors other than age and education together explained only 40 per cent of the gross unadjusted earnings differentials between high-school and graduates in the age-group 18-34, and only 12 per cent in the age-group 35-74.

Carnoy[61] conducted a study in Mexico based on a cross-sectional sample of 4,000 male wage-earners in 1963. The questionnaire provided data on other variables like wage/salary, years of completed schooling, age, father's occupation, type of industry wherein the respondent was employed and the city in which he was located. The results of the regressions were that, when schooling alone was used, 43 per cent of the income variance was explained, but when age and other independent variables were added, the schooling explanatory power dropped to 36 and 29 per cent respectively. Yet, schooling was found to be the largest single determinant of income differences. The non-standardised private rates range from 21.5 per cent for 3 years of schooling to 36.7 per cent for 15 years of schooling. His study shows that the socio-economic background at the early stages is much more important than the ability factor in later years.

60. Morgan et al : "Income and Welfare in the United States", New York, 1962, pp. 387-427.
61. Carnoy M. : 1967, op. cit.

Schultz[62] conducted a study in Bogota in 1965, based on a rather small sample of urban labour force, consisting of 684 men and 316 women, 10 years old or over. Earnings functions were estimated separately for men and women. The independent variables were schooling, age, years of residence, and other sources of income. Hourly earnings were used as the dependent variable. He adjusted for under-employment and the earnings of domestic servants to account for fringe benefits. Taxes were not deducted. His private returns on adjusted earnings for men were 18.4 per cent for primary, 34.4 per cent for secondary, as low as 4.4 per cent for university and 52.5 per cent for vocational secondary schooling. The highlight of the results is that the rates are higher for women than men for vocational secondary schooling and university education, but lower for primary and general secondary.

Lerner M.O.[63], in his study in Brazil, 1960, used data from the Brazilian Demographic Census. The sample size from which age-earnings data were used, was 4,700 Regression analysis yielded estimates of earnings by level of formal education. Variables other than education included sex, colour and place of residence. His estimate of the private rate of return to elementary schooling ($4^{+}$over 0 years) for females was more than double (38.6 per cent) the one for males (17.9 per cent). This is in contrast to Schultz's study in Bogota wherein the rates for females was less than that of males at the primary level.

Blaug[64] estimated rates of return to education in Thailand. A sample survey of 5,000 males and females was conducted in Greater Bangkok in 1970. Multiple regression analysis was used to estimate earnings functions. Earnings were standardised

62. Schultz T.W. : "Returns to Education in Bogota, Columbia," The Rand Corporation Memorandum, RM-5645, RC/AID, Sept. 1968.
63. Lerner M.O. : "Determinants of Educational Attainment", in G. Psacharopoulos and K. Hinchliffe, 1973, op. cit. p. 45.
64. M. Blaug : 1977, op. cit.

for age, sex, years of schooling, parents' education, origin, fathers' occupation, urban and rural, private or public school, vocational or academic school, hours of work, sector of employment, size of the firm and occupation. According to Blaug, this degree of standardisation corresponds to a coefficient of 0.55. The adjusted private rates to lower primary was 24 per cent ; upper primary 16 per cent ; lower and higher secondary 11 per cent and university education 11 per cent. Vocational secondary schooling yielded negative rates.

Pichai Charnsupharindr[65] estimates the rates of return to various types of education in Thailand. He estimated the earnings functions using multiple regression analysis to isolate the effects of the different independent variables on earnings. The independent variables included were age, education, hours of work, type of school, sex and size of firm. The contribution of education to the earnings of the Thai people was explained only by about 40 per cent, the remaining 60 per cent of the earnings being due to other factors. The education-age-earnings profiles were estimated setting all the independent variables except age, type of school and field of study at the mean values of their samples. This finding revealed that education contributed to the improvement of the earning power of the people—the longer the year of schooling, the higher the earnings profile, all other things being equal.

Thias and Carnoy's[66] study in Kenya based on a survey of 4,800 observations (1969) attempted to isolate the benefits of additional schooling from other socio-economic factors and ability and to project rates of return. Regression analysis was used. Adjustments were also made for unemployment, mortality

65. Pichai Charnsupharindr : "The Rate of return to Investment in Thai Education", The Philippine Economic Journal, No. 41, Vol. XVIII (3), 1979, pp. 289-327.
66. Thias H.H. and Carnoy M. : "Cost-benefit Analysis in Education : A Case Study of Kenya", International Bank for Reconstruction and Development, Report EC-173, Nov. 1969.

and taxation. His adjustments suggested values of $\alpha$ coefficient ranging from 0.3 for primary, 0.6 for secondary and 0.8 for university, i.e., lower the level of schooling, less of the income differential is due to education only.

Rogers[67] conducted a longitudinal study of 364 American males to generate data on the relationship between education, earnings and ability. He omitted variables such as occupation, self-employment, etc., in the earnings functions as they tend to distort the measured effect of education and they are to a great degree results of the education process. He used discount rates of 0, 4 and 8 per cent to evaluate the returns using the net present value method. Expenditure on education appeared to be a viable investment for all levels through college graduation, except for the post-graduate level which was not viable for individuals paying its full private costs. The highlight of his study is that ability differences are unlikely to have significant effects on the calculated rates of return.

Magnusson's[68] study in Sweden was based on income and earnings data of persons employed in private and State sectors. He made adjustments for taxes and costs borne by the state. It is interesting to note that he was reluctant to adjust the rates upwards for productivity growth. The reason he gave was, that he performed a sensitivity test which showed that the use of cross-sectional data over-estimates rather than under-estimates the time-series rates. This hypothesis usually underlies a rate of return correction for changes in productivity.

**Studies in India**

Studies on the profitability to investment in education in India are few and far between. Attempts made by the researchers to evaluate the economic rate of return to education have been mainly from the social point of view. Studies in

67. Daniel C. Rogers : 1969, op. cit.
68. Magnusson : in Pscharopoulos and K. Hinchliffe, 1975, op. cit.

this direction include those of Harberger[69], Nalla Gounden[70], Blaug et al[71], Kothari[72], Panchamukhi[73] and Ishrat Hussain[74]. Only Kothari[75] and Blaug et al[76] have estimated the private rates of return in their studies. Kothari, using the data in the Report on the Economic Survey of Bombay City, conducted by the Department of Economics, Bombay University, estimated the age-specific earnings data for each educational level. His estimate of the private monetary rates of return for college education (Arts and Science graduates) was 14 per cent and that for technical and engineering, 25 per cent.

Blaug et al attempted to diagnose the origin of graduate unemployment in India. The data were adjusted for unemployment and wastage. Using an $\alpha$ coefficient of 0.65 and growth (2 per cent/year) the private returns were found to be 18.7 per cent for primary, 10.4 per cent for the first degree after matriculation and 15.5 per cent for an engineering degree. The author explain graduate unemployment by the presistence of an advantageous private rate of return over time.

Apart from the studies cited above, various other researches have been referred to which do not refer to returns but have indirect bearing on the present study. They refer to studies on education and income distribution. A few of them are quoted

69. Harberger A. C. : "Investment in Men Verses Investment in Machines : The Case of India", in "Education and Eeonomic Development", (ed) C.A. Anderson & M J. Bowmen, Chicago, Aldine, 1965.
70. Nalla Counden A.M. : 1967, op. cit.
71. Blaug et al : 1969, op cit
72. Kothari V.N. : "Returns to Education in India", "Education as Investment" (ed) B. Singh, Meenakshi Press, Meerut, India, 1967.
73. V. R. Panchamukhi & P.R. Panchamukhi : "Socio-Economic Variables & Urban Incomes", in H.N. Pandit (ed), 1969, op. cit.
74. Ishrat Z. Hussain : "Returns on education in India : An Estimate", (ed) B. Singh, 1967 op. cit.
75. Kothari V.N. : 1967, op. cit.
76. Blaug et al : 1969, op. cit.

here. They are studies by Ahluwalia[77], Jain[78], Psacharopoulos[79], Psacharopoulos and Marvin[80], Sahota[81], Winegarden[82], Haim Ofek and Fredricka Pickford Santos[83], J. R. Moroney[84] and others.

In the light of the foregoing review of literature relating to private returns from education the following conclusions emerge :

1. Interest in the studies of returns to education is widespread and growing outside India. In India, it is still to catch the attention that it deserves by social scientists.
2. The studies done so far and reviewed here are concerned mainly with conceptual problems and methodological issues. Case-studies on returns from education are still wanting.
3. There are still conceptual and methodological difficulties in quantifying the non-monetary private returns from education.
4. Special attention has not been given to the returns from women's education.

The review has helped the researches to develop a frame-

77. Ahluwalia M.S. : 1976, op. cit.
78. Jain S. : "Size Distribution of Income : A Compilation of Data", Washington DC., World Bank, 1975.
79. Psacharoloulos G. : 1977, op. cit.
80. Psacharoloulos G. & Marvin A. : 1976, op. cit.
81. Sahota C.S. : "Theories of Personal Income Distribution : A Survey", Journal of Economic Literature 16, 1978, pp. 1-55.
82. Winegarden C.R. : 1978 op. cit.
83. Haim Ofek and Fredricks Pickford Santos "The Economic Attainment of Women : A Comparative Analysis of the Parental Role" Economica, Vol. 48 (184) Nov. 1979.
84. J. R. Moroney : "Do Women Earn less Under Capitalism", The Economic Journal, 89, Sept. 1979, pp. 601-613.

work of reference in terms of definitions, samples selection, measurement of returns and analysis.

In the following chapter, operational definitions of the terms used, universe and sample selected, tools and techniques of data collection and analysis are discussed in detail.

# CHAPTER 3

# Methodology

In this chapter, the procedure adopted for the study, the universe, sampling technique, tools for collecting information, method of data collection, statistical techniques used and the limitations of the study are discussed in detail.

For the purpose of clarity some of the key terms used in this study are defined operationally. The terms defined are Private Returns, Private Cost, Economic Returns and Non-Economic Returns from Education.

**Operational definitions of the key terms used**

1. *Private Returns from Education* : is defined as the benefits that accrue to women from investing in education. It considers the relation between costs incurred by them in obtaining a particular level of education and the benefits (both economic and non-economic) they as individuals derive from that level of education.

2. *Private Cost of Education* : is defined as the expenses incurred by women in acquiring a particular level of education. It comprises of the direct and indirect costs of education.

(i) The direct costs refer to those types of investment which are perceptible, regular and actually paid by the women for acquiring a certain level of education. They comprise of the tuition and non-tuition costs of education.

(ii) Indirect costs is the 'income foregone' by women while attending school or college. If woman joined the labour force instead of pursuing education, they would have profited by earning an income and not incurring any expenses on education. However, as they did not consider such an alternative to education, they incur a loss in the form of foregoing, earnings which is also referred to as the 'opportunity cost of education.'

3. *Private Economic Returns from Education*: It has the same connotation as used by other authors. It is the monetary or earning benefits that accrue to women by investing in a particular level of education. The two methods generally employed to evaluate the economic returns from education are the net present values and internal rates of return. Both these methods will be used in this study.

4. *Private Non-Economic Returns from Education*: Though there are innumerable non-economic benefits that accrue to women from education, in the present study only attitudes and behaviour of the women towards certain social institutions are taken to represent the non-economic benefits.

(i) *Attitude*: Thurstone has defined an attitude as "the intensity of positive or negative affect for or against a psychological object. A psychological object is any symbol, person, slogan or idea toward which people can differ as regards positive or negative effect."[1] Thus, an attitude is a feeling that an attitude object is good or bad, fair or unfair, etc.

1, Thurstone, L.L.: 'Comment' American Journal of Sociology, 52, 1946, p. 39.

Krech and Crutchfield defined an attitude as"... ... ........ an enduring organisation of motivational, emotional, perceptual and cognitive processes with respect to some aspect of the individuals' world"[2].

Allport felt that there is a common thread running through the diverse defiinitions, since, "in one way or another each (definition) regards the essential feature of attitude as a preparation or readiness for response"[3]. The definitions of attitude have stressed the behaviour implications of attitudes.

In this study an attitude is defined as the positive or negative feeling for or against a psychological object. They are measured in terms of verbal or written reports of the women towards the institutions of education, employment, marriage and family, politics, religion and social life.

(ii) *Behaviour* : is defined as the predisposition to act toward some aspect of the individual's world.[4] It is measured by either written/oral reports or observation of the overt behaviour of the respondents to 'real-life' situations.

In the present study, the behaviour of the respondents is defined in terms of how they have reacted to certain real-life situations which are provided as stimuli. The areas covered to measure the behaviour of women are social institutions of education, employment, marriage and family, politics, religion and social life.

2. Krech, D. and R S. Crutchfield : "Theory and Problems of Social Psychology". McGraw Hill, New York, 1948, p. 152.
3. Collins, E. Barry : 'Social Psychology', Addison Wesley Publishing Company, 1970, p. 72.
4. Krech, D. & R. S. Crutchfield : op. cit., 1948, p. 152.

**Universe and Sample Selection**

Economic returns from education to employed women is the focus of the present study. As such, employed women form the universe. Women who are both educated and employed are mostly found in large numbers in urban areas. This is because there are wide avenues of work in urban areas. In Karnataka State, Bangalore City holds the highest percentage of educated and employed women. Further, it is the largest city of the State and its capital. Also, there are employed women who have migrated from neighbouring States of Andhra Pradesh, Tamil Nadu and Kerala among the women labour force in the city. As such, Bangalore City has been chosen for the purposes of this research.

This study is confined to women working in the public and organised private sectors in Bangalore City. The un-organised sector has been deliberately omitted as systematic information about such establishments is not available. The organised sector comprises of :

(a) All public sector establishments, i.e., all services under the Central, State and Local Governments and occupations in public sector undertakings in the fields of industry, credit financing, public utilities, etc., and

(b) Non-agricultural private sector establishments which employ ten or more than ten persons. This connotation of the organised sector is important for two reasons :

1. The Directorate General of Employment and Training, Ministry of Labour, collects detailed data regarding employment from all these establishments under 'Organised Sector' and hence it is readily available.

2. This 'Organised Sector' is governed by certain laws and regulations referring to industries, services and other occupations. These laws and regulations provide a framework of requirements, procedures

and conditions on the part of the employers, ensure a degree of legal protection to workers in these establishments, and a relatively mechanised work-situation.

In Bangalore City, out of a total population of 7.72 lakhs women, 49,296 (6.4 per cent) are in the labour force and 41,028 (5.3 per cent of the total) therein are employed in the organised sector. In other words, 83.2 per cent of the employed women in Bangalore City are in the organised sector. Of those employed in the organised sector, 24,733 (60.3 per cent) are in the public sector and 16,295 (39.7 per cent) in the private sector. A list of establishments in both the public and private sectors employing more than 25 women[5] was collected from the Directorate of Employment and Training. This list was up-dated from 30th September, 1975 to 30th September, 1977, using the live registers maintained by the Sub regional Employment Exchange, Brigade Road, Bangalore. While the Directorate of Employment and Training provided information regarding the exact number of women employees in each of the public sector establishments, the same was not readily available for the organised private sector establishments. Hence, to derive at an estimate of the number of women employees in each of the private sector establishments, the Directorate was requested to group the establishments under ranges based on the number of women employed in each establishment. The size of the ranges suggested were as follows :

Range 1. Establishments employing 25 to 30 women :

Range 2. 51 to 100 ; Range 3. 101 to 150 ;

Range 4. 151 to 200 ; Range 5. 201 to 300 ;

Range 6. 301 to 500 and Range 7. 501 and above.

5. It was decided to take a five per cent sample of the women respondents from each establishment. As such, those establishments employing less than 25 women were precluded.

The Directorate obliged the researcher by giving this type of information. Having grouped the establishments, the midpoints of each range was taken to represent the number of women employed in an establishment belonging to the respective range. The sum of these midpoints for all the establishments employing more than 25 women gives an estimate of the total number of women employed in the organised private sector establishments. Thus, an estimate of 12,118 women are found to be employed in 129 establishments in the private sector which employed 25 and more than 25 women. This figure forms the universe of study in the organised private sector.

To maintain uniformity in sampling design, the public sector establishments were also classified rangewise on the basis of the number of women employees in each establishment. Thus, there are 17,177 women employed in the 98 public sector establishments employing more than 25 women. The criterion for classifying the establishments based on the number of women it employs has been to take as representative a sample of small and large establishments as is available in the universe of study.

Thus, the main list prepared comprised of 227 establishments with a working force estimate of 29,295 women. Of them, 17,177 women are employed in 96 public sector establishments and an estimate of 12,118 in 129 private sector establishments.

**Sampling Procedure**

A multistage stratified random sampling technique was used to draw the sample for the study.

It was decided to take a thirty per cent sample of the establishments for the study. The total number of establishments came to 70. However, 75 establishments were selected. This was done as there was a speculated possibility of non-cooperation of closure of some establishments. These 75 establishments were distributed between the public and private sectors in proportion to the total number of establishments,

As such, 35 public sector establishments and 40 private sector establishments were selected.

The establishments in the public and private sectors were listed alphabetically range-wise. In the public seetor[6], the various divisions such as Central Government ; Central Government Quasi ; State Government ; State Government Quasi and the City Corporation were also maintained. From these divisions of the public sector, 30 per cent proportionate random sample of the establishments based on the range-wise classification was made.

The following table presents the range-wise and division-wise distribution of establishments in the public sector and the proportion of the sample drawn for the study.

It may be observed from table 3.1 that majority of the establishments fall in the range-groups 25 to 50 and 51 to 100. Hence, 71.43 per cent of the establishments drawn were from these two ranges for all the divisions. The largest number of establishments drawn from the various divisions of the public sector are from State Government (13) and Central Government Quasi (11). These together form 48.57 per cent of the sample in this category (i.e., 24 out of 35 public sector establishments).

The same procedure was adopted for the selection of establishments from the private sector. The following table gives the range-wise distribution of establishments and the sample drawn from the private sector.

6. The connotation of the term 'public sector' is taken from the Employment Exchange Compulsory Notification of Vacancies Act, 1959, viz. : all establishments whose activity is wholly or partially controlled by the Government or regulated by an Act of Parliament. This includes establishments under Central and State Governments, Quasi Government establishments and the Local Bodies covering both the administrative and industrial wings of such establishments.

TABLE No. 3.1

**Total Number of Establishments and Sample Drawn in the Public Sector**

| Ranges | Central Govt. | | Central Govt. Quasi | | State Govt. | | State Govt. Quasi | | Corporation | | Total |
|---|---|---|---|---|---|---|---|---|---|---|---|
| | Total | Sample | Total | Sample | Total | Sample | Total | Sample | Total | Sample | Sample |
| 25— 50 | 9 | 3 | 10 | 4 | 20 | 6 | 3 | 1 | — | — | 14 |
| 51—100 | 9 | 3 | 9 | 3 | 12 | 4 | 2 | 1 | — | — | 11 |
| 101—150 | — | — | 3 | 1 | 1 | — | — | — | — | — | 1 |
| 151—200 | — | — | 2 | | 1 | 2 | — | — | — | — | 3 |
| 201—300 | — | — | 1 | 1 | 3 | | 1 | 1 | — | — | 1 |
| 301—500 | 1 | 1 | 2 | 1 | 1 | 1 | — | — | — | — | 4 |
| Above 500 | 1 | | 3 | 1 | 1 | | — | — | 1 | 1 | 1 |
| Total | 20 | 7 | 30 | 11 | 39 | 13 | 6 | 3 | 1 | 1 | 35 |

(Braces in the original group the Central Govt. totals for 301—500 and Above 500 (sample 1); the Central Govt. Quasi totals for 101—150 and 151—200 (sample 1); the State Govt. totals for 101—150, 151—200 and 201—300 (sample 2); and the State Govt. totals for 301—500 and Above 500 (sample 1).)

TABLE No. 3.2

**Total Number of Establishments and the Sample Drawn in the Private Sector**

| | Total No. of establishments | No. of establishments selected |
|---|---|---|
| 25— 50 | 72 | 22 |
| 51—100 | 26 | 8 |
| 101—150 | 9 | 3 |
| 151—200 | 10 | 3 |
| 201—300 | 4 | 1 |
| 301—500 | 5 | 2 |
| Above 500 | 3 | 1 |
| Total | 129 | 40 |

It is observed from the above table that majority of the establishments selected are from the range 25 to 50 (22). This forms 55.0 per cent of the total number of establishments selected from the private sector.

The next step consisted in drawing women employees from the public and private sector establishments selected for the study. It had been decided to take a five per cent sample of the total number of women employees. The figure for five per cent comes to 1463. However, a six per cent sample of 1758 women was taken. This was done as there was a possibility of non-return or return of schedules with incomplete information from the respondents. The 1758 women were distributed proportionately between the public and private sectors, which worked out to be 1031 in the public sector and 727 in the private sector. The 1031 women employees in the public sector

TABLE No. 3.3

**Total Number of Women Employees and Sample Drawn from the Public Sector**

| Ranges | Central Govt. Total | Central Govt. Sample | Central Govt. Quasi Total | Central Govt. Quasi Sample | State Govt. Total | State Govt. Sample | State Govt. Quasi Total | State Govt. Quasi Sample | Corporation Total | Corporation Sample | Total Sample |
|---|---|---|---|---|---|---|---|---|---|---|---|
| 25— 50 | 299 | 18 | 467 | 28 | 648 | 39 | 114 | 7 | — | — | 92 |
| 51—100 | 659 | 39 | 376 | 35 | 893 | 54 | 183 | 11 | — | — | 139 |
| 101—150 | — | — | 360 | 22 | 108 | 6 | — | — | — | — | 28 |
| 151—200 | — | — | 363 | 22 | 187 | 11 | — | — | — | — | 33 |
| 201—300 | — | — | 254 | 15 | 758 | 46 | 252 | 15 | — | — | 76 |
| 301—500 | 457 | 27 | 655 | 40 | 482 | 29 | — | — | — | — | 96 |
| Above 500 | 633 | 38 | 4074 | 244 | 1639 | 98 | — | — | 3112 | 187 | 567 |
| Total | 2042 | 122 | 6749 | 406 | 4715 | 283 | 549 | 33 | 3112 | 187 | 1031 |

were distributed proportionately to its various divisions. Table 3.3 gives the range-wise and division-wise distribution of women employees in the public sector and sample drawn.

The highest proportion of the sample was taken from the Central Government Quasi. As regards the City Corporation, the break-ups of the Corporation was got (i.e., General Administrative Block, Hospitals, Health Centres, Schools, etc.). The number of women to be interviewed in the Corporation was 187. These 187 women respondents were drawn from the above mentioned break-ups using the proportionate random sampling technique. In the case of the other sectors, the sample was distributed proportionately to the establishments selected for the study.

Next, the 727 women to be drawn from the private sector were distributed proportionately to the various ranges. As the exact figures regarding the strength of women employees in the private sector establishments were not available, the range-wise sample selected were evenly distributed among the randomly selected establishments in each range. The following table gives the range-wise estimation of the number of women employees in the private sector and the sample drawn.

TABLE No. 3.4

**Range-wise Distribution of Women Employees and their Sample in the Private Sector**

| Ranges | Total Number of Women Employees | Sample drawn |
|---|---|---|
| 25—50 | 2736 | 164 |
| 51—100 | 1976 | 119 |
| 101—150 | 1134 | 68 |
| 151—200 | 1760 | 106 |
| 201—300 | 1004 | 60 |
| 301—500 | 2005 | 120 |
| Above 500 | 1503 | 90 |
| Total | 12118 | 727 |

It may be observed from the above table that the largest number of women respondents (164) were drawn from the range 25 to 50. These 164 respondents were drawn in equal numbers from the 22 establishments selected in the range (refer Table No. 3.2).

From the registers maintained by each of the establishments, a random sample of women employees were drawn using the random digit technique. Since most of the establishments belonged to the size groups 25 to 50 and 51 to 100, the number of women respondents to be interviewed from these establishments were 7 and 15 respectively. Hence, data from the respondents was collected by meeting them in a group. Information was collected through the questionnaire and interview techniques depending upon the educational qualification of the respondent. While for respondents having an education above the matriculation level questionnaires were canvassed, for those with education below the matriculation level, the interview technique was used. The list of establishments visited ; the number of women employees in each establishment ; the sample drawn and the questionnaire returns from the establishments and respondents ; is given in Appendix A.

**The Questionnaire**

The tool used for collecting information regarding the economic and non-economic returns from education to employed women was a structured questionnaire. However, wherever necessary, questions were made open-ended in order to give more scope for individual responses. The questionnaire consists of three parts. Part 'A' deals with general information regarding the respondents and items relating to educational investment and economic returns from education. The section on general information consists of items on age, caste, mother-tongue, migration, marital status, socio-economic status of parents, etc. The section dealing with educational investment comprises of the private cost of education, i.e., tuition cost ;

non-tuition cost on items like books and stationery, hostel charges, transport etc., and information about fee-concessions, freeships and scholarships, as these reduce the expenditure borne by the individual. In addition, information was collected about variables having an influence on the private cost of education. The items included were the type of educational institution attended and the total number of years taken to complete the course (as costs increase for repeaters). The part dealing with economic returns from education comprises of items on earnings (monthly salary) and variables having an influence on earnings such as sector of employment ; nature of employment ; number of jobs changed ; experience ; and additional earnings.

Part 'B' relates to items on attitudes towards certain social institutions like education, employment, marriage and family, politics, religion and social life. The statements were worded in such a way as to require the respondents either to agree or disagree with the same, i.e., the respondent has to circle either "Agree" of "Disagree" for each statement depending on the response that suits her. The reason for the two-point responses is that the sample comprising of women with various levels of education including the illiterates would find it difficult to differentiate between the various degrees of agreement and disagreement towards the item. The "uncertain" category was also omitted because of its disadvantage. It was observed during the pilot study that the subjects who were not serious, tend to put most of their responses in this category, thus making the effort meaningless. Further, in the absense of this category it was observed, that the respondents tried hard to exert their minds in deciding one way or the other.

Part 'C' deals with behaviour of women respondents towards the same social institutions as dealt with in attitudes of Part 'B.' The items consist of specific life situations under each social institution and how they have behaved in the circumstances. Responses in Part 'C' will help in cross-checking the responses in Part 'B' as questions in Part 'B' deal with attitudes and those in Part 'C' deal with behaviours towards the same in life-situations. Further, it will help to highlight the degree of dissonance or consistency between the attitudes and behaviours of women with various levels of education.

After preparing a very comprehensive questionnaire, it was pre-tested on a ten per cent sample of the total number of women respondents taken for the final study. Care was taken to see that the pre-test was conducted on as representative a sample as possible. Simultaneously, copies of the questionnaires were sent to experts for their comments and suggestions.

**Pilot Study (or pre-tryout)**

The pilot study was carried out with the following objectives :

1. To find out if the questions included in the questionnaire are relevant and whether they needed re-wording or be dropped.

2. To find out if the alternatives provided for each item are appropriate and exhaustive.

3. To see whether the statements included in the attitudes towards the various social institutions are controversial. It is assumed that the non-controversial statements would not be reflecting any difference in attitudes between different groups of respondents.

4. To find out whether any grave ommissions have been made in the schedule.

5. In budgetting both time and cost for the final study.

Ten per cent representative sample of employed women respondents, i.e., 160 women employees were selected for the pilot study and interviewed. The questionnaires were then scored, tabulated and analysed. The results of the pilot study are given below :

1. Certain items in Part 'A' were modified in order to make them more meaningful and clear.

For example, the alternatives for the question 'Since when are you living in Bangalore City ?' has been modified from :

| | | |
|---|---|---|
| (i) Less than 5 years | | (i) Less than 5 years |
| (ii) More than 5 years | to | (ii) 6 to 10 years |
| | | (iii) 11 to 15 years |
| | | (iv) 16 to 20 years |
| | | (v) 21 to 25 years |
| | | (iv) More than 25 years |

This modification was made as the objective of the item was not to find out whether the respondent is a domicile of Bangalore City but to find out the number of years of stay is Bangalore City as this has bearing on her employment.

2. As the pre-tryout questionnaire consisted of a comprehensive list of times regarding attitudes in Part 'B', the pre-tryout study helped to reduce the total number of items. For this, the percentile distribution of responses for each item was obtained. Items below the 15th and above the 85th percentiles were omitted as they indicate almost complete agreement or disagreement of a statement. Further, such items do not reflect any difference in attitudes of respondents with different levels of education. However, in certain cases, such items were retained so as to give a meaningful perspective to the items following them.

For example : Item No. 7 under 'Marriage and family', i.e., 'The system of dowry should not be continued', was retained in the final questionnaire through according to the analysis, it was to be excluded as 99.5 per cent of the pre-tryout sample agreed with the view.

In certain other cases where a group of items carried a single idea, they were clubbed together to form multiplechoice items.

For example : Under 'Attituds towards Education', the first four items in the pretest, i.e. :

1. Girls should not be given any education.
2. Girls should be educated up to the primary level only.
3. Girls should be taught upto the secondary level only.
4. A girl should not be allowed to go for higher education even if she is very intelligent.

were clubbed to form a multiple-choice item in the final questionnaire.

The final format is :

Girls should be given :

1. No education at all.
2. Primary education only.
3. Secondary education.
4. College education.
5. Professional education.
6. Others (specify).

3. As regards Part 'C' of the questionnaire, the alternatives to the questions were made exhaustive. In some cases, the questions were re-worded.

The questionnaire was thus refined on the basis of the pilot-study. Opinion of experts were also kept in mind while refining the questionnaire. A copy of the final questionnaire is given in Appendix B.

## Field Work

The data was collected during the year 1978. The selected estabtishments were visited for the collection of data. The total number of establishments visited during the field-work was 75—40 in the Private sector and 35 in the public sector. The total number of women employees studied was 1465—553 in the private sector and 910 in the public sector. Since a large number of women respondents belonged to the small-size establishments, i.e., ranges 1 and 2, only seven and fifteen questionnaires respectively were to be canvassed at a time. Hence, the interview method in such onces was used. As this method ensured the definite return of questionaires, five per cent of the sample was taken instead of six. In the large-size establishments, the questionnaire method was adopted and hence a six per cent sample of women employees was taken in order to ensure five per cent returns. However, the interview technique was also used wherever the level of education of the respondents was below matriculation. Questions were explained in the regional language or mother-tongue to those respondents who did not follow English.

Simultaneously, data on pay-scales along with the allowances were collected from the managements of the establishments visited so as to compare and verify the salary data as given by the women respondents. Further, in such cases where there has been a change/s in the pay-scales, data on the previous scales were also collected from the managements, so as to cover a period of thirty years, i.e., from 1947 onwards. This helped in the calculation of life-time earnings of the respondents.

## Statistical Techniques used for the Analysis of Data

The present study was undertaken with the main purpose of identifying the private economic returns from various levels of education to women. Further, the study also attempts to examine the non economic returns from education in terms of the attitudes and behaviour of women towards the institutions of education, employment, marriage and family, politics, religion and social life. With these purposes in view, suitable statistical techniques have been selected for analysing the data.

In order to arrive at the relative importance of the independent variables in their relation to earnings, it was decided to use the Standard Partial Regression Coefficients (β coefficients) associated with the different independent variables fitted into a Regression Equation for different levels of education. This provided an indication about the relative importance of the variables compared.

**Computation of β — Coefficients for Factors in the Regression Equation**

To obtain information about the relative importance of the independent variables studied in relation to the criterion variable, multiple regression model was used. The model also helped in estimating the value of the dependent variable.

Multivariate regression analysis is made use of to predict the effect of more than one variable on the criterion variable or it may be used to determine the relative importance of a few variables in relation to the dependent variable. It is also made use of to estimate the value of the dependent variable. In order to arrive at the final regression equations, the correlation matrix involving the independent variables inclusive of the levels of education and earnings was drawn. The coefficients of correlation of the independent variables with earnings and between themselves were examined to determine the variables that should be included in the regression equation. According to Guodocor and Cochron, an equation based upon the best 3 or 4 variables might be a wise choice in fitting a regression equation. β coefficients are generally used for determining the relative importance of the independent variables in predicting the estimates of the dependent variables. This is because the β coefficients associated with different independent variables are expressed in terms of the unit of measure of the independent variables associated. They are the indices of change in the dependent variable with unit change in the respective independent variables. Consequently they do not indicate actual comparative significance of each independent variable. Hence, to derive at estimates of the dependent variable, these coefficients were standardised by multiplying them with the ratio of the standard deviation of independent variable by the standard deviation of dependent variable.

β-coefficients were computed for all the significant independent variables (inclusive of the various levels of education) in the final regression equation in respect to earnings. Thus, a set of nine regression equations were drawn to estimate the earnings of women with different levels of education, standardising for the influence of other wage-earner characteristics.

To evaluate the returns to alternative investments in education, both the net present values and the internal rates of return methods were used. The lifetime earnings were estimated making necessary adjustment for unemployment and taxes and standardising for the influence of independent variables other than education. The present values of the costs and benefits are compared as both differences and ratios at zero, five and six per cent discount rates. These estimates are from simple mean lifetime earnings figures and those from the estimates of lifetime earnings from the Final Regression. The internal rates of return are calculated from the regression estimates of the benefits.

The non-economic returns in terms of attitudes and behaviour towards the institutions of education, employment, marriage and family, politics, religion and social life are analysed using the descriptive method. Simple percentages are used to explain the differences in the attitudes and behaviour of women with different levels of education and also to explain the degree of consistency and dissonance between attitudes and behaviour among them.

**Scope and Limitations of the Study**

The study is concerned with the evaluation of the private

returns from education to employed women in Bangalore City, with regard to both economic and non-economic returns. The present investigation is different from other studies in the following respects :

In the estimation procedure of lifetime earnings, generally cross-sectional data, where average earnings of each age group in a given year are totalled, have been used, in this study, they have been estimated using data specific to the women respondents in the sample. These are supplemented by pay scale(s) collected from the establishments which facilitated the estimation of earnings of each of the women's working life.

Since the data for this study represent a much larger group of women belonging to various educational levels and occupation with diverse background, conclusions drawn from the analysis of these data will have general applicability.

Further, this study examines the non-economic returns from education that accrue to women while majority of the studies confine themselves to only the economic returns.

Inspite of the superiority of this study, a great number of assumptions had to be made in the processing of the data with respect to economic returns. In addition, only attitudes and behaviour of women have been considered to represent the non-economic benefits, though there are innumerable aspects to these returns.

In summary, this study has generated superior data which has allowed itself to multiple regression analysis of many factors as regressors to explain the variation in lifetime earnings. Consequently, the relationship between earnings and education can be specified to a greater extent than has been accomplished. Further, it has lent an insight into the non-economic returns from education which has hitherto been neglected.

## CHAPTER 4

# Profile of the Sample

In this chapter, information regarding the general characteristics of the respondents is presented. The variables included under general characteristics are age, religion, caste, mother-tongue, migration pattern, marital status, type of family, number of children, education, occupation and income of parents/husband/respondent. The data are presented and interpreted under the following sub-headings for the private, Central Government, Central Government Quasi, State Government, State Government Quasi and Corporation Sectors and comparisons made therein :

1. Characteristics of Employed Women.
2. Employment-pattern of Women.
3. Socio-economic Background of Employed Women.

## CHARACTERISTICS OF EMPLOYED WOMEN

### Age of the Respondents

TABLE No. 4.1

**Distribution of Respondents by Age**

| Organised Sectors | Below 20 Yrs. | 21-30 Years | 31-40 Years | 41-50 Years | 51-60 Years | Above 60 Yrs. |
|---|---|---|---|---|---|---|
| Private | 16.58 | 51.17 | 20.72 | 8.83 | 2.52 | 0.18 |
| Central Govt. | 1.90 | 56.10 | 24.76 | 15.24 | — | — |
| Central Govt. Quasi | 1.71 | 50.72 | 33.33 | 9.97 | 4.27 | — |
| State Govt. | 2.80 | 36.00 | 33.20 | 23.20 | 4.80 | — |
| State Govt. Quasi | — | 34.38 | 53.12 | 12.50 | — | — |
| Corporation | 12.21 | 34.88 | 31.98 | 18.02 | 2.91 | — |
| Total | 5.87 | 44.20 | 32.85 | 14.63 | 2.42 | 0.03 |

It may be observed from Table No. 4.1 that majority of the women employed in Bangalore City fall in the age-range 31 to 40 years. The total percentage in this range is 77.05. While the Central Government Sector has the highest proportion of respondents belonging to the age-range 21 to 30 (63.1 per cent), the Private and Central Government Quasi Sectors have an almost equal distribution of women in this age-group (51.17 and 50.72 per cent respectively). As high as 53.12 per cent of the respondents in the State Government Quasi fall in the age-range 31 to 40 years.

Among respondents in the various sectors of the organised sector, only the Private and Corporation indicate a high proportion of respondents below 20 years i.e., 16.58 and 12.21 per cent respectively. One explanation for this is that women employed in these sectors have either no education or less education, and hence were able to join the labour force at an younger age. Further, their occupation is either unskilled or semi-skilled in nature.

When the respondents are categorised into two groups on the basis of their ages : below and above 30 years of age, a higher proportion of respondents are above 30 years in the State Government and State Government Quasi Sectors than the others. This is because participation of women in the State services must have taken place earlier than their participation in other services. Further, their participation in the Private Sector appears to be a recent phenomenon as majority of the respondents in this sector are below 30 years of age. The high percentage of respondents below 30 years in this sector may also be due to the fact that it is easier to get jobs in the private than the public sectors.

In general, it is seen that more than 80 per cent of the women in the labour force are below 40 years of age.

**TABLE No. 4.2**

**Mean Age of Respondents by Sector of Employment**

| Organised Sectors | Mean Age |
|---|---|
| Private | 28.50 |
| Central Govt. | 30.50 |
| Central Govt. Quasi | 31.50 |
| State Govt. | 34.50 |
| State Govt. Quasi | 33.50 |
| Corporation | 32.50 |
| Total | 31.80 |

The above table reveals that the mean age of working women in Bangalore City is 31.8 years. The mean age of the respondents in the private sector is 28.5 years indicating that the proportion of women employees of the younger age-groups are concentrated here. In all the other sectors, the mean ages of the respondents range between 30.5 and 34.5 years.

This indicates that participation of women in the labour force is quite recent.

**Religion and Sect**

The population breakup by religion in Bangalore City[1] indicates that the Hindus form the largest group, the percentage being 76.84 per cent. Muslims and Christians form 14.62 per cent and 7.47 per cent respectively. Other religions form only 1.07 per cent of the total population. The following table gives the distribution of respondents by religion.

TABLE No. 4.3

**Distribution of Respondents by Religion**

| Sectors | Hindus | Christians | Muslims | Others |
|---|---|---|---|---|
| Private | 59.28 | 31.53 | 9.01 | 0.18 |
| Central Govt. | 89.52 | 10.48 | — | — |
| Central Govt. Quasi | 86.90 | 11.40 | 1.70 | — |
| State Govt. | 76.80 | 15.60 | 6.80 | 0.80 |
| State Govt. Quasi | 71.87 | 28.13 | — | — |
| Corporation | 92.44 | 6.98 | 0.58 | — |
| Total | 79.47 | 17.35 | 3.01 | 0.16 |

1. As the break-up of religions for women separately is not available, the break-up for the total population has been taken to make comparisons.
Source : Census of India (Mysore) 1971, Part 1-A, Vol. II, General Report.

It may be observed from the above table that as high as 79.47 per cent of the employed women in Bangalore City are Hindus. The Christians form the next highest proportion of the employed women, the percentage being 17.35 per cent. Only 3.01 per cent of the respondents are Muslims.

Among the various sectors, the proportion of Hindus is highest in the Corporation (92.44 per cent), followed by Central and Central Government Quasi Sectors (i.e., 89.52 and 86.9 per cent respectively). The Christians form 31.63 per cent and 28.13 per cent respectively of the respondents in the Private and State Government Quasi Sectors. There were no Muslim respondents in the Central and State Government Quasi Sectors.

The data shows that the proportion of Christian employed women to Christian women in Bangalore City is quite high (7.47 : 17.35), that of Hindus is almost the same (76.84 : 79.47) and that of Muslim women is quite low (14.62 : 3.01).

The following table gives the proportion of respondents in the labour force by religion to their respective proportion in the total population.

TABLE No. 4.4

**Distribution of Respondents in the Labour Force to the Total Population by Religion**

| Religions | Percentage of respondents in the work force | Percentage to the total population | Ratio |
|---|---|---|---|
| Hindus | 79.47 | 76.84 | 1.03 |
| Christians | 17.35 | 7.47 | 2.32 |
| Muslims | 3.01 | 14.62 | 0.21 |
| Others | 0.16 | 1.07 | 0.15 |

It may be observed from the above table that the proportion of Christians entering the labour force is twice that of their proportion in the population. While the ratio of Hindu respondents to their distribution in the total population is almost equal, i.e., 1.03, that of the Muslims is very low, 0.21. The high participation of the Christian women perhaps is due to the less inhibitions Christians have in entering the labour force than the others.

The table no. 4.5 is confined only to the Hindu respondents. As can be observed from the table, Brahmins form the highest proportion of the employed women in all services in Bangalore City, except that of the Corporation, the total percentage being 42.58. The next highest percentage is that of the Scheduled Castes and Scheduled Tribes, 20.31 per cent. The remaining six castes other than the Brahmins and the Scheduled Castes and Tribes together form only 37.21 per cent of the sample.

Brahmins form the majority among all the sectors, except the Corporation where only 9.32 per cent are Brahmins. As high as 72.34 per cent of women in the Central Government Sector are Brahmins. In the Corporation, the proportion of women belonging to the Scheduled Castes and Scheduled Tribes is highest. They form 74.53 per cent of the sample. While the percentage of women who are Lingayats is highest in the State Government Quasi (17.4 per cent), that of the Trading and Agricultural Castes are highest in the Private Sector (20.6 per cent and 18.51 per cent respectively).

In general, Brahmins and Scheduled Castes and Tribes form the highest proportion of the sample. One explanation for this is that Brahmins have been exposed to education and urban working life for a long period. In the case of SC/ST, their high percentage especially in the Corporation is due to the relation caste has with their occupation i.e., scavenging. They have been doing this job for centuries, while other castes rarely do it.

TABLE No. 4.5

Distribution of Respondents by Caste[2]

| Sectors | Brahmins | Lingayats | Trading Caste | Agricultural Caste | Warrior Soldier Caste | Artisan Servicing Caste | SC/ST | Other Castes |
|---|---|---|---|---|---|---|---|---|
| Private | 37.91 | 4.78 | 20.60 | 18.31 | 4.48 | 6.56 | 4.78 | 2.38 |
| Central Covt. | 72.34 | — | 8.51 | 4.25 | 2.13 | 3.19 | 7.45 | 2.13 |
| Central Govt. Quasi | 40.45 | 5.82 | 8.74 | 11.65 | 8.18 | 9.39 | 15.53 | 3.24 |
| State Govt. | 47.98 | 12 63 | 8.06 | 8.08 | 6.06 | 8.08 | 11.11 | — |
| State Govt Quasi | 47.83 | 17.40 | 8.69 | 8.69 | 4.35 | 4.35 | 8.69 | — |
| Corporation | 9.32 | 3.10 | — | 3.73 | 3.73 | 5.59 | 74 53 | — |
| Total | 42.58 | 7.23 | 8.75 | 9.09 | 4.75 | 6.11 | 20.31 | 1 28 |

2. The caste codes followed here are taken from the Bangalore City Survey Project of the Institute for Social and Economic Change, Bangalore, 1974.

**Mother-tongue of the Respondents**

The percentage break-up of the general population in Bangalore City indicates that the mother-tongue of 34 per cent of the population is Kannada, 25 per cent Tamil, 17 per cent Telugu, 10 per cent Urdu and 14 per cent other languages like Malayalam, Marathi, Tulu, Hindi, etc. The table no. 4.6 gives the distribution of the respondents by mother-tongue.

It may be observed from the table no. 4.6 that the mother-tongue of 32.66 per cent of the sample is Kannada. The next highest percentage is of those whose mother-tongue is Tamil (29.58 per cent), followed by Telugu (21.1 per cent). Respondents whose mother-tongue comprises of these three languages together form 83.34 per cent of the sample.

As would be expected, the mother-tongue of majority of the respondents in the State and State Govt. Quasi Sectors is Kannada. The proportion of Kannada speaking respondents in each of these sectors is around 47 per cent. In the Private Sector, the percentage of those whose mother-tongues are Tamil and Telugu is higher than that of Kannada. The percentage difference between Tamil and Telugu speaking respondents and Kannada speaking respondents is in the order 19.28 and 2.7 per cent respectively. In the Corporation, the mother-tongue of as high as 67.44 per cent of the respondents is Telugu. It means that two out of every three women (Scavengers) in Bangalore City are Telugu-speaking. The proportion of respondents whose mother-tongue is Urdu is highest in the private sector ; the percentage being 9.01. Over 8 per cent of the respondents whose mother-tongue is Malayalam are from the private and Central Government Quasi Sectors. Nearly 10 per cent of the respondents in the Central Government Quasi Sector belong to the other mother-tongue groups.

TABLE No. 4.6

Distribution of Respondents by Mother-tongue

| Sectors | Kannada | Tamil | Telugu | Urdu | Malayalam | Marathi | Others |
|---|---|---|---|---|---|---|---|
| Private | 17.12 | 36.40 | 19.82 | 9.01 | 8.65 | 1.44 | 7.56 |
| Central Govt. | 37.14 | 40.00 | 8.57 | — | 5.71 | 1.91 | 6.66 |
| Central Govt. Quasi | 31.34 | 34.19 | 12.54 | 1.43 | 8.26 | 2.28 | 9.97 |
| State Govt. | 47.20 | 25.20 | 12.00 | 6.80 | 3.20 | 2.00 | 3.60 |
| State Govt. Quasi | 46.88 | 31.25 | 6.25 | — | 6.25 | 3.13 | 6.24 |
| Corporation | 16.28 | 10.47 | 67.44 | 0.58 | 0.58 | 4.07 | 0.58 |
| Total | 32.66 | 29 38 | 21.10 | 2.97 | 5.44 | 2.47 | 5.77 |

TABLE No. 4.7

**Place of Birth and Present Address of the Respondents**

| Sectors | Place of birth | | Present address | |
|---|---|---|---|---|
| | Within Bangalore City (Residents) | Outside Bangalore City (Migrants) | Within Bangalore City | Outside Bangalore City |
| Private | 64.14 | 35.86 | 96.40 | 3.60 |
| Central Govt. | 42.86 | 37.14 | 96.19 | 3.81 |
| Central Govt. Quasi | 43.31 | 56.68 | 90.60 | 9.40 |
| State Govt. | 53.60 | 46.40 | 98.80 | 1.20 |
| State Govt. Quasi | 43.75 | 36.25 | 96.88 | 3.12 |
| Corporation | 58.14 | 41.86 | 100.00 | — |
| Total | 50.97 | 49.03 | 96.32 | 3.68 |

It is observed from the above table that nearly fifty per cent of the respondents are in-migrants to Bengalore City. While more than fifty per cent of the respondents in the Public Sector belonged to places outside Bangalore City, in the Private Sector as high as 64.14 per cent respondents belong to Bangalore City by birth. It is seen that labour migration is least for private sector jobs (35.86 per cent).

Considering their present address, majority of the respondents live in Bangalore City. A negligible percentage live in the outskirts of Bangalore City, it being the highest among Central Government Quasi respondents, 9.4 per cent. They commute every day for work from outside the City.

## Migration

According to a study in demography, "Mobility in India is quite considerable, about one-third of a total population was enumerated outside their place of birth[3]". A study of the previous table (Table No. 4.7) also reveals that nearly 50 per cent of the respondents are from places other than Bangalore City. At this stage, it would be interesting to study the migration pattern of the respondents—migration within the district, States, inter-state and rural-urban and urban-urban. A migrant, as defined in this study, "is one who was not born in Bangalore City, but was residing the City"[4]. Tables 4.8, 4.9 4.10 indicate the migration pattern of the respondents.

TABLE No. 4.8

**Urban-Urban and Rural-Urban Migration of the Respondents**

| Sectors | Urban-Urban Migration | Rural-Urban Migration |
|---|---|---|
| Private | 55.27 | 44.73 |
| Central Govt. | 44.99 | 55.01 |
| Central Govt. Quasi | 47.24 | 52.76 |
| State Govt. | 76.72 | 23.28 |
| State Govt. Quasi | 88.89 | 11.11 |
| Corporation | 33.33 | 66.67 |
| Total | 58.41 | 41.59 |

It may be observed from the above table that of those who are in-migrants to Bangalore City, 58.41 per cent of the respondents

3. Ashish Bose : "Studies in Inaia's Urbanisation, 1901-1971" 1973, p. 148.
4. Institute for Social and Economic Change, 1974, op. cit.

have migrated from urban areas and 41.50 per cent from the rural areas. The highest proportion of urban-urban migrants are found in the State Government Quasi and State Government Sectors ; the percentages being 88.89 and 78.72 respectively. In the Corporation as high as 66.67 per cent of the migrants have a rural-base. However, it is surprising to note that the percentages of rural-urban migration is higher than the urban-urban migration in the Central Government and Central Government Quasi Sectors.

Table No. 4.9 indicates the intra and inter-district migration of respondents.

TABLE No. 4.9

**Intra and Inter-district Migration of Respondens**

| Sectors | Within Bangalore District | Out-side Bangalore District |
|---|---|---|
| Private | 13.08 | 86.92 |
| Central Govt. | 9.99 | 90.01 |
| Central Govt. Quasi | 15.06 | 84.94 |
| State Govt. | 13.79 | 86.21 |
| State Govt. Quasi | — | 100.00 |
| Corporation | 9.72 | 90.28 |
| Total | 11.99 | 88.01 |

As can be observed from the above table, 88 per cent of the migrants are from districts other than Bangalore District. Only around 12 per cent of them have migrated from within district. In all the sectors, more than 85 per cent of the in-migrants are from outside Bangalore District. In the State Government Quasi Sector, there is cent per cent migration from outside Bangalore District. The highest proportion of migration within the district is found in the Central Government Quasi (15.06 per cent).

The following table gives the intra-and inter-state migration of the migrants.

TABLE No. 4.10

**Intra and Inter-State Migration of Migrants**

| Sectors | Migration within Karnataka State | Migration from outside Karnataka | | | |
|---|---|---|---|---|---|
| | | Tamil Nadu | Andhra Pradesh | Kerala | Others |
| Private | 45.23 | 21.11 | 6.03 | 20 60 | 6.03 |
| Central Govt. | 55.00 | 20.00 | 6.67 | 11.66 | 6.67 |
| Central Govt. Quasi | 57.28 | 15.58 | 7.54 | 15 58 | 4.02 |
| State Govt. | 75.00 | 10.34 | 8.62 | 2 59 | 3.45 |
| State Govt. Quasi | 66.68 | 5.55 | 5.55 | 11.11 | 11 11 |
| Corporation | 36.11 | 8.33 | 54.17 | 1.39 | — |
| Total | 56.05 | 13 49 | 14.76 | 10.49 | 5.21 |

Of the respondents who have migrated to Bangalore City, it is observed that 56.05 per cent have done so from within the State. Around 39 per cent of the migrants are from the other three South Indian States—Tamil Nadu, Andhra Pradesh and Kerala. Only 5.21 per cent are from rest of India. For all the sectors except Corporation, majority of the migrants are from within the State, the percentage being the highest for State Government and State Government Quasi Sectors i.e., 75 and 66.68 per cent respectively. In the Corporation, as high as 54.17 per cent of the migrants are from Andhra Pradesh.

While the proportion of migrants from Tamil Nadu is highest in the Private (21.11 per cent) and Central Government Sectors (20 per cent), for those from Kerala it is highest in the Private Sector (20.6 per cent).

One of the reasons for the high rate of migration may be the availability of jobs in Bangalore City.

**Stay in Bangalore City**

TABLE No. 4.11

**Migrants by Number of Years in Bangalore City**

| Sectors | Less than 5 Year | 6-10 Years | 11-15 Years | 16-20 Years | 21-25 Years | More than 25 Yrs |
|---|---|---|---|---|---|---|
| Private | 23.13 | 20 61 | 13.08 | 16.55 | 9.04 | 15 39 |
| Central Govt. | 17.14 | 20.00 | 10.48 | 10.48 | 17.14 | 24.76 |
| Central Govt. Quasi | 23.36 | 9.97 | 11.68 | 8.55 | 7.41 | 39.03 |
| State Govt. | 48.00 | 9.60 | 10.40 | 10 00 | 4 80 | 17.20 |
| State Govt. Quasi | — | 38.90 | 5.56 | 27.77 | 22 22 | 5.56 |
| Corporation | 5.57 | 6.95 | 12.68 | 11.49 | 10.11 | 53.20 |
| Total | 19.87 | 17.67 | 10.65 | 14.14 | 11.78 | 25 89 |

While nearly 55 per cent of the migrants have stayed in Bangalore City between 6 and 25 years, around 25 per cent have lived in Bangalore City for more than 25 years and another 20 per cent for less than 5 years. In the Corporation, as high as 53 2 per cent of the migrants have lived in Bangalore City for more than 25 years. The next highest proportion in this group is in the Central Government Quasi Sector (39.03 per cent). In the State Government, 48 per cent of the migrants have stayed in Bangalore City for less than 5 years. Around 45 per-cent in the Private Sector have stayed for less than 10 years.

**Marital Status of the Respondents**

TABLE No. 4.12

**Distribution of Respondents by their Marital Status**

| Sectors | Un-married | Married | Widowed | Div-orced | Sepa-rated |
|---|---|---|---|---|---|
| Private | 43.78 | 47.57 | 6.49 | — | 2.16 |
| Central Govt. | 46.67 | 46.67 | 6.67 | — | — |
| Central Govt. Quasi | 35.90 | 52.42 | 10.26 | — | 1.43 |
| State Govt. | 28.80 | 59.20 | 10.40 | — | 1.60 |
| State Govt. Quasi | 28.13 | 58 75 | 3.13 | — | — |
| Corporation | 11.05 | 66.86 | 21.51 | — | 0.58 |
| Total | 32.39 | 56.01 | 9.74 | — | 0.96 |

As can be observed from the above table, majority of the respondents are married (56.91 per cent). Over 32 per cent of the respondents are unmarried and nearly 10 per cent are widowed. While there are only 0.96 per cent separated, there are no divorcees in the sample.

The proportion of unmarried women is highest in the Central Government (46.67 per cent) and Private Sector (43.78 per cent). This may be due to the higher percentage of respondents of the younger age-groups in these sectors, i.e., below 30 years (refer Table No. 4.1). In the Corporation, though around 47 per cent of the respondents are below 30 years of age, only 11.05 per cent are unmarried. This is due to the early age at marriage of the respondents in this sector (refer Table No. 4.13). However, a majority of the respondents are married. More than 52 per cent of the respondents in all the sectors except the Central Government Quasi and Private Sectors are married. The highest percentage of widowed respondents are in the Corporation, 21.51 per cent. While the percentage of separated women is negligible in all the sectors, it is highest in the Private Sector (2.16 per cent or 11 respondents). There are no divorcees in all the sectors. This may be due to the practice of divorce being an unacceptable norm among Indian women. They prefer to be forced to be separated than divorced.

## Age at Marriage

One of the major social evils sought to be curbed by legislation is child marriage. The first legislation in this direction was the Civil Marriage Act, 1872, which laid down the age at marriage is 14 years. As only a very small section of the people married under this Act, the problem of child marriage continued. In 1929, the Sarda Act or the Child Marriage Restraint Act was passed. The minimum age according to this Act for males was 18 and for females 14. This was further amended in 1949 raising the age for females to 15 years. While there are many personal laws like the Hindu Marriage Act, 1955 ; the Parsi Marriage and Divorce Act, 1936 ; the Christian Marriage Act, 1872, etc., having their own minimum age of marriage, it is only the Special Marriage Act of 1954, a post-independence legislation which provides for a secular marriage regulation irrespective of the religious affiliation of the parties. It fixes the minimum age at 21 and 18 for males and females respectively. The table no. 4.13 gives the age at marriage of respondents.

Though the Special Marriage Act had fixed the minimum age of marriage for a female at 18 years, 31.17 per cent of the respondents have married below this age. Of them, around 8 per cent have married when below 13 years of age (Sarda Act). Majority of the respondents have married between ages 18

TABLE No. 4.13

**Distribution of Respondents by Age at Marriage**

| Sectors | Below 13 Yrs | 14-17 Yrs | 18-24 Yrs | 25-30 Yrs | Above 31 Yrs | Mean age at marriage |
|---|---|---|---|---|---|---|
| Private | 7.69 | 29.9 | 52.64 | 6.98 | 1.60 | 19.71 |
| Central Govt. | 3.57 | 7.14 | 59.14 | 24.79 | 3.36 | 22.77 |
| Central Govt. Quasi | 4.00 | 26.33 | 41.78 | 24.00 | 4.89 | 21.67 |
| State Govt. | 5.06 | 18.66 | 57 18 | 18.73 | 3.37 | 21.24 |
| State Govt. Quasi | — | 8.70 | 60.87 | 26.08 | 4 35 | 23.07 |
| Corporation | 29.41 | 48.37 | 19.61 | 2.61 | — | 16 25 |
| Total | 8.29 | 22.88 | 48.54 | 17.03 | 3.26 | 20.78 |

and 24, i.e., 48.54 per cent. Only 3.26 per cent of the women married when they were 31 years and above.

It is observed that as high as 77.78 per cent of the respondents in the Corporation have married when they were below 17 years of age. Of them, 48.37 per cent have married between ages 14 and 17, and 29.41 per cent below 13 years. In the State Government Quasi Sector, there was not a single respondent who had married at the age of 13 and below.

Majority of the respondents in all the sectors except the Corporation have married between ages 18 and 24 In the Corporation only 19.61 per cent of the respondents married between these ages. In the State Government Quasi, Central Government and Central Government Quasi Sectors, 26.08 per cent, 24.79 per cent and 24 per cent respectively of the respondents have married between ages 25 and 30 years. Those who have married at the age of 31 years and above form a very negligible percentage, it being the highest among Central Government respondents, i.e., 5.36 per cent.

**Mean Age at Marriage** (refer Table No. 4.13)

Normally in an urban setting, due to the lengthening of the period of education, and the relative occupational, economic and social independence of women, one would expect a higher mean age at marriage. The national mean for urban females is 19.20 years[5]. It may be observed from Table No. 4.13 that the mean age at marriage for all the respondents is 20.78 years, which is higher than the national average. The difference is of the order of 1.58 years.

The average age at marriage is around 23 years for State Government Quasi and Central Government respondents and 21.5 years for those in Central Government Quasi and State Government Sectors. While the mean age is 19.71 years for those in the Private Sector, it is as low as 16.25 years for those in the Corporation.

**Respondents by Number of Children**

Among the married respondents in the sample an almost equal proportion of about 27 per cent have one and two children respectively. They together form around 55 per cent of the married respondents. The next highest percentage is of those having three children (14.3 per cent).

More than 50 per cent of the respondents in all the sectors except the Corporation have one or two children. While the percentage of respondents having three children is highest in the Corporation and Private Sectors, it ranges between 8.93 per cent and 13.04 per cent in the other sectors. In the Corporation, 15.03 per cent and 24.84 per cent of the respondents have

5. Towards Equality, Report of the Committee on the Status of Women in India, ICSSR, 1974, p. 23.

**TABLE No. 4.14**

**Distribution of Respondents by Number of Children**

| Sectors | No. Children | One | Two | Three | Four | Five and above | Mean No. of Children |
|---|---|---|---|---|---|---|---|
| Private | 14 10 | 28.68 | 26.92 | 19.55 | 8.01 | 6.73 | 2.44 |
| Central Govt. | 12.50 | 23.57 | 37.50 | 8.93 | 5.36 | 7.14 | 2.00 |
| Central Govt. Quasi | 13.78 | 33.33 | 28.00 | 11.11 | 4.00 | 9.78 | 2.20 |
| State Govt. | 11.80 | 31.46 | 26.97 | 12.92 | 10.52 | 6.33 | 2.39 |
| State Govt. Quasi | 21.74 | 30.43 | 26.09 | 13.04 | 8.70 | — | 2.13 |
| Corporation | 3.92 | 18.30 | 17.65 | 20.26 | 15.03 | 24.84 | 3.76 |
| Total | 12.97 | 27.80 | 27.19 | 14.30 | 8.60 | 9.14 | 2.40 |

four, five and more children respectively, i.e., nearly 40 per cent have four and more than four children.

The mean number of children for all the sectors together is 2.49. The average number of children is highest among respondents in the Corporation, (3.76), followed by those in the private and State Government Sectors (2.40). In the remaining sectors the mean ranges are from 2 to 2.2.

**Education of the Respondents**

It may be observed from the table no. 4.15 that illiterates form 15.43 per cent of the sample. 17.33 per cent of the respondents have secondary education. While 19.88 per cent of the respondents have school level vocational and technical education, 16.52 per cent have college level professional and technical education. Over 15 per cent of the sample are graduates.

Among the various sectors, the proportion of respondents with primary education only is highest in the Private Sector, the percentage being 27.92 per cent.

38.10 per cent of the respondents in the Central Government are graduates. In the Central Government Quasi Sector, as high as 38.18 per cent of the respondents have high school education. The next highest percentage of respondents in this sector are those with vocational education 18.52 per cent.

In the State Government, 38.00 per cent and 26 per cent of the respondents have school level vocational and technical education and college level professional and technical education respectively.

In the State Government Quasi Sector, as high as 96.87 per cent of the respondents are secondary educated and above. Of them nearly 22 per cent and 25 per cent have secondary education and school level vocational education respectively. Another 21.83 per cent and 28.13 per cent are graduates and professional and technical educated respectively.

TABLE No. 4.15

**Educational Qualification of the Respondents**

| Sectors | Illiterates | Lower Primary | Upper Primary | Secondary | Vocational Edn. | Inter /PUC | Graduates | Post-Graduates | Prof./Tech. Edn. |
|---|---|---|---|---|---|---|---|---|---|
| Private | 7.39 | 10.08 | 17.84 | 19.64 | 18.02 | 2.16 | 4.69 | 4.32 | 13.68 |
| Central Govt. | 0.95 | 1.91 | 1.91 | 18.10 | 12.38 | 8.56 | 38.10 | 4.76 | 13.33 |
| Central Govt. Quasi | 14.53 | — | — | 38.18 | 18.52 | 5.70 | 13.39 | 1.42 | 8.26 |
| State Govt. | 3.20 | 2.40 | 4.40 | 4.00 | 38.00 | 2.00 | 12.00 | 7.60 | 26.00 |
| State Govt. Quasi | 3.13 | — | — | 21.86 | 25.00 | — | 21.88 | — | 28.13 |
| Corporation | 63.37 | 11.06 | 4.07 | 2.33 | 6.98 | 1.16 | 1.74 | 1.74 | 7.56 |
| Total | 15.43 | 4.24 | 4.70 | 17.33 | 19.88 | 3.26 | 15.30 | 3.32 | 16.52 |

The proportion of illiterates is highest in the Corporation. (63.37 per cent), or nearly two out of every three respondents are unskilled workers (i.e., scavengers). About 11 per cent of the respondents in this sector have lower primary education.

As revealed in Table No. 4.7, nearly 50 per cent of the respondents belong to places other than Bangalore City. However, on a further analysis it was observed that among the literate women, more than 70 per cent received their education in Bangalore City. This shows that not all women have migrated to Bangalore City for purposes of employment. Around 20 per cent of the employed women might have migrated for education and secured jobs also.

**Place of Study**

TABLE No. 4.16

**Distribution of Respondents by Place of Study**

| Sectors | Within Bangalore City | Outside Bangalore City |
|---|---|---|
| Private | 76.65 | 23.35 |
| Central Govt. | 68.27 | 31.73 |
| Central Govt. Quasi | 73.67 | 26.33 |
| State Govt. | 76.86 | 23.14 |
| State Govt. Quasi | 58.06 | 41.94 |
| Corporation | 71.43 | 28.57 |
| Total | 70 82 | 29.18 |

Nearly 70 per cent of the respondents have received their education in Bangalore City. Of those who have received their education in Bangalore City, around 20 per cent have migrated for purpose of education. The rest (29.18 per cent) who have migrated to Bangalore City after receiving their education, mainly consisted of those whose main purpose was to secure employment. The proportion of the respondents who have received their education outside Bangalore City is highest in the State Government Quasi and Central Government Sectors. Their respective percentages are 41.94 per cent and 31.73 per cent.

**Respondents by Type of Educational Institution Attended**

TABLE No. 4.17

**Distribution of Respondents by Type of Educational Institution Attended**

| Sectors | Government | Corporation | Private | Missionary/Convent |
|---|---|---|---|---|
| Private | 44.53 | 2.34 | 50.19 | 2.92 |
| Central Govt. | 27.88 | 1.92 | 66.35 | 3.85 |
| Central Govt. Quasi | 36.00 | 1.67 | 57.67 | 4.67 |
| State Govt. | 39.67 | — | 58.26 | 2.07 |
| State Govt. Quasi | 38.71 | — | 58.06 | 3.23 |
| Corporation | 49.21 | 11.11 | 39.68 | — |
| Total | 39.34 | 2.84 | 55.04 | 2.78 |

Majority of the respondents have received their education from private institutions (55.04 per cent). While 39.34 per cent are from Government Institutions, a meagre 2.84 per cent and 2.78 per cent are from Corporation and Convent/Missionary Institutions respectively.

In all the sectors except the Corporation, more than 50 per cent of the respondents have attended private institutions, the percentage being the highest in the Central Government Sector

(66.35 per cent). Of the respondents who attended Government institutions, the proportion is highest in the Corporation (49.21 per cent), followed by the Private Sector (44.55 per cent). About 11 per cent of the respondents in the Corporation Sector have attended Corporation institutions. Thus, as high as 60.32 per cent of the respondents in the Corporation have attended Government and Corporation institutions. This may be due to the lower economic status of the parents of the respondents (refer Table No. 4.17) and their inability to send their children to private institutions. However, 39.68 per cent have attended private institutions, which surprisingly is a high figure for their background.

The high concentration of respondents in the private educational institutions may be explained through the assumption that quality education is basically imparted by private institutions.

**Respondents by Class Obtained**

TABLE No. 4.18

**Distribution of Respondents by Class Secured**

| Sectors | Distinction | 1st Class | 2nd Class | 3rd Class | Failures |
|---|---|---|---|---|---|
| Private | 2.18 | 20.71 | 32.70 | 31.06 | 13.35 |
| Central Govt. | 1.98 | 26.73 | 47.52 | 22.77 | 0 99 |
| Central Govt. Quasi | 1.33 | 21.00 | 36.33 | 40.33 | 1.00 |
| State Govt. | 1.73 | 22.08 | 38.53 | 35.07 | 2.60 |
| State Govt. Quasi | — | 16.13 | 38.71 | 45.16 | — |
| Corporation | 1.56 | 2.56 | 51.28 | 38.46 | 6.13 |
| Total | 1.46 | 18.20 | 40.85 | 35.48 | 4.01 |

Table No. 4.18 refers to those who have taken public examinations only, i.e., matriculation and above, since class-wise breakups is given only from this level. Further, it refers only to the highest examination taken by the respondents. It may be observed from the above table that majority of the respondents have passed their highest examination with a second class (45.85 per cent). While 35.48 per cent have passed with a third class, only 18.2 per cent have done so with a first class.

The percentage of first class holders is highest among the Central Government respondents, 26.73 per cent. In the private, Central Government Quasi and State Government Sectors, the proportion of first class holders range between 20.71 per cent and 22.08 per cent. Though the respondents from the Corporation have the highest percentage of second classes (51.28 per cent), a comparison with other sectors could not be made as only 21.51 per cent of the respondents in this sector have taken public examinations.

The percentage of distinction holders and failures form a negligible percentage of 1.46 and 4.01 respectively. The proportion of failures is highest among respondents in the private sector (13.35 per cent).

## 2. EMPLOYMENT-PATTERN OF WOMEN

In this part, the employment pattern of working women with regard to sector of employment, nature of employment, hours of work, occupation, income, number of jobs changed and earnings through other means is presented.

**Sector of Employment**

TABLE No. 4.19

**Distribution of Respondents by Sector of Employment**

| Private | Central Govt. | Central Govt. Quasi | State Govt. | State Govt. Quasi | Corporation | Total |
|---|---|---|---|---|---|---|
| 37.88 | 7.17 | 23.96 | 17.07 | 2.18 | 11.74 | 100 00 |

The private sector appears to be the single largest employer of women in Bangalore City. 37.88 per cent of employed women belong to the private sector. The next highest percentage of respondents are from the Central Government Quasi establishments. A major share of the establishments in this sector consists of public undertakings in the sphere of industry. Next in absorption are the State Government and Corporation which together provide for 28.81 per cent of the total employment for women. However, when the categories of the public sector are considered together, they provide for 62.12 per cent of the total employment for women in Bangalore City, the rest i.e., 37.88 per cent being provided by the private sector.

**Nature of Employment**

TABLE No. 4.20

**Distribution of Respondents by Nature of Employment**

| Sectors | Permanent | Temporary | Stipendary and Apprenticeship | Contract | Daily wages |
|---|---|---|---|---|---|
| Private | 91.35 | 7.39 | 1.26 | — | — |
| Central Govt. | 96.33 | 3.67 | — | — | — |
| Central Govt. Quasi | 98.86 | — | 1.15 | — | — |
| State Govt. | 97.60 | 0.80 | 0.80 | 0.80 | — |
| State Govt. Quasi | 100.00 | — | — | — | — |
| Corporation | 98.84 | 0 58 | 0.58 | — | — |
| Total | 97.16 | 2 07 | 0.63 | 0.13 | — |

On an average, around 97 per cent of the employed women hold permanent jobs. 2.07 per cent of the respondents hold temporary jobs and a negligible percentage of 0.63 and 0.13 are on stipendary/apprenticeship and contract respectively.

All the respondents hold permanent jobs in the State Government Quasi Sector. In the other sectors, barring the private sector, more than 96 per cent are permanent employees. In the private sector, a relatively less percentage of the respondents hold permanent jobs, 91.35 per cent. The proportion of respondents who hold temporary jobs is highest in the private sector, the percentage being 7.39 per cent.

**Occupation[6] of the Repondents**

From the table no. 4.21 it may be observed that majority of the employed women are engaged in clerical and related occupations and in production oriented jobs. The percentage of women in these occupations are 29.47 and 29.62 respectively. 22.57 per cent of the employed women are engaged in professional and technical occupations. While around 17 per-cent are service workers, a negligible percentage of 1.28 and 0.18 are involved in administrative/executive and sales occupations respectively.

In the private, Central Government and Central Government Quasi Sectors majority of the respondents are employed as production and related workers, transport and communication equipment operators and labourers. Their respective percentages in these sectors are 55.68, 55.24 and 64.39. While the bulk of these respondents in the private sector are labourers, in the Central Government sector they are telephone operators and labourers. In the Central Government Quasi sector majority are production and related workers in industries.

6. The classification of occupations followed here are as those followed by the Bangalore City Survey Project of the Institute for Social and Economic Change. The classified list of occupations is given in Appendix C.

TABLE No. 4.21

**Distribution of Respondents by their Occupation**

| Sectors | Professional Technical etc. | Administrative Executive, etc. | Clerical and related workers | Sales workers | Service workers | Production, Transport & Equipment Operators & Labourers |
|---|---|---|---|---|---|---|
| Private | 29.55 | — | 9.91 | 1.08 | 3.78 | 55.68 |
| Central Govt. | 5.71 | 1.91 | 32.38 | — | 4.76 | 55.24 |
| Central Govt. Quasi | 5.41 | 3.42 | 24.79 | — | 1.99 | 64.39 |
| State Govt. | 57.20 | 1.20 | 33.20 | — | 6.00 | 2.40 |
| State Govt. Quasi | 21.88 | — | 71.88 | — | 6.24 | — |
| Corporation | 15.70 | 1.16 | 4.65 | — | 78.49 | — |
| Total | 22.57 | 1.28 | 29.47 | 0.18 | 16.88 | 29.62 |

In the State Government Sector, 57.2 per cent of the respondents are engaged in professional and technical occupations. The next highest percentage of respondents in this category are from the private sector, 29.55 per cent. Majority of these respondents are teachers and nurses.

Around 72 per cent of the respondents in the State Government Quasi Sector are clerical and related workers.

As high as 78.49 per cent of the respondents in the Corporation are service workers. The bulk of these respondents constitute the sweepers and the ayahs.

A comparison of Tables 4.21 and 4.15 reveals that while the illiterates and primary educated respondents in the Corporation are service workers, those in the private sector are labourers. The tables also reveal a tendency for educated women to aspire for jobs in production, clerical and professional/technical occupations.

It may be observed from the table no. 4.22 that more than 98 per cent of the employed women work six days a week. Only in the private sector nearly 7 per cent work for five days a week.

As for the number of working hours per week, as high as 82.43 per cent of the employed women work between 43 and 48 hours/week.

Among the various sectors, majority of the respondents work between 43 and 48 hours/week. The proportion of respondents who work for less than 36 hours/week is highest in the State Government Sector, 27.6 per cent. They constitute the teachers Nearly 20 per cent of the respondents in the private sector work for more than 48 hours/week. They constitute the production labourers who work betwen 54 and 60 hours/week. Around 12 per cent of the respondents in the Private, Central Government Quasi and State Government Sectors work between 37 and 42 hours per week.

TABLE No. 4.22

Distribution of Respondents by Number of Working Days and Working Hours per Week

| Sectors | Working days/week | | Working hours/week | | | |
|---|---|---|---|---|---|---|
| | Five | Six | Less than 36 hrs. | 37 to 42 hrs. | 43 to 48 hrs. | More than 48 hrs. |
| Private | 6.67 | 93.33 | 9.19 | 11.71 | 59.28 | 19.82 |
| Central Govt. | — | 100.00 | — | 2.86 | 97.14 | — |
| Central Govt. Quasi | — | 100.00 | — | 11.11 | 88.89 | — |
| State Govt. | 0.80 | 99.20 | 27.60 | 12.40 | 56.00 | 2.00 |
| State Govt. Quasi | — | 100.00 | — | — | 100.00 | — |
| Corporation | — | 100.00 | 0.58 | 6.40 | 91.28 | 1.74 |
| Total | 1.24 | 98.76 | 6.23 | 7.41 | 82.43 | 3.93 |

**Income**

It may be observed from Table 4.23 that the maximum percentage of employed women fall in the income ranges Rs. 301-500/- and 501-750/- per month. The percentages of women who fall in these ranges a 30.52 per cent and 34.03 per cent respectively. Thus, about 65 per cent of the working women get an income ranging between Rs. 301/- and Rs. 750/- per month. While there is a steady increase in the percentange of women who fall in the successively increasing income ranges from less than Rs. 150/- to Rs. 501-750/-, there is a decline in the percentages from the range Rs. 751-1000/- and beyond that.

In the private Sector, 41.44 per cent of the respondents earn less than Rs 150/- per month, and 27.39 per cent between Rs. 150/- and 300/-. Thus, when the percentages are combined, nearly 69 per cent of the respondents earn less than Rs. 300/- per month.

44.76 per cent and 39.05 per cent of the respondents in the Central Government Sector fall in the income ranges Rs. 301-500/- and Rs. 501-750/- respectively. Thus, 83.81 per cent of the Central Government respondents earn between Rs. 301/- and 750/- per month.

As high as 61.54 per cent of the Central Government Quasi respondents fall in the Rs. 501-750/- income range.

In the State Government and State Government Quasi Sectors majority of the respondents earn between Rs. 301/- and 750/-. The percentage for the State Government is 78.40 per-cent, whereas it is 65.63 per cent for the State Government Quasi Sector. The percentage of respondents who earn Rs. 751-1,000/- and Rs. 1,001-1,500/- is highest in the State Government Quasi. The percentages in these income ranges are 25.00 and 9.38 per cent respectively.

More than 85 per cent of the respondents in the Corporation earn between Rs. 150/- and Rs. 500/-. Of them, 37.21 per cent fall in the range Rs. 150-300/- and 48.26 per cent fall in the Rs. 301-500/- income range.

## TABLE No. 4.23

### Distribution of Respondents by Income

| Sectors | Less than Rs. 150/- | Rs. 151/- to Rs. 300/- | Rs. 301/- to Rs. 500/- | Rs. 501/- to Rs. 750/- | Rs. 751/- to Rs. 1000/- | Rs. 1001/- to Rs. 1500/- | More than Rs. 1500 | Mean Income |
|---|---|---|---|---|---|---|---|---|
| Private | 41.44 | 27.39 | 13.15 | 11.53 | 5.05 | 1.25 | 0.18 | 234.00 |
| Central Govt. | — | — | 44.76 | 39.05 | 10.48 | 4.76 | 0.95 | 625.50 |
| Central Govt. Quasi | 0.57 | 11.68 | 15.67 | 61.54 | 5.98 | 4.56 | — | 613.00 |
| State Govt. | — | 4.00 | 30.00 | 48.40 | 11.60 | 6.00 | — | 638.00 |
| State Govt. Quasi | — | — | 31.25 | 34.38 | 25.00 | 9.38 | — | 875.50 |
| Corporation | — | 37.21 | 48.26 | 9.30 | 4.65 | 0.58 | — | 389.00 |
| Total | 7.00 | 13.38 | 30.52 | 34.03 | 10.46 | 4.42 | 0.19 | 562.50 |

A negligible percentage of 0.95 per cent and 0.18 per cent of the respondents in the Central Government and Private Sectors earn more than Rs. 1,500/- per month.

**Mean Income of Respondents**

The mean income of an employed woman in Bangalore City is Rs. 562.50 per month.

An analysis of the mean income of respondents in the various sectors indicate that the average is very low for those employed in the Private Sector. The mean Income of those working in the Private Sector is only Rs. 234/- per month. The low average may be due to the generally low wages paid by the private Sector establishments, especially the small size establishments. Besides, those working in the private sector are not protected with respect to labour laws regarding wages, facilities and work conditions to the extent public sector employees are protected. The next lowest average is of those employed in the Corporation, i.e., Rs. 389/-. This is because most of them are illiterates and are engaged in unskilled work. While the mean ranges from Rs. 613/- to Rs. 638/- in the Central Government, Central Government Quasi and State Government Sectors, it is highest in the State Government Quasi, Rs. 875.50.

**Job Mobility**

TABLE No. 4.24

**Number of Jobs Changed by the Respondents**

| Sectors | Job not changed | Changed the Job | | | |
|---|---|---|---|---|---|
| | | Once | Twice | Thrice | Four times and above |
| Private | 85.05 | 8.65 | 3.06 | 1.62 | 1.62 |
| Central Govt. | 80.95 | 9.52 | 7.62 | — | 1.91 |
| Central Govt. Quasi | 86.90 | 7.69 | 3.99 | 0.57 | 0.86 |
| State Govt. | 75.20 | 16.00 | 5.20 | 2.40 | 1.20 |
| State Govt. Quasi | 68.75 | 28.13 | 3.13 | — | — |
| Corporation | 91.86 | 5-81 | 1.74 | 0.58 | — |
| Total | 81.43 | 12.63 | 4.12 | 0.86 | 0.93 |

It is evident from Table No. 4.24 that majority of the employed women have not changed their jobs at all. 12.63 per cent of the women have changed their job once ; 4.12 per cent twice and nearly one per cent each have done so thrice and four times and above.

The proportion of respondents who have changed their jobs is highest in the State Government Quasi and State Government Sectors. The percentage of respondents who have changed their job once in these sectors are 28.13 and 16.00 per cent respectively. In the Central Government Sector 7 62 per cent of the respondents have changed their job twice. Those who have changed their job more than twice form a negligible minority in all the sectors.

**Other Earnings**

TABLE No. 4.25

**Distribution of Respondents by Extra Earnings**

| Sectors | Yes | No |
|---|---|---|
| Private | 7.39 | 92.61 |
| Central Govt. | 2.86 | 97.14 |
| Central Govt. Quasi | 0.29 | 99.71 |
| State Govt. | 2.40 | 97.60 |
| State Govt. Quasi | — | 100.00 |
| Corporation | 10.47 | 89.53 |
| Total | 3.90 | 96.10 |

As can be observed from Table No. 4.25, majority of the employed women do not have extra earnings.

TABLE No. 4.26

**Education of the Parents of the Respondents**

| Sectors | | Illiterates | Lower Primary | Upper Primary | Secondary | Vocational Edn. | Inter/ PUC | Graduates | Post-Graduates | Prof/ Tech. Edn. | No Response |
|---|---|---|---|---|---|---|---|---|---|---|---|
| Private | F* | 20.18 | 8.11 | 16.40 | 27.75 | 2.52 | 8.11 | 7.03 | 1.08 | 3.24 | 5.58 |
| | M* | 45.23 | 15.32 | 14.41 | 14.23 | 1.08 | 1.44 | 1.98 | — | 0.54 | 5.77 |
| Central Govt. | F | 9.52 | 2.86 | 20.00 | 32.38 | 3.81 | 14.29 | 10.48 | 0.95 | 3.81 | 1.90 |
| | M | 38.10 | 25.71 | 17.14 | 13.33 | — | 0.95 | 2.86 | — | — | 1.91 |
| Central Govt. Quasi | F | 29.06 | 4.27 | 13.96 | 25.93 | 3.70 | 6.55 | 5.13 | 0.86 | 6.84 | 3.70 |
| | M | 56.13 | 11.97 | 14.25 | 10.54 | — | 0.29 | 1.71 | — | — | 5.11 |
| State Govt. | F | 6 80 | 4.80 | 13 20 | 37.20 | 8.80 | 6.80 | 11.20 | 0.40 | 6.40 | 4.40 |
| | M | 35.20 | 17.60 | 24.40 | 14.40 | 3.20 | — | — | 0.40 | 1.20 | 3.60 |
| State Govt. Quasi | F | 6.25 | 3.13 | 6.25 | 43.75 | — | 6.25 | 9.38 | — | 12.50 | 12.50 |
| | M | 21.88 | 15.63 | 29.13 | 28.13 | — | — | — | — | — | 6.23 |

| | | | | | | | | | | | |
|---|---|---|---|---|---|---|---|---|---|---|---|
| Corporation | F | 73.84 | 4.07 | 6.40 | 9.30 | 0.58 | 2.33 | 2.91 | — | 0.58 | — |
| | M | 84.88 | 4.07 | 9.30 | 1.16 | — | 0.58 | — | — | — | — |
| Total | F | 24.28 | 4.54 | 12.70 | 29.39 | 3.24 | 7.39 | 7.69 | 0.55 | 5.54 | 4.58 |
| | M | 46.90 | 15.05 | 17.94 | 13.63 | 0.71 | 0.54 | 1.09 | 0.07 | 0.29 | 3.77 |

* F—Fathers of the respondents.
M—Mothers of the respondents.

Among the various sectors, 10.47 per cent and 7.39 per cent of the respondents in the Corporation and Private Sectors respectively have earnings through other means. This is perhaps due to the low income they get from their regular jobs (refer Table No. 4.23).

**Socio-Economic Background of Employed Women**

In this part, the family background of the respondents is presented and discussed.

**Education of Parents**

It may be observed from Table No. 4.26 that between the parents of the respondents, illiteracy is more prominent among the mothers. 45.9 per cent of the mothers are illiterates as against 24.28 per cent of the fathers. In the lower and upper primary levels, a higher percentage of mothers than fathers are educated. While 32.99 per cent of the mothers have primary education, 17.24 per cent of fathers have such education. However, at the high school stage and beyond, the fathers dominate over the mothers. The percentage difference between the parents at the high school stage is of the order of 15.76.

Illiteracy is highest among the parents of the respondents employed in the Corporation, it being 73.84 per cent among the fathers and 84.88 per cent among the mothers. They are the parents of respondents who are mostly sweepers. The other sectors where illiteracy is high are the Central Government Quasi (29.06 and 56.13 per cent of the fathers and mothers are illiterates respectively) and the Private Sectors (20.18 and 45.23 per cent of the fathers and mothers are illiterates respectively).

27.75 per cent of the fathers of the respondents in the Private Sector have secondary education, while around 15.00 per cent of the mothers here are lower and upper primary educated. In the Central Government Quasi Sector, while

25.93 per cent of fathers are secondary educated, 11.97 and 14.25 per cent of mothers are lower and upper primary educated respectively.

In the Central Government, while majority of the fathers are secondary (32.38 per cent) and upper primary educated (20.00 per cent), majorty of the mothers are illiterates (38.1 per cent) and lower primary educated (25.71 per cent). In this sector as high as 14.29 per cent and 10.48 per cent of the fathers are intermediates and graduates.

37.20 per cent of the fathers are secondary educated in the State Government Sector. 35.20 and 24.40 per cent of the mothers are illiterates and upper primary educated respectively.

Majority of the fathers in the State Government Quasi are secondary educated. The next highest percentage is of those having college level professional/technical education, 12.50 per cent. Among the mothers, an equal percentage of 28.13 per cent are upper primary and secondary educated.

In general, the fathers are better qualified than the mothers in all the sectors. Further, a comparison of Table No. 4.26 with Table No. 4.15 reveals that the respondents are more qualified than their parents, indicating educational mobility among the respondents.

**Occupation of Parents**

As can be observed from the table no. 4.27, a vast majority of the mothers of the employed women are house-wives. Among the fathers, the highest percentage, 20.52 per cent, are in the service sector. 16.78 per cent and 14.75 per cent are engaged in professional/technical and clerical work. While nearly 14 per cent are farmers, agricultural workers, etc, around 11 per cent each are production and sales workers.

As regards the sectoral break-up of the occupation of fathers of the respondents, it is observed that in the private sector as high as 21.44 per cent are production and related

TABLE No. 4.27

Occupation of Parents of the Respondents

| Sectors | | Professional, Technical etc. | Administrative, Executive, etc. | Clerical & related workers | Sales workers | Service workers | Farmers agricultural workers | Production, Transport & Equipment Operation & Labourers | Workers not classified | Unemployed | No response | Housewives |
|---|---|---|---|---|---|---|---|---|---|---|---|---|
| Private | F* | 10.27 | 2.70 | 12.07 | 17.30 | 18.02 | 10.81 | 21.24 | 2.70 | 0.18 | 4.51 | — |
| | M* | 5.77 | — | — | — | 2.15 | 2.88 | 3.24 | — | — | 0.97 | 84.98 |
| Central Govt. | F | 20.97 | 18.10 | 20.00 | 5.71 | 15.24 | 6.67 | 10.48 | — | 0.95 | 1.90 | — |
| | M | — | — | 0.95 | — | 0.95 | — | — | — | — | 0.96 | 97.14 |
| Central Govt. Quasi | F | 11.40 | 6.55 | 13.96 | 14.25 | 16.24 | 17.93 | 11.68 | 2 28 | 1.71 | 3.98 | — |
| | M | 2.28 | — | — | 0.29 | 2.28 | 6.27 | 3.13 | — | — | 5.12 | 80.63 |

| | | | | | | | | | | | | |
|---|---|---|---|---|---|---|---|---|---|---|---|---|
| State Govt. | F | 19.60 | 8.00 | 22.40 | 16.00 | 14.00 | 6.40 | 7.60 | 1.20 | — | 4.80 | — |
| | M | 7.20 | — | 0.40 | 0.40 | 0.80 | 0.80 | — | — | — | 3.60 | 88.80 |
| State Govt. Quasi | F | 36.13 | 9.38 | 12.50 | 8.25 | 12.50 | 12.50 | 3.13 | 3.13 | — | 2.48 | — |
| | M | 3.13 | — | — | — | — | — | — | — | — | 0.24 | 96.63 |
| Cor-poration | F | 2.33 | 1.16 | 7.56 | 4.65 | 74.09 | 28.49 | 8.14 | 0.58 | — | — | — |
| | M | 1.16 | — | — | — | 39.54 | 14.54 | 2.91 | — | — | — | 41.86 |
| Total | F | 16.78 | 7.65 | 14.75 | 11.03 | 20.32 | 13.80 | 10.41 | 1.65 | 0.47 | 2.95 | — |
| | M | 3.26 | — | 0.23 | 0.12 | 7.62 | 4.08 | 1.55 | — | — | 1.81 | 81.34 |

* F—Fathers of the respondents.

M—Mothers of the respondents.

## TABLE No. 4.28

### Income of the Parents of the Respondents

| Sector | | Less than Rs. 150/- | Rs. 151/- to Rs. 300/- | Rs. 501/- to Rs. 500/- | Rs. 501/- to Rs. 750/- | Rs. 751/- to Rs. 1000/- | Rs. 1001/- to Rs. 1500/- | More than Rs. 1500/- | Mean income in Rs. | Mean Difference in in income |
|---|---|---|---|---|---|---|---|---|---|---|
| Private | F* | 16.40 | 22.52 | 32.61 | 14.96 | 9.19 | 2.52 | 1.80 | 397.50 | 280.50 |
| | M* | 65.00 | 22.00 | 11.00 | — | 2 00 | — | — | 117.00 | |
| Central Govt. | F | 11.43 | 11.43 | 38.32 | 14.29 | 20.00 | 2.86 | 7.62 | 538.00 | 357.50 |
| | M. | 36.33 | 20.33 | — | 43.33 | — | — | — | 180.50 | |
| Central Govt. | F | 21.94 | 12.25 | 22.79 | 20.51 | 13.68 | 5.41 | 3.42 | 425.50 | 312.50 |
| Quasi | M | 75 00 | 19.12 | — | 2.94 | 1.47 | — | 1.47 | 113.00 | |
| State Govt. | F | 20.80 | 19.60 | 26.00 | 13.80 | 14.40 | 4.00 | 1.60 | 400.50 | 279.00 |
| | M | 39.39 | 18.18 | 30.30 | 12.12 | — | — | — | 121.50 | |
| State Govt. | F | 15.63 | 25.00 | 34.38 | 6 25 | 12.50 | 3.13 | 3.13 | 413.00 | 283.50 |
| Ouasi | M | 66.67 | — | 33.33 | — | — | — | — | 129.50 | |

| | | | | | | | | | | |
|---|---|---|---|---|---|---|---|---|---|---|
| Corporation | F | 26.16 | 57.56 | 9.30 | 2.33 | 3.49 | — | 1.16 | 230.88 | 100.30 |
| | M | 37.00 | 60.00 | 3.00 | — | — | — | — | 130.50 | |
| Total | F | 18.73 | 24.73 | 26.24 | 11.99 | 12.21 | 2.99 | 3.12 | 400.88 | 268.88 |
| | M | 53.23 | 23.27 | 12.94 | 9.73 | 0.58 | — | 0.23 | 132.00 | |

* F—Fathers of the respondents.

*M—Mothers of the respondents.

workers. There is an equal distribution in the sales and service categories (around 17.5 per cent).

In the Central Government Sector, over 20 per cent each are in the professional/technical and clerical categories. 18.1 per cent are administrators, executives and managers.

17.95 per cent and 16.24 per cent of the fathers of the respondents in the Central Government Quasi Sector are agricultural labourers and service workers respectively. An almost equal percentage of around 12 per cent of the fathers are clerks, sales-workers, production and professional/technical workers.

While in the State Government Sector, 22.40 per cent and 19 60 per cent of the fathers belong to the clerical and professional/technical group respectively, majority in the State Government Quasi Sector are professional/technical workers. Their proportion is as high as 36.13 per cent.

As high as 75 58 per cent of the fathers in the Corporation are unskilled workers, i e , they are either sweepers or agricultural labourers. While 47 09 per cent are sweepers, 29.49 per cent are agricultural labourers.

Amongst the mothers of the respondents, it is seen that more than 80 per cent of them are house-wives, except in the Corporation where around 58.12 per cent of them are employed. They constitute mainly the unskilled labourers in the area of service and agriculture. While 39.54 per cent of them are sweepers, 14.54 per cent are agricultural labourers.

**Income of the Parents**

It may be observed from the table no. 4.28 that majority of the fathers of the employed women fall in the income ranges Rs. 151-300/- and Rs. 301-500/-. Their respective percentages are 24.73 and 26.24. 18.73 per cent earn less than Rs. 150/- per month. While around 12 per cent fall in the income ranges of

Rs. 501-750/- and Rs. 751-1,000/-, a negligible percentage of 6.11 earn more than Rs. 1,000/- also.

Though only 16.85 per cent of the mothers of the respondents are employed, it is observed that among them as high as 53.23 per cent earn less than Rs. 150/- per month. The next highest percentage is of those in the income range of Rs. 151-300/. 23.27 per cent belong to this income group. While 12.94 per cent earn between Rs. 301 and Rs. 500/-, about 10 per cent earn Rs. 501/- to Rs. 750/- and a negligible 0.83 per cent earn more than Rs. 750/-.

As regards the fathers of the respondents in the various sectors, it is seen that in the private sector 32.61 per cent and 22.52 per cent fall in the income ranges of Rs. 301-500 and Rs. 151-300/- respectively. Thus, over 55 per cent earn between Rs. 151/- and Rs. 500/-.

In the Central Government Sector, the highest proportion of fathers fall in the income-range Rs. 301-500/-, the percentage being 32.38. 20.0 per cent fall in the income category Rs. 751-1,000/-. The proportion of those who earn more than Rs. 1,500/- is highest in this sector (7.62 per cent) compared to the same in other sectors.

An almost equal percentage of the fathers of the respondents in the Central Government Quasi Sector fall in the income ranges less than Rs. 150/- ; Rs. 301-500/- and Rs. 501-750/. Their percentages range between 20.51 and 22 79 in these income groups.

26.0 per cent of those in the State Government earn between Rs. 301 and Rs. 500/-. About 20.0 per cent each fall in the categories less than Rs. 150/- and Rs. 151-300/-. In the State Government Quasi Sector, 34.38 per cent and 25.0 per cent fall in the income ranges Rs. 301-500/- and Rs. 151-300/- respectively. Thus, over 59 per cent earn between Rs. 151/- and Rs. 500/-.

As high as 83.72 per cent in the Corporation earn less than Rs. 300/- per month. While 57.56 per cent earn between Rs. 151/- and 300/-, 26.16 per cent earn less than Rs. 150/-.

As the percentage of mothers employed in the various sectors except the Corporation is very low (refer Table 4.27), no generalisation could be drawn. However, it is observed that majority of them in all the sectors earn less than Rs. 150/-. In the Corporation 60.0 per cent earn between Rs. 151 and 300/-.

In the Corporation, parents earning less than Rs. 300/- are those engaged in service and agricultural labour, while in the private and Central Government Quasi Sectors, they are unskilled and semi-skilled labourers. In all the sectors, majority balonging to the Rs. 301-500/- income range do clerical and related work. Those belonging to the category Rs 501-750/- (Central Government Quasi) are involved in administrative, executive supervisory managerial occupations. Those earning more than Rs. 750/- (especially in the Central Government) do either middle level/high level managerial jobs or business.

The mean income of the fathers of the working women is Rs. 400.88, while that of their mothers is Rs. 132/- only.

The average for the various sectors reveal that it is highest for the fathers of the respondents employed in the Central Government, i.e., Rs. 638.00. The mean income of fathers in the Central Government Quasi, State Government and State Government Quasi Sectors are Rs. 425.50, Rs 400.50 and Rs. 413 00 respectively. On an average in these sectors, their mean income is Rs. 413.00. While the mean in the private sector is Rs. 397.50, it is least in the Corporation, Rs. 230.80.

For mothers, the mean is highest in the Central Government Sector, Rs. 180.50. The mean income in the State Government Quasi and Corporation is around Rs. 130.00. The means are lowest in the Central Government Quasi and Private Sectors. They are Rs. 113.00 and Rs. 117.00 respectively.

The difference in the mean income of parents (fathers and mothers of respondents) for the whole sample is Rs. 268.88. The sector-wise mean difference is higher than the overall mean for all sectors except the Corporation. Participation of women in labour force is also highest in the Corporation (refer Table No. 4.27). In the Corporation sector the mean difference is only Rs. 100.30, which is very much below the overall mean. As such, there appears to be a greater parity in the relative incomes of fathers and employed mothers in the families of respondents employed in the Corporation.

**Married Women and their Husbands**

The table no. 4.29 refers to respondents who are married inclusive of those who are widowed, separated or divorced.

As can be observed from the table 4.29, among the married women, the proportion of husbands having secondary education is highest. Nearly 25.0 per cent of them are secondary educated. 18.81 per cent and 14.36 per cent of the husbands have graduate and college level professional/technical education respectively. 12.46 per cent of husbands are illiterates.

In the Private, Central Government Quasi and State Government Sectors, highest percentage of the husbands of the respondents are secondary educated, their respective percentages being 28.16, 20.25 and 27.53. In all these three sectors, the next highest proportion is of those having college level professional/technical education. 17.42 per cent and 13.92 per cent of husbands are graduates in the State Government and Private Sectors. In the Central Government Quasi Sector, 16.62 per cent are illiterates.

In the Central Government and State Government Quasi Sectors, higher percentage of husbands are graduates. They form 28.07 per cent and 39.13 per cent respectively. Respondents whose husbands are secondary educated form the next highest proportion in these two sectors (26.32 and 30.43 per cent respectively). Further, 19.3 per cent of husbands in the

TABLE No. 4.29

**Education of Husbands of the Respondents**

| Sectors | Illiterates | Lower Primary | Upper Primary | Secondary | Vocational Edn. | Inter/ PUC | Graduates | Post-Graduates | Prof/ Tech. Edn. |
|---|---|---|---|---|---|---|---|---|---|
| Private | 11.00 | 3.24 | 12.30 | 28.16 | 2.91 | 8.41 | 13.92 | 4.20 | 15.87 |
| Central Govt. | 1.75 | 3.51 | — | 26.32 | 5.26 | 12.28 | 28.07 | 3.51 | 19.30 |
| Central Govt. Quasi | 16.62 | 3.96 | 2.64 | 20.26 | 13.22 | 8.81 | 13.66 | 3.08 | 17.75 |
| State Govt. | 4.49 | 0.56 | 4.49 | 27.53 | 11.24 | 6.74 | 17.42 | 3.93 | 23.59 |
| State Govt. Quasi | — | — | — | 30.43 | 4.35 | 13.04 | 39.13 | 4.35 | 8.70 |
| Corporation | 39.87 | 22.22 | 13.75 | 16.99 | 3.27 | 1.31 | 0.65 | — | 1.96 |
| Total | 12.46 | 5.58 | 5.53 | 24.95 | 6.71 | 8.43 | 18.81 | 3.18 | 14.36 |

Central Government Sector are professionally/technically qualified.

In the Corporation nearly 40.0 per cent are illiterates and 35.95 per cent are primary educated. 16.99 per cent are secondary educated. Only 7.19 per cent of the husbands have more than sccondary education.

Thus, the husbands of the respondents in the Corporatio n are the least educated as compared to those in the other sectors.

It may be observed from the table no. 4.30 that majority of the husbands of the respondents are production workers, 23.90 per cent. The other major occupations are in the order of professional/technical (21.46 per cent), service (18.13 per cent) and clerical and related occupations (17.26 per cent).

In the Private Sector, majority of the husbands are production workers (32 04 per cent). 17.8 per cent and 16.5 per cent of them are engaged in professional/technical and service occupations respectively.

40 35 per cent of the respondents' husbands in the Central Government Sector have professional/technical jobs. Around 23 per cent are clerical and related workers.

Around 42.0 per cent of those in the Central Government Quasi are production workers, followed by about 18.0 per cent employed in professional and technical jobs.

In the State Government Sector, 34.66 per cent and 23.30 per cent are professional/technical and clerical and related workers respectively.

An equal proportion of 28.09 per cent in the State Government Quasi are clerical and production workers. The next major proportion of husbands of respondents in this sector hold administrative, executive and managerial jobs.

TABLE No. 4.30

**Occupation of Husbands of the Respondents**

| Sectors | Professional, Technical, etc. | Administrative, Executive, etc. | Clerical and related Workers | Sales Workers | Service Workers | Farmers Agricultural Workers | Production, Transport Equipment Operators & Labourers | Unemployed |
|---|---|---|---|---|---|---|---|---|
| Private | 17.80 | 3.56 | 11.97 | 12.62 | 16.50 | 3.24 | 32.04 | 2.27 |
| Central Govt. | 40.35 | 7.02 | 22.81 | 12.28 | 3.51 | 1.75 | 12.28 | — |
| Central Govt. Quasi | 17.70 | 3.54 | 14.16 | 7.52 | 10.18 | 0.44 | 42.03 | 4.42 |
| State Govt. | 34.66 | 7.39 | 23.30 | 7.95 | 10.23 | 0.57 | 15.91 | — |
| State Govt. Quasi | 13.04 | 21.74 | 26.09 | 8.70 | 4.34 | — | 25 09 | — |
| Corporatian | 5.23 | 0.65 | 5.23 | 1.31 | 64.05 | — | 15.03 | 8.50 |
| Total | 21.46 | 7.32 | 17.26 | 8.40 | 18.13 | 1.00 | 23.90 | 2.53 |

As high as 64.05 per cent of the husbands in the Corporation are service workers. They comprise of the sweepers and Class IV workers in this sector. Around 15.0 per cent are production workers.

The highest proportion of unemployed husbands are in the Corporation, 8.5 per cent.

In all the sectors where husbands are farmers and agricultural labourers, the figures are negligible.

As can be observed from Table No. 4.31, majority of the husbands of the employed women fall in the income range Rs. 501-750/- per month. Nearly 23.0 per cent of the husbands belong to this range. The other major income-ranges to which the husbands belong are Rs. 751-1,000/- (20.02 per cent), Rs. 301-500/- (19.38 per cent) and Rs. 151-300/- (18.1 per cent). While 12.55 per cent earn more than Rs. 1,000/-, only 7.08 per cent earn less than Rs. 150/- per month.

In the Private Sector, 22.98 per cent and 19.74 per cent fall in the income ranges Rs. 151-300/- and Rs. 301-500/- respectively. They together form 42.72 per cent. There is a decline in the percentage of husbands who fall in the successively increasing income ranges except for the range Rs. 751-1,000/- where it is higher than the previous range.

An equal percentage of 24.56 per cent of the husbands of the respondents in the Central Government Sector fall in the income-ranges Rs. 501-750/- and Rs. 751-1,000/-. About 14 0 per cent fall in the ranges Rs. 301-500/- and Rs. 1,001-1,500/-. The percentage of those who earn more than Rs. 1,500/- is highest in this sector, 10.53 per cent.

In the Central Government Quasi Sector, 32.74 per cent and 25.66 per cent respectively fall in the income ranges Rs. 501-750/- and Rs. 751-1,000/. Nearly 14.0 per cent earn less than Rs. 150/-.

## TABLE No. 4.31

**Income of Husbands of the Respondents**

| Sectors | Less than Rs. 150/- | Rs. 151/- to Rs. 300/- | Rs. 301/- to Rs. 500/- | Rs. 501/- to Rs. 750/- | Rs. 751/- to Rs. 1,000/- | Rs. 1001/- to Rs. 1,500/- | More than Rs. 1,500/- | Mean income in Rs. |
|---|---|---|---|---|---|---|---|---|
| Private | 10.36 | 22.98 | 19.74 | 15.21 | 18.45 | 7.77 | 5.50 | 575.00 |
| Central Govt. | 3.51 | 8.77 | 14.04 | 24.56 | 24.56 | 14.04 | 10.33 | 780.80 |
| Central Govt. Quasi | 13.72 | 8.41 | 11.06 | 32.74 | 25.66 | 4.42 | 3.98 | 618.15 |
| State Govt. | 5.11 | 6.82 | 21.59 | 28.41 | 22.73 | 9.09 | 6.25 | 689.85 |
| State Govt. Quasi | — | 8.70 | 21.74 | 30.43 | 26.09 | 13.04 | — | 688.54 |
| Corporation | 9.80 | 52.94 | 28.10 | 5.88 | 2.61 | 0.65 | — | 307.15 |
| Total | 7.08 | 18.10 | 19.38 | 22.87 | 20.02 | 8.17 | 4.38 | 609.92 |

In both the State Government and State Government Quasi Sectors, maximum percentage fall in the income range Rs. 501-750/-. While nearly 22.0 per cent belong to the Rs. 301-500/- income range in each of the sectors, 22.73 and 26.09 per cent respectively belong to the income range Rs. 751-1,000/-. In the State Government Quasi Sector, there is not a single respondent whose husband earns less than Rs. 150/- per month.

As high as 52.94 per cent in the Corporation fall in the Rs. 151-300/- income range. The next highest percentage is of those who earn between Rs. 301/- and Rs. 500/-. While 5.88 per cent fall in the income range Rs. 501-750/-, the percentages are very negligible for the income categories Rs. 751-1,000/- and Rs. 1,001-1,500/. There is nobody in the Rs. 1500/- and above category.

Among respondents whose husbands earn Rs. 501/- and above, the percentage is highest for the Central Government Sector, 73.69 per cent 69.56 per cent in the State Government Quasi and about 66.0 per cent of the Central Government Quasi and State Government Sectors earn more than Rs. 500/-. This percentage falls significantly in the Private and Corporation Sectors. Thus, 46.93 per cent of the husbands of respondents in the Private Sector and only 9.14 per cent in the Corporation belong to this group. The overall proportion in this category is 55.44 per cent.

The mean income of the husbands of the working women is Rs. 609.92, The mean is highest for respondents in the Central Government Sector, Rs. 780.80. The average for the State Government and State Government Quasi Sectors is almost equal. The means are Rs. 689.85 and Rs. 688.54 respectively. The average for those in the Central Government Quasi Sector is Rs. 618.15. The mean is lower than the overall mean for the Private and Corporation Sectors. It is quite low for the Corporation Sector, While the mean for the husbands in the

Private Sector is Rs. 575/-, it is only Rs. 307.15 for those in the Corporation.

**General Characteristics of the Respondents**

The main characteristics of the sample of employed women in Bangalore City is given below :

The mean age of a working woman in Bangalore City is 31.8 years. Majority of the respondents in the sample fall in the age groups 21-30 and 31-40 years. They together form 77.05 per cent of the sample. Nearly 80.0 per cent of the working women are Hindus. Of them, Brahmins form the highest proportion, 42.58 per cent. Scheduled Castes and Scheduled Tribes form the second highest group with 20.31 per cent. Nearly one-third of the sample are Kannadigas. The other major mother-tongue groups are the Tamil and Telugu speaking respondents. Around 49.0 per cent of the respondents are in-migrants to Bangalore City. Of them, 58.41 per cent are from urban areas and 41.59 per cent are from rural areas. Of those who are in-migrants, 88.0 per cent are from outside Bangalore District. Further, the migration pattern reveals that while 56.05 per cent have migrated to Bangalore City from within the State, the rest are from Tamil Nadu, Andhra Pradesh and Kerala. Majority of the respondents are married. 32.39 per cent are not married and 9.74 per cent are widowed. While 0.96 per cent are separated, there are no divorcees in the sample.

Of those who are married, majority of them have married between ages 19 and 24. As high as 31.17 per cent have married below the age of 18 which is the minimum age at marriage for a female according to the Special Marriage Act. The mean age at marriage for the respondents is 20.78 years. Majority of the married respondents who have children fall within the family planning limit set by the Government which is taken to be two or less than two children. Nearly 48.0 per cent of the sample have one or two children.

The distribution of the sample on the basis of education reveals that 15.43 per cent are illiterates ; 8.94 per cent are primary educated ; and 17.35 per cent are secondary educated. Out of the 58.28 per cent who have received more than secondary education, 19.88 per cent and 16.52 per cent have vocational (school level) and Professional education (college level) respectively. About 15.0 per cent of the sample are graduates. Those who have PUC/Intermediate and Post-Graduate education form a negligible three per cent each. Among the literate women, 70.82 per cent have received their education in Bangalore City. Majority of the respondents have attended private educational institutions followed by the Government institutions.

The employment data reveals that the public sector provides for 62.12 per cent of the total employment for women in Bangalore City. The remaining 37.88 per cent are employed in the private sector. More than 97.0 per cent of the employed women held permanent jobs. The proportion of respondents who hold temporary jobs is highest in the private sector, the percentage being 7.39 per cent. Majority of the respondents are engaged in clerical and related occupations and in production oriented jobs. They together form 59.09 per cent of the sample. 22.57 per cent and 16.88 per cent of the employed women are engaged in professional/technical and service occupations respectively. The proportion engaged in administrative/executive and sales occupations is negligible. As high as 98.76 per cent of the respondents work six days a week. Only in the private sector around 7.0 per cent work five days a week. Majority of the respondents work between 43 and 48 hours a week. The income data reveals that the maximum percentage of employed women fall in the income ranges Rs. 301-500/- and Rs. 501-750/- per month. They together form 65.0 per cent of the sample. The mean income of an employed women is Rs. 562.50 per month. While the mean is highest for the respondents working in the State Government Quasi Sector (Rs. 875.50), it is very low for the Corporation and Private

Sectors (Rs. 389.00 and Rs. 234.00 respectively). 81.45 per cent of the respondents have not changed their jobs at all. Out of the 18.53 per cent of the sample who have changed jobs, the percentage of those who have changed their job once, twice, and four times and above are 12.63, 4.12, 0.86 and 0.93 per cent respectively. About 96.0 per cent of the respondents do not have earnings other than their regular income. However, 10.47 per cent and 7.39 per cent in the Corporation and Private Sectors have extra earnings. This may be due to the low income they get from their regular jobs and the additional opportunities that are available to them.

Data on the family background of the respondents reveals that participation of women in the labour force is from middle class families except for the Corporation Sector. While women from upper middle class families have openings in Central Government and State Government Quasi Sectors, women from lower middle class families have openings in the State Government, Central Government Quasi and Private Sectors in the order followed. Women employed in the Corporation come from lower class families. It is interesting to note that there is virtually no participation of women in the labour force coming from upper class families (refer Appendix D for a detailed discussion of the derivation of the class categories).

The education, occupation and income data of the husbands of the respondents reveal that the proportion having secondary education is highest. The next highest percentage is of the graduates followed by those with professional and technical education. 51.49 per cent of the husbands have more than secondary education. Majority of the husbands are production workers. The other major occupations are professional/technical, service and clerical and related occupations. Their respective percentages are 21.46, 18.13 and 17.26. The mean

**income of the husbands is Rs. 609.92 per month. While 22.87 per cent fall in the income range Rs. 501-750/-, about 20.0 per cent fall in the Rs. 301-500/- and Rs. 751-1,000/- income categories. Thus, 62.27 per cent earn between Rs. 301/- and Rs. 1,000/-. 55.44 per cent earn more than Rs. 500/- and 12.55 per cent earn more than Rs. 1,000/-. Those who earn less than Rs. 150/- form about 7.0 per cent of the sample.**

CHAPTER 5

# Analysis and Interpretation

The data collected from the women employed in the organised sector of Bangalore City, following the methodology discussed in Chapter III, are analysed and interpreted in the present chapter.

The main objective of the present investigation is to study the returns from education in terms of both economic and non-economic returns. Data collected from the women are analysed and interpreted under two sections. Section 1, deals with the private costs of education as incurred by the respondents in acquiring education. Section 2 deals with the returns that accrue to the individuals from investing in various levels of education. Section 2 is further divided into two parts—A and B. While Part A discusses the economic returns from education from the investment point of view, Part B discusses the non-economic returns from education in terms of attitudes and behaviour of women towards the institutions of education, employment, marriage and family, politics, religion and social life.

## I. PRIVATE COST OF EDUCATION

In this section, the private cost of education, broadly defined as the expenses incurred by respondents in getting their education is discussed. An analysis of private costs of education can be viewed at from two angles.

1. The direct costs ; and

2. The indirect costs.

1. *The Direct Costs* : of education refer to those types of investment which are perceptible, regular and actually paid by the respondents for acquiring a certain level of education. The direct costs comprise of two major components :

(a) Tuition costs ; and

(b) Non-tuition costs.

(a) *Tuition Costs* ; may be taken to mean payment of fees. In computing tuition costs, scholarship amount received from Government or private agencies and fee-concessions are considered and the net amount paid is taken as tuition cost.

(b) *Non-tuition Costs* : are expenses incurred by the respondents on items like books and stationery, transport, hostel-stay, etc.

2. *The Indirect Costs* : referred to also as the opportunity cost of the student's time, i.e , respondent's "foregone earnings" while attending school or college. If instead of pursuing education, the respondent had preferred to go for employment, secured employment and earned an income, then she would have profited in two ways :

(a) By earning an income ; and

(b) By not spending on education.

However, as the respondent did not consider such an opportunity as an alternative to go in for education, the loss that must have occured therein is referred to as opportunity cost. Although no actual cost is involved, opportunity cost is an important item of the private cost of education, because if the respondent chooses to continue her education instead of entering the work force, it is a real cost to her, since it also means foregoing earnings during her schooling (net income after deducting taxes which would have been levied on those earnings).

**Collection of Data Regarding Private Costs of Education**

Information regarding private costs of education was collected from women respondents through an interview schedule. The schedule consisted of items relating to fees paid, expenses on non-tuition aspects such as books/stationery, transport, hostel-stay, etc. Information relating to scholarships, fee-concessions and freeships was also collected. As costs to the individual depend on the management of the educational institution attended and the total number of years taken to complete a given level of education, information regarding these two variables were also collected. The information given by the respondents (especially those relating to tuition costs and books, scholarships and fee-concessions) were cross-checked with the help of records maintained by both the public and private schools/colleges. Further, information collected from the respondents was also checked among themselves by grouping them on the basis of their age, level of education and the type of educational institution attended. The information was found to be quite reliable and consistent. The cost values are presented in 1960-61 Rupee Value (1960-61=100).[1]

Information regarding foregone earnings were taken from the age-education-earning profiles of respondents, net of taxes. The foregone earnings estimate was further adjusted for unemployment, for the existence of unemployment reduces the opportunity cost of the respondent's time just as it reduces the economic benefits from education.

Foregone earnings were estimated for all levels of education except the primary level because in view of the Constitutional

1. The Consumer Price Index with 1960-61=100 is given in Appendix E.

Directive of Article 45 for free and compulsory education and the prohibitive stricture on children to participate actively in the labour force before the age of 14, it is assumed that no earnings are foregone by those who attend primary schools. However, when discussing the causes of school dropout in India, as early as in 1966 the Education Commission had stated : 'after the age of 9 or 10, the child becomes an economic asset because he works at home or earns some-thing outside'[2]. Therefore, the estimate of foregone earnings of upper primary school children should be made especially in under-developed and developing countries as the time of even such children does have some money value. While the researcher was aware of the importance of estimating the foregone earnings for those with upper primary education also, in this study it was omitted for mainly two reasons :—

1. The number of respondents in the sample who entered the labour force before the age of 14 was negligible, i.e., only eight out of a total of 1465 respondents.

2. The full implementation in a future date of the Constitutional Directive of Article 45 for free and compulsory education and forbidding the entry of children into the labour force before the age of 14 would only put to waste the computation of foregone earnings for this level.

Thus, the total private costs of primary level educated respondents will consist of only tuition and non-tuition costs, whereas for all other levels it will consist of foregone earnings in addition to tuition and non-tuition costs.

An adjustment in the estimate of the total private cost is also made for repeaters, as repeating a class means additional expenses for the individual.

2. Report of the Indian Education Cmomission, New Delhi, 1966, p. 159.

Thus, estimates of private costs of education are presented at constant prices, i.e., in 1960-61 rupee values.

The following table gives an estimate of the net private tuition cost of education by levels of education at constant prices.

TABLE No. 5.1

**Net Tuition Cost of Education per Pupil at Constant 1960-61 Prices in Rupees**

| Levels of Education | In Rupees | |
|---|---|---|
| | Annual Private Tuition Cost | Total Private Tuition Cost |
| Lower Primary | 34.06 | 136.25 |
| Upper Primary | 111.52 | 334.56 |
| Secondary | 156.47 | 469.34 |
| Vocational Edn. | 183.75 | 551.26 |
| Inter/P.U.C. | 268.59 | 537.19 |
| Graduates | 311.40 | 934.21 |
| Post-Graduates | 387.59 | 775.18 |
| Prof/Tech. Edn. | 455.25 | 2726.25 |

It is observed from the above table that the annual and total net tuition cost increases with an increase in the level of education. While this trend is to be expected, the only aspect that needs to be highlighted is that the annual tuition cost of obtaining vocational education is less than that of the intermediate/P.U.C. level. This may be due to the divergent courses combined in this level i.e., nursing, typing and shorthand and teacher training programmes. While nursing is a stipendary course, tuition cost for typing and shorthand is very low. Thus, the estimate of the tuition cost for this level is over-estimate as it consists of mainly the cost incurred by respondents who attended teacher training institutions. Further, it is observed from Table No. 5.1, that the total tuition cost of graduate education is higher than that of post-graduate education. It is because the duration of graduation courses is longer than that of post-graduation courses ; they being 3 years and 2 years respectively.

The tuition costs given in the table are slightly over-estimated due to the following two reasons :—

1. Inclusion of repeaters in all the levels of education. Thus, the average number of years taken to complete each level of education as against the prescribed number of years are as follows :

| Levels of Education | Average No. of years taken | Prescribed No. of years |
|---|---|---|
| Lower Primary | 5.50 | 4 |
| Upper Primary | 9.52 | 7 |
| Secondary | 12.30 | 10 |
| Vocational Edn. | 13.96 | 13 |
| Inter/P.U.C. | 13.40 | 12 |
| Graduates | 17.50 | 15 |
| Post-Graduates | 20.10 | 17 |
| Prof/Tech. Edn. | 18.78 | 17 |

2. Inclusion of respondents from both Government and private educational institutions.

The following table presents the annual private tuition cost of education by levels of education and type of institution the respondents attended.

TABLE No. 5.2

**Aunual per Pupil net Tuition Cost of Education by Levels and Type of Institution the Respondents Attended (In Rupees)**

| Levels of Education | Government/ University | Private | Total |
|---|---|---|---|
| Lower Primary | 11.40 | 56.72 | 34.06 |
| Upper Primary | 53.67 | 169.38 | 111.52 |
| Secondary | 85.09 | 227.84 | 156 47 |
| Vocational Edn. | 150 37 | 217.13 | 183.75 |
| Inter/P.U.C. | 200.23 | 336.95 | 268.59 |
| Graduates | 204.40 | 418.41 | 311 40 |
| Post-Graduates | 300.76 | 474.33* | 387.59 |
| Prof/Tech. Edn. | 302.74 | 607.76 | 455.25 |

*This figure relates to respondents who have completed their post-graduation through correspondence courses.

It is observed from table No. 5.2 that the annual tuition cost of education at all levels is higher in private institutions than in Government/University institutions. At the lower primary stage, the tuition cost in private institutions is five times that in Government institutions. At the upper primary stage it is three times the cost in Government institutions ; two and a half times at the secondary stages : twice that at the graduate and professional levels ; and around one and a half times at the vocational, intermediate and post-graduate levels. The vast difference in the net tuition costs between the Government and Private institutions may be due to the high subsidization of the tuition cost in the Government institutions in the form of freeships, fee-concessions and scholarships to a greater extent than in private institutions. Further, infrastructure facilities in Government institutions are provided for by the Government,

As such, tuition fees itself is quite low. On the other hand, private institutions collect, through additional tuition fees, funds to build up infrastructure facilities.

The respondents even in Government institutions have incurred tuition cost at the primary level because some of the respondents received their education before the enactment of free education at this stage. The average tuition cost for private institutions may be considered as slightly under-estimated due to the inclusion of aided educational institutions.

On the basis of the estimated expenditure on non-tuition items, the annual per pupil non-tuition cost of education at constant 1960-61 prices is given in Table No. 5.3 by levels of education and managements.

TABLE No. 5.3

**Estimated Annual per Pupil Non-tuition Costs by Levels of Education and Types of Management**

(in Rupees)

| Levels of Education | Government | Private | Total |
|---|---|---|---|
| Lower Primary | 41.73 | 153.85 | 97.79 |
| Upper Primary | 118.64 | 276.84 | 197.74 |
| Secondary | 225.40 | 412.30 | 318.35 |
| Vocational Edn. | 209.84 | 259.60 | 234.72 |
| Inter/P.U.C. | 289.95 | 396.50 | 343.23 |
| Graduates | 493.20 | 696.29 | 594.75 |
| Post-Graduates | 685.98 | 593.17 | 639.58 |
| Prof/Tech. Edn. | 1089.10 | 1734.97 | 1412.04 |

From the above table it is observed that the estimated annual non-tuition costs increased with successive levels of education, except at the vocational level where it is less than that of the secondary level. One of the reasons for the low non-tuition costs for the vocational level may be a low requirement of books and costs therein, availability of boarding and lodging for nursing being met from stipends given to the respondents, while the non-tuition costs for those who did shorthand and typing is very low as they do not have to spend on books and other heads.

Barring the post-graduate level, at all other levels of education, the annual non-tuition cost is higher for those who attended private institutions than Government institutions. This is because they constitute respondents who did their post-graduation through correspondence courses As such, their non-tuition costs included only expenditure on attendance at contact seminar programmes and examinations and cost on books ; while for the University students, apart from them, daily transport itself constituted a major item of expenditure. The margin of difference in per pupil non-tuition costs between post-graduate regular (University) and correspondence (private) is Rs. 92.81 per annum. It is seen that the difference in the annual non-tuition costs between the Government and private institutions is greater at the lower levels of education. This is because the pursuit of higher e lucation requires a minimum economic standard, a threshold, which the large majority cannot reach. Those who pursue higher education may be supposed to have reached that threshold. In contrast, lower levels of education can be acquired by the general population irrespective of their economic status. Here, there is a provision for high cost-quality education (real or imaginary) provided by private educational institutions which run parallel to low-cost Government organised primary education. Thus, while the disparity in the economic back-ground of respondents who pursue higher education is less, at the lower levels the disparity is large and hence the greater difference in the non-tuition costs in Government and private institutions. Thus, at the lower primary stage, the annual non-tuition cost in private institutions is nearly four times that of Government institutions ;

about 2.3 times at the upper primary stage ; nearly 1.77 times at the secondary level. While it is almost equal at the vocational and post-graduate levels, it is nearly one and a half times at the intermediate, graduate and professional levels.

Estimates of the earnings that respondents have foregone were made in the following manner : Age-earnings streams of respondents with different levels of education were first drawn. From these streams the annual earnings foregone by the respondents were estimated for different stages of education. An adjustment was also made on the estimated earnings foregone for un-employment. Data regarding un-employment for respondents with various levels of education was estimated from the survey data on the basis of the actual waiting period between leaving school/college and getting their first job.

As it was decided earlier to estimate foregone earnings only for those with secondary education and above, information on the duration of un-employment among respondents who had completed primary education and above was collected.

The estimated period of un-employment for the various levels of education is as follows :

| Level of Education | Estimated period of Un-employment in months |
|---|---|
| Upper Primary | 6.9 |
| Secondary | 6.7 |
| Vocational Edn. | 7.8 |
| Inter/P.U.C. | 5.8 |
| Graduation | 8.06 |
| Post-Graudation | 3.3 |
| Prof/Tech. Edn. | 7.5 |

The above information reveals that the waiting period is least for the post-graduates, followed by those who are under-graduates. The un-employment period for the vocational and professional level educated respondents is higher than that of upper primary and secondary level educated respondents. The graduates face the longest un-employment period, an average of 8 months. One explanation for a relatively shorter waiting period among intermediates as against matriculates and post-graduates as against graduates may be due to matriculates and intermediates ; and graduates and post-graduates competing for similar jobs. Under the circumstances, it is the intermediates and post-graduates who get preference over the matriculates and graduates respectively.

Using the education-earnings profiles, the number of years for which earnings foregone for every level of education making it the terminal point for the next level of education is given below :

| Levels of Education | Terminal Level of Education | Number of years Foregone Earnings were estimated |
|---|---|---|
| Secondary | Primary | 3 |
| Inter/P.U.C. | Secondary | 2 |
| Vocational Edn. | Secondary | 3 |
| Graduates | P.U.C. | 3 |
| Post-Graduates | Graduates | 2 |
| Prof/Tech. Edn. | PUC/Graduates | 5 |

After adjusting for un-employment, the total estimated foregone earnings was divided by the appropriate number of years to arrive at estimates of annual foregone earnings for the various levels.

The following table gives the total and annual earnings

foregone as constant prices by levels of education of respondents. The earnings foregone are presented : (i) unadjusted, and (ii) adjusted for un-employment.

TABLE No. 5.4

**Total and Annnal Income Foregone, Unadjusted and Adjusted for Un-employment in Constant Prices (1960-61 =100), in Rupees.**

| Levels of Education | Total Earnings Foregone | | Annual Earnings Foregone | |
|---|---|---|---|---|
| | Unadjusted | Adjusted | Unadjusted | Adjusted |
| Secondary | 6644.46 | 2823.90 | 2214.82 | 941.30 |
| Vocational Edn. | 11990.88 | 5295.96 | 3996.96 | 1765.32 |
| Inter/P.U.C. | 7327.26 | 3256.20 | 3663.63 | 1628.10 |
| Graduates | 16313.64 | 8428.71 | 5437.88 | 2809.57 |
| Post-Graduates | 18965.70 | 6227.08 | 9482.85 | 3113.54 |
| Prof/Tech. Edn. | 28189.45 | 11910.05 | 5637.89 | 2382.01 |

From the above table it is seen that both the unadjusted and adjusted annual foregone earnings is highest for the post-graduates. However, when the estimate of total earnings foregone is considered, it is at the professional level where earnings foregone is highest, i.e., nearly double that of the post-graduate level. The vast difference in the total and annual earnings foregone at all levels of education is due to the influence of the number of years of the course on earnings foregone.

It is further observed that at almost all levels of education, the earnings foregone falls by more than 50 per cent when adjusted for un-employment.

Having estimated the major components of the private cost of education, in the following table is given the annual private cost of education by components for the various levels of education in constant prices. It is in the annual costs of schooling that the magnitude of earnings foregone can be highlighted. Hence, the table also presents the earnings foregone as a proportion of the total private cost.

TABLE No. 5.5

**Estimated Annual Private Cost of Education by Major Components and Levels of Education at Constant Prices (In Rupees)**

| Levels of Education | Net tuition cost | Non-tuition cost | Adjusted income foregone | Total private | Income foregone as % of total private cost |
|---|---|---|---|---|---|
| Lower Primary | 34.06 | 97.79 | — | 131.85 | — |
| Upper Primary | 111.52 | 197.74 | — | 309.26 | — |
| Secondary | 156.47 | 318.35 | 941.30 | 1416.12 | 66.47 |
| Vocational Edn. | 183.75 | 234.72 | 1765.32 | 2183.79 | 80.84 |
| Inter/P.U.C. | 268.59 | 343.23 | 1628.10 | 2239.92 | 72.69 |
| Graduates | 311.40 | 594.75 | 2809.57 | 3715.72 | 75.61 |
| Post-Graduates | 387.59 | 639.58 | 3113.54 | 4140.71 | 75.19 |
| Prof/Tech. Edn. | 455.25 | 1412.04 | 2382.01 | 2449.30 | 56.06 |

It is observed from the above table that the annual total private cost of education increases with successive levels of education. Income foregone is seen as a major component of cost even after adjusting for un-employment. It forms about

80 per cent of the total private costs for these with vocational education; around 75 per cent for the graduates and post-graduates ; 72.69 per cent for the intermediates ; 66.47 per cent for the matriculates and about 56 per cent for those with professional and technical education. The high share of foregone earnings in the total private cost implies that student contribution in terms of their own time and effort is both prominent and important in the estimation of private costs of education.

## II. A. ECONOMIC RETURNS FOR EDUCATION

This section analyses the economic returns from education to employed women in Bangalore City. A detailed conceptual discussion (Chapter I) and operational definitions (Chapter III) of concepts used are presented in earlier parts of this thesis. For the present, it may be suffice to recall that economic returns is considered as the monetary benefits that accrue to individuals with any given level of education. Data about economic returns are collected from women employed in the organised sector of Bangalore City. Data are in the form of earnings from different cross-sections of employed women. The sample for the data consisted of 1465 working women stratified by size of establishment, sector (public and private) and divisions of the public sector (Central Government, Central Govt. Quasi, State Government, State Govt. Quasi and the Corporation). Information regarding earnings was collected through the questionnaire developed for collecting data regarding the economic and non-economic returns from education. Direct interviews with the women employees were held in order to facilitate cent per cent return of the questionnaires. The Questionnaire consisted of items relating to the women's scale of pay, basic salary, net earnings per month (after deducting Provident Fund subscription and taxes. Net earnings data were used by the researcher to cross-check computations of earnings of the respondents on the basis of salary scales and basic pay), monthly earnings through means other than their salary, etc. Information regarding age, sector of employment, experience, period of un-employment, details about job(s) held prior to the presents one and some background variables was also collected. The data on returns to given level of education collected here a are analysed in the light of costs of education for the same level. (Data on costs of education are presented in the previous section.) All the data used for computing returns to education—the development of correlation matrix for the selection of independent variables, the regression equations for the estimation of the contribution of the various independent variables and education to earnings—was analysed using the computor. However, lifetime earnings were estimated through manual analysis.

**Estimation of Lifetime Earnings**

Estimation of lifetime earnings is beset with a number of conceptual problems. The basic data available from the information schedules collected from the respondents for estimating their lifetime earnings consisted of scale(s) of pay, basic salary and not monthly earnings at the time of interview, experience, details about previous job(s), duration of un-employment and average monthly extra earnings through means other than their full-time- occupation (e.g., tuitions, consultancy, private service, part-time job, etc.). Additional data about pay scales (present and prior) by sector of employment, occupations and grades were collected from the various establishments visited. Further. information regarding allowances admissible and deductions including taxes effected for the various income slabs were obtained from the respective establishments.

No set pattern could be adopted for the estimation of lifetime earnings of the respondents. Depending upon the sector of employment (Public and Private), and the variation in the earnings data obtained, different techniques were adopted for the estimation procedure. As such, the derivation of the estimates for respondents working in establishments where earnings were fixed on regular pay scales were different from those working either on consolidated salaries or according to the quantum of production, as in the case of agarbathi workers.

The estimates for those fixed on regular scales were derived as follows :

1. The current scales of pay (1978) were obtained individually from the respondents and also from the managements.

2. Scale(s) that were in use prior to the implementation of the current scale was/were also obtained from the establishments along with the particulars of allowances, deductions, etc.

3. The position of respondents on their respective current scales of pay was determined by means of their basic salary at the time of interview.

4. With the help of the current and previous scales of pay and job experience of the respondents, annual net earnings from the time of entry into the labour force upto 1978 was estimated. Wherever there was a change in the scale(s) of pay, their relative position on those scale(s) were also determined in estimating the net earnings. Necessary adjustments were also made for those who had a change in job(s). Example : the respondent could have been on stipend, honorarium, an employee in a private establishment or a consolidated salary before being fixed on a scale.

5. For the years 1979 onwards, until the age of retirement of the respondents, net earnings were estimated on the basis of the current scale. The estimation for the latter years was made on the assumption that the current scale of pay would continue upto the retirement age of the respondents. It is possible that there may be pay revisions in future. It would be futile to assume the exact nature of such revisions. However, it may

be presumed that the revision effected will cover all categories of employed and relative differentials in returns would continue to be the same. This would be by and large very true of respondents working in public sector establishments.

The estimates for those whose earnings were either on consolidated basis or on that of the quantum of production (e.g., incense stick rollers) were derived in the following way :

1. Data about those who are on consolidated salary (e g , weavers, dress makers) were collected from the respondents and the managements regarding increments, periodicity of such increments, allowances, etc.

2. Data about those whose wages were tagged to the quantum of their produce/work (agarbathi workers) were collected from both the respondents and the establishments. Data about changes in daily wages over the years were also collected.

3. Net annual earnings and lifetime earnings were estimated using the above data.

The age at retirement varies by the type of establishments the respondents work in. Hence, the age at retirement for those working in the public sector was taken to be 55 years for State Sector employees. Age of employees working in the private sector was fixed at 60 years. Sixty years may be considered to be the average age at which women retire from service in the private establishments, though there are exceptions of women who work beyond this age.

In the estimation of lifetime earnings, while adjustments in earnings were effected for allowances, increments, Provident Fund deductions, taxes, extra earnings from other part-time jobs, etc., no adjustment for promotions was made for the following reasons :

1. The researcher did not come across a single respondent

who had been promoted among as large a sample of 1465 women, though there were women who changed jobs because of better financial prospects. The reason given by the respondents themselves and the managements was that women rarely get a promotion. Further, some of the respondent women reported that men were promoted by the establishments even though they themselves were equal to the opportunity.

2. Further, it is assumed following the earlier finding that the omission of an adjustment for promotion among those, who might have got a promotion in the universe of study would not affect the results as they would perhaps form a negligible proportion.

No adjustment was made for mortality (probability of survival) for the following reason :

> This is a study of returns to private investments in education. Such adjustments are often made and are useful in the estimation of social returns. Individuals, however, do not consider their probability of survival while deciding on investments in education.

Adjustment for growth in the economy was not incorporated, as cross-sectional data for rate-of-return analysis would take care of such growth variations. This hypothesis has been tested and verified to be correct by Magnusson* who showed that cross-sectional data will have a tendency to overestimate rates while time-series has a tendency to underestimate. Adjustment for un-employment** has been incorporated IN THE COST EARNINGS STREAMS. Information regarding the period of un-employment was obtained from the respondents themselves, by asking them the number of months they had to wait between leaving school/college and procuring their first

*Refer Pscharopoulas and K. Hinchliffe, 1973, op. cit.

**Un-employment is defined as the duration of time between leaving school/college and beginning the first job.

employment. However, for the illiterates and lower primary educated respondents the duration of un-employment was accounted for only after the age of 14 years. Even in cases where respondents entered the labour force before 14 years of age (i.e., 8 respondents), their earnings were estimated from 14 years onwards only for the following reasons :

The full implementation in future of the Constitutional Directive prohibiting the entry of children into the work-force before the age of 14 years would put to waste the computation of earnings before the specified age group for these few exceptional cases.

It may be recalled that estimation of the costs of education is made in terms of direct costs (tuition and non-tuition costs) and indirect costs (opportunity costs or foregone earnings). The magnitude of the earnings foregone by women with different levels of education has also been demonstrated.

Thus, in the life cycle cost-earnings streams are presented the flows of cost incurred during schooling and the subsequent flows of earnings that can be attributed to that schooling after all the adjustments referred to earlier were made. The cost-earnings streams, thus, drawn were adjusted by the Consumer Price Index and presented in constant 1960-61 Rupee Value. 1960-61 was preferred as the base year as a great majority of respondents had joined the work-force after 1961.

Since the monetary benefits of education accrue over a period of time, it is necessary to use some discount factor to take account of the fact that the value of money earned in future is less than that in the present. It would be hazardous to guess the inflationary trends in future periods and therein choose the appropriate discount factors. Moreover, the cost-earning streams are highly sensitive to the discount factors.

Thus, in choosing the most appropriate discount rates*, random sample of the cost-earnings streams for the various level of education was taken and discounted for a number of rates. The rates which exhibited the highest internal consistency were selected for the current study. The discount rates obtained thus are five and six per cents. The life-cycle cost-earnings streams were then discounted at zero, five and six percents to reflect the effect of time preferences on the value of future money. As such, a fairly accurate estimate of the costs incurred and life-time earnings for the respondents was obtained.

As the main objective of the study is to find out the economic returns keeping education as 'the' independent variable, the earnings should be estimated standardising for independent variables, other than education. For this, the independent variables were subjected to multi-variate regression analysis to estimate the earnings functions.

Table No. 5. A. 1 gives a list of the independent and dependent variables initially considered for inclusion in the regression analysis including education with their respective notations. It may be noted in passing that occupation of the respondent is not considered as an independent variable. This is because, when people with different levels of education are being studied, occupation will tend to distort the measured effect of education since it is to a greater degree result of the education process and hence, does not have completely independent effect on earnings. Further, by and large, the relation between education and occupation was found to be quite high for any given level of education and as such, the inclusion of education as an independent value was considered enough to take care of the effect of occupation.

*The determination of an appropriate discount rate is to some degree subjective because of the differences in individual time preferences and risk assessment. Various discount rates have been used more or less arbitrarily in rate of return studies in education. Rates of 0, 3, 3½, 4, 5, 6, 8 and 10 per cent have been used by other researchers.

Type of educational institution attended was also omitted as it was covered in the estimation of costs. Nature of employ- and sector of establishments were not considered for regression analysis as they were covered in the life-time earnings estimation.

TABLE No. 5.A.1

**Variables and their Notations**

| Sl. No. | Variables | Notations* |
|---|---|---|
| **I.** | **Independent variables** | |
| 1. | Age | AG |
| 2. | Religion | R |
| 3. | Caste | C |
| 4. | Mother-tongue | MT |
| 5. | Present address | PA |
| 6. | Place of birth | PB |
| 7. | Duration of stay in Bangalore City | DSB |
| 8. | Marital Status | MS |
| 9. | Education of Father | EF |
| 10. | Occupation of Father | OF |
| 11. | Income of Father | IF |
| 12. | Education of Mother | EM |
| 13. | Income of Mother | IM |
| 14. | Socio-economic status | SES |
| **Education of the respondent** | | |
| 15. | Education in general | E |
| 16. | Illiterate | $E_1$ |

* These notations are preferred rather than $X_1, X_2, X_3 \ldots X_n$ as it is felt that it may be easier to recall the expanded term for the variables from the above used notations.

| | | |
|---|---|---|
| 17. | Lower Primary | $E_2$ |
| 18. | Upper Primary | $E_3$ |
| 19. | Secondary | $E_4$ |
| 20. | Vocational Edn. | $E_5$ |
| 21. | Inter/P.U.C. | $E_6$ |
| 22. | Graduate | $E_7$ |
| 23. | Post-Graduate | $E_8$ |
| 24. | Prof/Tech. Edn. | $E_9$ |
| 25. | Place of study | PS |
| 26. | Class obtained | CO |
| 27. | Dependence while studying | DS |
| 28. | No. of working hours/week | WHW |
| 29. | Earnings through other means | EOM |
| **II.** | **Dependent variables** | |
| | Life-time earnings— | |
| 30. | Discounted at 0 per cent | $Y_0$ |
| 31. | " " 5 per cent | $Y_5$ |
| 32. | " " 6 per cent | $Y_6$ |

The procedure adopted for determining the variables to be included in the estimation of earnings in the regression equations, at the outset the correlation matrix was drawn for the independent variables. (The correlation matrix showing intercorrelations in a 32 × 32 table is given in appendix F.) A value of ±0.062 for 'r' and above that will be significant at 0.05 level and for 1,000 degree of freedom. Those values obtained in the present analysis which are significant at 'atleast' one of zero per cent or five per cent or six per cent discount rates are given in Table No. 5.A.2. By doing so, it was observed that of the 29 correlations obtained, seven were rejected. The table presents the value of the coefficients of correlation between independent and dependent variables. However, the coefficient values for levels of education as independent variables and lifetime earnings as dependent variables are retained irrespective of their significance. This is because levels of education happen to be the main foci of analysis and they need to be subjected to deeper analysis.

TABLE No. 5.A.2

**Correlations between Select Independent and Dependent Variables (earnings)**

| Sl. No. | Correlations of: With | Lifetime Earnings: Zero per cent | Five per cent | Six per cent |
|---|---|---|---|---|
| 1. | AG | 0.54* | 0.56* | 0.56* |
| 2. | R | −0.13* | −0.16* | −0.18* |
| 3. | PB | 0.22* | 0.21* | 0.19* |
| 4. | DSB | 0.57* | 0.57* | 0.56* |
| 5. | MS | −0.09* | 0.10* | 0.14* |
| 6. | EF | 0.08* | 0.08* | 0.07* |
| 7. | OF | 0.20* | 0.23* | 0.21* |
| 8. | IF | 0.27* | 0.03 | −0.01 |
| 9. | E | 0.60* | 0.16 | 0.10* |
| 10. | $E_1$ | −0.25* | 0.16* | 0.23* |
| 11. | $E_2$ | −0.27* | −0.19* | −0.20* |
| 12. | $E_3$ | −0.33* | −0.29* | −0.30* |
| 13. | $E_4$ | −0.05 | −0.05 | −0.05 |
| 14. | $E_5$ | 0.02 | −0.04 | −0.06 |
| 15. | $E_6$ | 0.03 | 0.01 | 0.01 |
| 16. | $E_7$ | 0.24* | 0.11* | 0.11* |
| 17. | $E_8$ | 0.23* | 0.09* | 0.09* |
| 18. | $E_9$ | 0.36* | 0.14* | 0.11* |
| 19. | PS | 0.12* | 0.12* | 0.12* |
| 20. | CO | 0.34* | 0.05 | 0.01 |
| 21. | WHW | −0.46* | −0.28* | −0.27* |

* Significant at 0.05 level.

From Table No. 5.A.2, it is observed that education in general (E) is positively correlated with lifetime earnings at all the discount rates. Age (AG) is seen to be significant and positively related with earnings. This is because increased age is associated with an increase in earnings. The co-efficient of correlation between earnings and place of birth (PB) and the duration of stay in Bangalore City (DSB) are both positive and significant. Education of father (EF) is positively correlated with earnings and is significant at all the three discount rates. While occupation of father (OF) is significant but negatively correlated with earnings, income of father (IF) is found to be positive and significant at the zero discount rate, but insignificant at 5 and 6 per cent discount rates. It is observed that marital status (M/S) is significantly related to earnings. However, the relationship is negative for earnings discounted at zero per cent but positive at the 5 and 6 per cent levels. A negative and significant value at zero per cent level for marital status may be explained by the entry of women at a relatively earlier period (late 50's and early 60's) into less paying jobs (Corporation). The positive and significant values at the 5 and 6 per cent discount rates may be attributed to the entry of women into highly paying jobs in recent years (late 60's and early 70's) and also due to the revision of pay scales in both low and high paid jobs. It is observed that a lifetime earning of a person (lifetime taken to be around 35 years assuming 20 years as entry for service and 55 years as exit from service in State Sector employment and 38 years if Central Sector is considered) who entered service in the late 60's or early 70's when pay revisions were effected, would be higher than that of a person who entered service in the late 50's or early 60's. While education of the father is positively related with earnings, occupation is negatively correlated. The relationship between income of father and earnings is positive and significant at the zero per cent discount rate only. Class obtained is significant and positive with earnings at zero per cent, while with earnings at five and six per cent discount rates, the correlations though positive are insignificant. Number of working hours per week is negatively correlated with earnings at all discount rates.

It may be observed that the obtained values for the coefficient of correlations given in Table No. 5.A.2 between educational levels and earnings show : negative and significant values at $E_1$ (only at zero per cent level), $E_2$ and $E_3$ levels ; are not significant at $E_4$, $E_5$ and $E_6$ levels ; but are positive and significant at $E_1$ (5 and 6 per cent discount rates), $E_7$, $E_8$ and $E_9$ levels. The correlations obtained indicate that independent variables such as age, place of birth, duration of stay in Bangalore City, education of father, and place of study apart from higher levels of education have shown positive and significant values at all discount rates. The correlations for variables such as religion, occupation of father and number of working hours per week apart from the lower levels of education (except $E_1$ level) indicate negative and significant values at all the discount rates. The coefficients are insignificant at all the discount rates for education levels $E_4$, $E_5$ and $E_6$ of the rest, education in general has shown positive and significant correlation with earnings, while the other variables have shown inconsistent correlations at the different discount rates ($E_1$ level of education, marital status, father's income and class obtained).

The procedure followed in determining the selection of independent variables for inclusion in the regression equations setup for the final estimation of earnings is as follows :

Age (AG) has been retained for the final equation as it is significantly correlated with earnings. Religion (R) i.e., being a Hindu or not is also found to be significantly correlated with earnings and hence it was also retained. Place of birth (PB), duration of stay in Bangalore City (DSB) and place of study (PS) are found to be highly inter-correlated. Further, all these variables have a significant relationship with earnings. However, only duration of stay in Bangalore City (DSB) is retained for the final estimation. This is because, of all the three variables, duration of stay in Bangalore City (DSB) has the highest correlation with earnings. Marital status (MS) of the respondents has been omitted as it is inter-correlated with age (AG), of the family background variables, education (EF), occupation (OF) and income of father (IF), it was decided to feed only income of father (IF) into the equation as income of father (IF) may be considered as the net effect of his education and occupation. (This hypothesis that father's income rather than education or occupation is the appropriate measure of family background (SES) has been verified by Hanser and Bowles.*) All the levels of education have been retained as the main objective, is to study the returns to investment for these levels of education in depth. Class obtained (CO) being inter-correlated with education (E) is also withdrawn Number of working hours per week (WHW) is retained as it is highly correlated with earnings.

Hence, the independent variables considered for inclusion in the regression equation are age (AG), religion (R), duration of stay in Bangalore City (DSB), income of father (IF) and number of working hours per week (WHW), apart from the nine levels of education.

**The Regression Model**

Data of education on costs and returns to it are analysed using a linear multiple regression model. Such a model estimates the controlled effect of each independent variable (considered for regression) on the dependent variable (earnings). To account for variation in earnings with wage-earner characteristics including education, a simple equation expressing the dependency of earnings on the independent variables was constructed. Here, earnings is a function of (age, education, religion, father's occupation, father's income, duration of stay,.......... etc.).

* Hanser and Bowles—"Schooling and Inequality from Generation to Generation," *Journal of Political Economy*, Part II, May/June 1972.

The equation can be expressed using mathematical notations as :

$$Y = F(X_1 + X_2 + X_3 + X_4 + \ldots\ldots\ldots + X_n)$$

Once the regression equation has been setup, the earnings associated with each level of education after adjustments for the obtained measures of all the independent variables can be estimated. The predictive form of the equation, obtained by least squares, is used to estimate the earnings :

$$Y = K + \beta_1 X_1 + \beta_2 X_2 + \beta_3 X_3 \ldots\ldots\ldots + \beta_n X_n$$

where Y = Predicted value of Y

K = The intercept or a constant that may be taken as the residual factor in explaining earnings.

$\beta_1, \beta_2, \beta_3 \ldots\ldots \beta_n$ = The least square estimator of the independent variables $X_1, X_2, X_3, \ldots\ldots\ldots X_n$.

In the derivation of the final regression equation, the independent variables selected from the correlation matrix were further tested for significance by regressing them against the three dependent variables (lifetime earnings discounted at zero, five and six per cent). The following table presents the regression coefficients along with their respective 't' values.

TABLE No. 5.A.3

**Regression Coefficients and 't' Values for the Variables Selected**

| | Lifetime earnings discounted at | | |
|---|---|---|---|
| | 0% | 2% | 6% |
| **Intercept** | 3.86030 | 0.89756 | 0.73561 |
| **Variables** | | | |
| 1. $E_1$ | 0.16508<br>(0.00008) | 0.41794<br>(0.00058) | 0.28688<br>(0.00062) |

Table No. 5.A.4 presents the regression coefficients of the lifetime earnings for each level of education or no education after regressing the effect of the various independent variables including the particular level of education. The intercept values are also presented. The 't' values for the various coefficients are given in parenthesis.

In each equation a given level of education was introduced individually along with other independent variables against lifetime earnings of that particular level of education. As may by observed from Table No. 5.A.4, the obtained values of regression coefficients for various levels of education and their corresponding lifetime earnings ($Y_1$ to $Y_9$) when subjected to 't' test analysis showed very high values for all levels indicating that education is a significant factor influencing the lifetime earnings of respondents at all levels.

It was hypothesized that an increase in age, considered as a proxy for experience in the job, would be associated with higher earnings. This was found to be true only at the secondary level. The coefficient is significant even at the 0.01 per cent level. This may be perhaps due to the fact that women with secondary education enter the labour force very much earlier than those with other higher levels of education. Another possibility is that majority of women with secondary education are in industrial establishments. The promotional opportunities for women who work in the shop floor of industries as operators will be quite frequent. They move from lower grades to higher grades in a shorter duration than it would be possible for those who work in clerical posts. However, age is a significant factor in influencing earnings positively at the 0.10 level for graduates.

Religion of the respondents has a significant and positive influence on earnings at the illiterate, lower primary, upper primary and vocational levels. The value of the regression coefficient for the professional level is found to be significant only at 0.10 level. The positive and significant influence of

## TABLE No. 5.A.4

**The Values of Intercepts, Regression Coefficients and t-values in Parenthesis**

| | Intercept | $\beta_1 E_1$ to $E_9$ | $\beta_2$ AG | $\beta_3$ R | $\beta_4$ DSB | $\beta_5$ IF | $\beta_5$ WHW |
|---|---|---|---|---|---|---|---|
| $Y_1$ | 0.15803 | 1.71249 | −0.01447* | 0.0550 | 0 01110 | −0 0045* | −0.05852 |
| (M=226) | | (72 6334 ) | (−1.60671) | (2.04329) | (2.82355) | (−0.85221) | (−5.15041) |
| $Y_2$ | 0.02924 | 1 07414 | −0.00186* | 0.02278 | 0.00254* | −0 00017* | −0.01723 |
| (M=62) | | (56 22954) | (−0.33492) | (2.27116) | (1 08917) | (−0.05763) | (−2.59440) |
| $Y_3$ | 0.08408 | 1.05975 | 0.00175* | 0.02716 | 0.00152* | −0 00724* | −0.03309 |
| (M=69) | | (52.26364) | (0 27012) | (2 17200) | (0.52434) | (−1.95356) | (−4.02192) |
| $Y_4$ | −0.37178 | 2.37546 | 0.06511 | 0.02788* | 0 08505 | 0 01913 | −0.00725* |
| (M=254) | | (70.85255) | (4.11355) | (0.92146) | (7.96563) | (2.12697) | (−0.36226) |
| $Y_5$ | 0.05001 | 2.56708 | 0.01489* | 0.08512 | 0.02259 | −0 00357* | −0.07568 |
| (M=291) | | (88.29538) | (1.06025) | (5.13919) | (3.61283) | (−0.44461) | (−4.26942) |
| $Y_6$ | −0.00921 | 2.68227 | −0.00407* | 0.01228* | 0.01041 | −0.00268* | −0.00324* |
| (M=48 | | (97.88941) | (−0.68894) | (1.08542) | (3.96295) | (−0.79687) | (−0.43510) |

| | | | | | | | |
|---|---|---|---|---|---|---|---|
| $Y_7$ (M=234) | 0.07263 | 3.43908 (109.43587) | 0.01898 (1.66327) | −0.01735* (−0.78780) | 0.00209* (0.41169) | −0.00627* (−0.9512) | −0.03380 (−2.34023) |
| $Y_8$ (M=49) | 0.07959 | 4.00579 (122.16439) | 0.00055* (0.00735) | −0 00137* (−0.9579) | −0.00598* (−1.79988) | 0.00208* (0.48838) | −0.02469 (−2.57259) |
| $Y_9$ (M=242) | 0.00332 | 7.64055 (107.1303) | −0.01726* (−1.30473) | 0.04272 (1.68202) | −0 00021* (−0.03721) | 0.00664* (0.85808) | −0 00344 (−0 19442) |

*Not significant at the 0.05 level of significance.

religion on earnings at the lower levels of education ($E_1$ to $E_3$) may be explained thus : A large majority of illiterate and primary educated employed women are Hindus, working in public sector establishments. For instance, a large majority of women who work in Bangalore City Corporation are the Hindus. The highest percentage of the Christian illiterate and primary educated employed women work in the private sector. It is possible that women at these levels working in the private sector relatively earn lower wages and salaries than those in the public sector. The size of the sample of Muslim women in the sample of the study is quite small and negligible. The explanation is a little different for significance at the vocational level. Quite a high percentage of Christian women take to nursing which is a low paid occupation in contrast to Hindu women who take to teaching in schools which is relatively better paying. Hence religion works out to have a significant influence on lifetime earnings at the vocational level.

It was hypothesized that the duration of stay in Bangalore City would be associated with higher earnings. The coefficients are significant at the illiterate, secondary, vocational and intermediate levels. The reason for this is at these levels, majority of the respondents work in the public sector establishments where earnings increase on the basis of continuing in the same place (experience). But at other levels of education, the duration of stay has not influenced the lifetime earnings.

It was hypothesized that the coefficient of the regression between the income of father of the respondent and lifetime earnings would be positive and significant i.e., a higher economic status of the father would be associated with higher earnings of the respondent. The coefficient is positive and significant only at the secondary level. This may be explained thus : A large number of secondary educated women are in production (industry). Their fathers' occupation has also been by and large in the 'production-sector'. Further, the lifetime earnings of an industrial woman-worker is observed to be quite high as compared to other jobs for the secondary level. Perhaps, the fathers' of the respondents who themselves get a relatively high income, have been able to use to their contacts in getting jobs for their daughters in industry.

The coefficients for the regression between number of working hours per week and lifetime earnings was found to be negative and significant at all levels barring the secondary, intermediate and professional levels. At the lower levels of education, the reason for negative coefficients may be that with an increase in the number of hours of work/week their efficiency falls (e.g., agarbathi workers and weavers). It is common knowledge that illiterate and primary educated women, most of whom work in the Corporation (voluntary work outside their regular working hours is also considered) and the private sector (sales, agarbathi production, weaving, dress-manufacturing, etc.) put in longer hours of work and their wages/salaries are not matched to their hours of work. At the vocational, graduate and post-graduate levels also, there has been no increase in the earnings with an increase in hours of work. With respect to vocational level, it is observed that most of the nurses and teachers do not earn salaries adequate to their hours of work. This is true of graduate and post-graduate levels also where most women are in clerical jobs. The co-efficients, however, are not significant at the secondary, intermediate and professional levels.

Using the regression coefficients presented in Table No. 5.A.4 and setting the independent variables, along with levels of education ($E_1$ to $E_9$) at their mean values*, the predictive form of the regression equations were set up to arrive at the earnings estimate for each level of education.

* Rogers Daniel C., op cit (1969) :—He used national means for the estimation of earnings as the size of the sample for his study was very small (364). In the current study the size of the sample was large enough (1465) to use their mean values for the estimation process.

**Results of the Statistical Analysis**

There are two methods employed in evaluating the returns to alternative investments in various levels of education. They are : (i) The Net present value method and (ii) the Internal rate of return method. Net present values for various levels of education are computed in terms of differences and ratios. In this study both these methods are used. The internal rate of return is used in addition to, or as an alternative to the net present values.

The analysis of the data collected in this study on economic returns to education are presented under two sections here. Section 1 : deals with the comparison of costs and benefits by the net present value method. Data about net present values are in the unregressed form at zero, five and six per cent discount rates. Further, the unregressed data at zero per cent discount rate are compared with similar data which are regressed. Section 2 : deals with the internal rates of return to alternative investment.

**1. Present Values of Educational Investment**

Both educational costs and the earnings advantage attributable to education must be quantified in order to estimate the present value of the gain from education. Benefits from education are estimated in terms of the average earnings-increment associated with an educational increment only and other than earning-benefits (the external benefits) are omitted because of the inability to quantify them. The earnings estimates presented and discussed here are those from the simple mean earnings figures, which are merely the set of unregressed average lifetime earnings figures for all those at each educational level. While the cost estimates of the previous section are used to compare costs and benefits of alternative investments, the following table presents the total private costs of education in Rs. 1,000's for the various levels of education at zero, five and six per cent discount rates.

TABLE No. 5.A.5

**Total Private Costs of Education at zero, five and six per cent Discount Rates (Rs. 1,000's)**

| Level of Education | Zero per cent | Five per cen | Six per cent |
|---|---|---|---|
| Lower Primary | 0.53 | 0.50 | 0.50 |
| Upper Primary | 0.93 | 0.77 | 0.75 |
| Secondary | 4.25 | 3.24 | 3.08 |
| Vocational Edn. | 6.55 | 4.71 | 4.58 |
| Inter/P.U.C. | 4.48 | 3.32 | 3.03 |
| Graduates | 11.15 | 7.32 | 6.77 |
| Post-Graduates | 8.28 | 4.87 | 4.41 |
| Prof/Tech. Edn | 21.25 | 13.29 | 11.52 |

The cost estimates of the above table are used to compare with the benefits provided in later sections. It is observed from the table that the cost estimates decrease with each discount rate used.

The table no. 5.A.6, gives the unregressed simple mean lifetime earnings of respondents discounted at zero, five and six per cents for the various levels of education.*

It is observed from Table No. 5.A.6 that at zero discount rate the earnings are highest for the professional educated respondents followed by those with vocational and secondary education. The earnings of graduates are found to be higher than that of post-graduates. The earnings falls considerably at all levels when discounted at five and six per cents. When

* Illiterates form the omitted category as this study deals with the returns from investment in various levels of education.

TABLE No. 5.A.6

**Unregressed Mean Earnings by Education Discounted at zero, five and six per cents (Rs. 1,000's).**

| Levels of Education | Zero per cent | Five per cent | Six per cent |
|---|---|---|---|
| Lower Primary | 60.2 | 21.5 | 19.0 |
| Upper Primary | 84.6 | 25.5 | 21.3 |
| Secondary | 458.8 | 124.3 | 98.7 |
| Vocational Edn. | 513.5 | 118 3 | 98.8 |
| Inter/P.U.C. | 188.0 | 46.0 | 38.5 |
| Graduates | 359.2 | 83.7 | 61.2 |
| Post-Graduates | 253.9 | 50.9 | 37.9 |
| Prof/Tech. Edn. | 542.4 | 112.1 | 80 8 |

earnings are discounted at five per cent, the lifetime earnings of the secondary educated is the highest, with the professional level falling into the third position. At this discount rate, the vocational level also scores over the professional level. All other levels of education hold the same placement as at the zero discount rate. At the six per cent discount rate, all levels have the same ranking as at the five per cent discount rate with the exception of the intermediates who score marginally over the post-graduates. The figures in the table implies that while at the zero per cent discount rate the life time earning returns is highest for the professional educated, at the five and six per cent discount rates the secondary educated seem to have the highest returns.

The unregressed lifetime earnings for various levels of education at zero per cent discount rate (presented earlier in Table No. 5.A 6) also include the contribution of independent variables considered in this study other than education.

As such, the unregressed data on lifetime earnings at zero per cent discount rate are compared here with the regressed data. This will enable one to understand the contribution of the independent variables considered in this study on lifetime earnings.

TABLE No. 5.A.7

**Unregressed and Regressed Estimates of Life-time Earnings at Zero Discount Rate (in Rs. 1,000's)**

| Levels of Education | Unregressed life-time earnings | Regressed life-time earnings |
|---|---|---|
| Lower Primary | 60.2 | 17.2 |
| Upper Primary | 84.6 | 35.4 |
| Secondary | 458.8 | 294.8 |
| Vocational Edn. | 513.5 | 296.2 |
| Inter/P.U.C. | 188.0 | 81.4 |
| Graduate | 359.2 | 132.9 |
| Post-Graduate | 253.9 | 81.4 |
| Prof/Tech. Edn. | 542.4 | 140.7 |

From the above table, it can be observed that when the independent variables other than education (age, religion, duration of stay in Bangalore City, income of father, number of working hours per week) which are considered to influence earnings are regressed for their potential contribution with education, the earnings associated with more education is markedly reduced in every case. But the fall is not so much for secondary and vocational levels as it is for other levels of education. The percentage fall is of the order of 35.75 and 42.32 respectively. It is least for employed women educated upto the secondary level while it is highest for the professional educated respondents. It is observed that in several production oriented concerns such as industries and other manufacturing establishments there is an insistence on secondary education as minimum level of education for recruitment. It is also observed that lifetime earnings are quite high among women employed in the said concerns. This might be a strong reason for a relatively marginal differential effect on regression at the secondary level. Further, the percentage of employed women with secondary and vocational levels of education are quite high in this sample. As such, lifetime earnings regressed for the independent variables including education appear to be quite high for secondary and vocational levels of education.

Table No. 5.A.8, presents the net earnings advantage at zero, five and six per cents for the various levels of education. The difference in the earnings between a given level of education and an educational increment (Table 5.A.6.), net of costs (Table 5.A.5.) gives the earning advantage from an educational increment.

From the table no. 5.A.8, it is observed that the lifetime earning advantage net of costs is highest for the secondary educated over the upper primary educated at all discount rates. The next in order is that of the professional educated over the intermediates. While the vocational level has a net earning advantage of Rs. 48, 150 over the secondary level at the zero discount rate, they represent a loss at the five and six per cent discount rates. The net earning advantage of intermediates over secondary educated and post-graduates over graduates represent a loss at all the three discount rates. At the remaining levels of education there is a positive net earning advantage at all discount rates.

The table no. 5.A.9, presents the unregressed and regressed net earning advantage at zero discount rate (in Rs. 1,000's).

From Table No. 5.A.9, it is observed that all levels of education have a positive net earning advantage over the lower

| | | | | | | | |
|---|---|---|---|---|---|---|---|
| Post-Graduate | 185.42 (56.92) | 161.02 (8.32) | 196.62 (—205.12) | 251.32 (—205.52) | 57.62 (8.28) | 113.53 (45.22) | |
| Prof/Tech. Edn. | 480.95 (103.25) | 436.55 (54.85) | 62.33 ( 132.85) | 7.65 ( 134.25) | 333.15 (38.05) | 161.95 ( 13.45) | 267.25 (38.05) |

**Note : First set of figures represent the unregressed values. Figures in parenthesis represent the regressed values.**

and upper primary levels. Vocational and professional levels have a positive net earning advantage over secondary when unregressed, but represent a loss when regressed. There are no earning advantage for the intermediates, Graduates and Post-graduates over the secondary educated, both when unregressed and regressed. The professional educated have a positive net earning advantage over the vocational educated only when unregressed. The earning advantage is negative for all other levels over vocational both when unregressed and regressed. The graduates, post-graduates and the professional educated have an earning advantage over the intermediates, except the post-graduates whose earnings are negative when regressed. While the post-graduates have no earnings advantage over the graduates, the professional educated have an advantage over the graduates and the post-graduates. However, when the earnings are regressed, the professional educated have a negative earning advantage over the graduates.

In the following table is given the ratios of earnings by education.

TABLE No. 5.A.10

**Ratios of Earnings at the Zero, Five and Six per cent Discount Ratios**

| Levels of Education | Earnings at discount rates | | |
|---|---|---|---|
| | Zero | Five | Six |
| **Earnings** of Lower Primary (Base level of Edn.) | 59.67 | 21.00 | 18.50 |
| **Ratios of :** | | | |
| Upper Primary / Lower Primary | 1.40 | 1.18 | 1.11 |
| Secondary / Upper Primary | 5.43 | 4.90 | 4.65 |

| | | | |
|---|---|---|---|
| Vocational / Secondary | 1.12 | 0.94 | 0.99 |
| Inter/P.U.C. / Secondary | 0.40 | 0.35 | 0.40 |
| Graduates / Inter/P.U.C. | 1.90 | 1.79 | 1.41 |
| Post-Graduates / Graduates | 0.71 | 0.60 | 0.62 |
| Prof/Tech. Edn. / Inter/P.U.C. | 2.83 | 2.32 | 1.80 |

From Table No. 5.A.10 it is observed that the earning advantage from educational increment is highest for the secondary level followed by the professional and graduate levels. The earnings associated with intermediate education and post graduate education is less respectively than that of secondary and graduate education. The same ranking holds good even at the five and six per cent discount rates.

**Earnings Advantages**

A comparison of Tables 5.A.5, 5.A.6 and 3.A.8 reveals that the unregressed and undiscounted lifetime earnings advantage to the average secondary educated over the upper primary educated is Rs. 3,74,000 (Rs. 3,70,880 net of total (Direct and opportunity costs) and Rs. 98,800 when a five per cent discount rate is applied (Rs. 96,330 net of costs). A professional degree holder has a Rs. 35,400 undiscounted advantage over those who completed only intermediate education (Rs. 3,37,600 net of costs) and Rs. 42,000 (Rs. 30,800 net of costs) when discounted at six per cent. Post-graduate education represents a loss of Rs. 1,05,300 (Rs. 1,02,400 net of costs) undiscounted and a loss of Rs. 23,300 (Rs 20,900 after costs) at the six per cent discount rate. Vocational education fetches Rs. 54,700 more than secondary education, undiscounted (Rs. 52,400 net of costs) though it would mean a loss of Rs. 6,000 at a five per cent discount rate (Rs. 7,470 net of costs.)

Thus, data on lifetime unregressed earnings obtained through the net present value method indicates that while lifetime undiscounted earnings (even net of costs) is most profitable for the professional educated, still at the five and six per cent discount rates, it is the secondary level which is most profitable. While vocational education seems more profitable than secondary education at zero per cent discount rate, it shows a marginal loss at the five and six per cent levels. However, intermediate and post-graduate levels of education are less profitable than the preceding levels at all the three discount rates.

The regressed and undiscounted lifetime earnings advantage (comparison of Tables 5.A.7 and 5.A.9) of a secondary educated over a upper primary educated is Rs. 2,30,200 (Rs. 2,25,950 net of costs), which is the highest positive advantage in comparison to all other levels of education. The next highest earning advantage is that of the professional educated over the post-graduate, Rs. 59,300. However, net of costs the upper primary and graduate levels have a higher earning advantage than that of the professional level. The earning advantage of a vocational educated is Rs. 1,400 over the secondary educated but, net of costs it means a loss of Rs. 5,150. Both the intermediate and post-graduate levels have negative earning advantages over secondary and graduate levels respectively.

Thus, data on the lifetime regressed earnings indicate that secondary education is the most profitable, followed by that of the professional level. While vocational education is marginally profitable over secondary eduation, it shows a loss when costs are deducted. Intermediate and post-graduate levels represent a loss and are thus not profitable,

## 2. Private Internal Rates of Return to Education

The internal rate of return is defined as that discount rate which equates the present values of costs to the present values of benefits. Alternately, it is also defined as that rate of interest on costs which would equate to zero the discounted net benefits. Interpolation is the commonly used technique to arrive at that discount rate which will equate costs with benefits. But, this is a technique involving trial and error exercises. As such, it is a time-consuming computational exercise. There is an improvisation of this technique by Frank H. Lamson Scribner.* In this improvised technique interpolation by trial and error is avoided by the use of the following six steps :

**Step 1**

Estimate the internal rate of return by dividing average annual benefits by total initial costs and express it as a decimal.

$$\frac{\text{Average Annual Benefits}}{\text{Total initial Costs}} = \text{Estimated internal rate of return.}$$

**Step 2**

Reduce the estimated internal rate of return by subtracting the amount indicated in the following table against the duration of benefits stream.

| Duration of the Benefit stream (Years) | Estimated value in Step 1 | | | |
|---|---|---|---|---|
| | Less than 0.1 | 0.1 to 0.2 | 0.2 to 0.3 | More than 0 3 |
| Five | — | — | 0.18 | 0.13 |
| Ten | 0.08 | 0.07 | 0.05 | 0.02 |
| Fifteen | 0.05 | 0 03 | 0.02 | 0.00 |
| Twenty | 0.02 | 0 01 | 0.00 | 0.00 |
| Twenty five | 0.02 | 0.01 | 0.00 | 0.00 |
| More than 25 | 0.00 | 0.00 | 0.00 | 0 00 |

* Scribner has used it for calculation of internal rates of return in projects of the Economic Development Institute, IBRD (now World Bank). For details refer Gittinger, Price J., "Economic Analysis of Agricultural Projects," The Johns Hopkins University Press, Baltimore, London, 1972, pp. 71-78.

**Step 3**

Considering the adjusted estimate obtained in Step 2 as E, then reduce E by the amount indicated in the following table for the number of years in the investment period.

| Investment period (years of schooling/college for a given level of education) | Formula to be used for reduction to be effected on E |
|---|---|
| 1 | $(E - 0 \times E)$ |
| 2 | $(E - 0.5 \times E^2)$ |
| 3 | $(E - 1 \times E^2)$ |
| 4 | $(E - 1.5 \times E^2)$ |
| 5 | $(E - 2 \times E^2)$ |

**Step 4**

Consider the Estimate obtained in Step 3 as $E^1$, then reduce $E^1$ by the amount indicated for the lapse between the end of the investment period and the time of the first benefits.

| Lapse (in years) Adjustment for unemployment period | Formula to be used for effecting the reduction on $E^1$ |
|---|---|
| 1 | $E^1 - (E^1)^2$ |
| 2 | $E^1 - 2\,(E^1)^2$ |
| 3 | $E^1 - 3\,(E^1)^2$ |
| 4 | $E^1 - 4\,(E^1)^2$ |
| 5 | $E^1 - 5\,(E^1)^2$ |

**Step 5**

(a) If benefits are larger in early years than laters, increase the step 4 estimate.

(b) If benefits are greater in later years than in early years, decrease the step 4 estimate.

For effecting adjustments to such increased or decreased benefits, use the standard table of annuity factor estimates.

**Step 6**

Shift the decimal point two places to the right to obtain the estimated internal rate of return in percentage terms (i.e., Step 5 estimate × 100).

The above procedure was adapted for estimation of internal rates of return in the present study. The average annual benefits was calculated by dividing the average lifetime earnings of the respondents, education-wise by the total number of years of workspan Herein average annual earnings were estimated using the regressed value of earnings after standardising the regression coefficients for the independent variables which (the variables) had earlier been expressed in differing units.* The total costs (direct costs—tuition and non-tuition costs) incurred by the respondents to acquire a given level of education was taken to represent the total initial costs of education. In this study, the estimated internal rate of return was not adjusted for at the Step 2 level, as all the respondents fall beyond the 'more than 25 years' benefit stream. Thus, the estimated internal rate of return was adjusted only for the number of years in the investment period. Step 4 represents the period of unemployment. It was omitted as it had already been adjusted for in the calculation of lifetime earnings. Step 5 was also dropped, since actual benefits were accounted for in the lifetime earning estimation for each year of earning. Thus, the main steps followed in this study for the derivation of internal rates of return estimates were steps 1, 2, 3 and 6.

* The method used to standardise has been explained in Chapter III under "Statistical Techniques used for the Analysis of Data".

The private internal rates of return, thus, estimated for the various levels of education are presented in Table No. 5.A. 11.

**TABLE No. 5.A.11**

**Private Internal Rates of Return to Levels of Education in Percentage Points**

| Levels of Education | Private Internal Rate of Return |
|---|---|
| Lower Primary | 15.49 |
| Upper Primary | 23.30 |
| Secondary | 24.44 |
| Vocational Edn. | 17.99 |
| Inter/P.U.C. | —31.56 |
| Graduates | 5.26 |
| Post-Graduates | —6.30 |
| Prof/Tech. Edn. | 7.41 |

These private internal rates of return were obtained after effecting adjustments on lifetime earnings for the independent variables. For this purpose, the independent variables had been set at the mean values of the respective sample. Along with this, adjustments on lifetime earnings had also been effected for tax deductions, unemployment, etc. The private internal rate of return on lifetime earnings obtained, thus, shows that secondary education gets the highest private internal rate of return (24.44 per cent). However, it is closely followed by upper primary education (23.30 per cent). Even vocational education (17.99 per cent) and lower primary education (15.06 per cent) have displayed relatively higher returns. The returns to professional level (7.41 per cent) is higher than that of the graduate level (5.26 per cent). However, the returns to these levels of education are quite low even though positive. But surprisingly the post-graduate and intermediate levels of education bring about negative returns. The performance of Pre-University education is most disappointing in this regard. Private internal rate of return to graduate education is quite low as the opportunity cost (foregone earnings) for getting graduate education is quite high apart from the direct costs involved.

Secondary education has yielded the highest returns as women who go for employment after matriculation normally get placements in industries in Bangalore which is essentially an industrial city. The income of industrial workers normally includes incentives, overtime and annual bonus apart from monthly salaries. As such, the income in any year will be relatively quite high. Further, this income will also work as an advantage over the next higher level of education for that period as those who go for the higher level will loose the said income during that period (foregone earnings). These advantages are in addition to the savings on costs of higher education.

The high return to vocational education may be due to the lower costs of such education. The costs are lower because of the size of the subsidy which is channeled directly into such training schools (e.g. nursing schools) is quite high, so that not all the private costs of procuring vocational education are privately financed. Further, the high returns may also be due to the low direct costs of procuring vocational training, this is true for courses in typing, short-hand and general secretarial training. The negative returns to post-graduates over graduates and intermediates over matriculates can be partly explained by the fact that on the one hand the private costs for getting these levels of education are high, and on the other hand, the opportunity cost is also quite high. Added to these, employment market for intermediates is the same as that for matriculates and similarly, the market for post-graduates is relatively the same as that for graduates. Professional education has yielded lower returns because teachers are included in the professional category along with doctors and engineers.* Moreover, teachers form the large majority in this category.

**Conclusion**

The data on economic returns from education to employed women were analysed using both the net present value and internal rate of returns methods. The highlights of the results using the net present value methods are as follows :

1. The unregressed mean earnings of the professional educated are highest followed by those with vocational and secondary education at the zero discount rate. But when earnings are discounted at the five and six per cent levels, the secondary educated get the highest returns.

2. The unregressed lifetime earning advantage from an educational increment, net of costs is highest for the secondary educated over the upper primary educated at all discount rates (i.e., zero, five and six per cent). While the vocational level has an earning advantage over the secondary level at the zero discount rate, at the five and six per cent levels they show a lose. The net earning advantage of intermediates and post-graduates over secondary educated and graduates respectively, show a loss at all discount rates.

3. When earnings are regressed for the influence of the indedendent variables (age, religion, duration of stay in Bangalore City, income of father, number of working hours/week) with levels of education as the variant variable, the lifetime earnings associated with more education is considerably reduced in every case.

4. The regressed and undiscounted lifetime earnings adventage, net of costs, is highest for the secondary

* *Note* : The returns to professional education obtained in this study are compared with returns obtained in other studies. The comparative account is given in Appendix.

educated over the upper primary educated. There is an apparent earning advantages for a vocational educated over a secondary educated, but net of costs, it shows a loss. Both intermediate over secondary and post-graduate over graduate levels have negative earning advantages.

5. Thus, data on the lifetime unregressed and regressed earnings indicate that secondary education is the most profitable (even net of costs) levels of education. Intermediate and post-graduate levels represent negative earning advantages and, are thus, not profitable over the preceding levels.

The internal rates of return from educational increments reveal that :

1. Secondary education over upper primary education yields the highest private internal rate of return, followed closely by the upper primary over the lower primary educated.

2. Above the secondary level, it is the vocational level which yields the highest rate of return.

3. The rate of return to professional education is higher than that of graduate education. However, both these levels yield quite low returns.

4. The internal rates of return indicate that secondary education yields the highest returns, followed by the upper primary level, and is hence considered to be a profitable personal investment. Intermediate and post-graduate levels bring about negative returns and are hence unprofitable.

In general, secondary education shows considerably high returns as compared to other levels of education and hence, should be considered as the most profitable level for private investment.

## II. B. NON-ECONOMIC RETURNS FROM EDUCATION

### Attitudinal and Behavioural Returns

In this part, information collected from the employed women regarding the non-economic returns from education, i.e., attitudinal and behavioural returns are presented in the form of simple percentage and interpreted. As education affects the attitude and behaviour of individuals, it is assumed that there is a difference in the attitudes and behaviour of employed women with different levels of education towards various social institutions such as Education, Employment, Marriage and Family, Religion, Politics and Social Life. Further, it is assumed that higher the level of education of the individuals, there will be less inconsistency between their attitudes and behaviour towards the above social institutions.

### I. Attitudes and Behaviour of Women towards 'Education'

In this section, attitudes and behaviour of respondents towards education are analysed. Items on attitudes refer to the level upto which girls should be educated, co-education, girls being taught by female teachers only, girls taking up a male-dominated course like engineering, girls staying in hostels and going out of their home towns to receive education and girls receiving education under economic constraints. Corresponding questions on behaviour for all items on attitudes were not asked due to two reasons :

1. As parents generally take decisions for their children, especially the daughters, behaviour items on the education of the respondents depict the behaviour pattern of the respondents' parents and not that of the respondents themselves.

2. As the percentage of respondents having daughters who have completed their education is very low, corresponding behaviour items for all the attitude items was not possible.

However, wherever possible, the behaviour of respondents in terms of their daughters' education has been elicited.

Attitude of respondents towards the level upto which girls should be educated indicate that nearly 5.42 per cent of the employed illiterate women believe that girls do not need any education. A reference to the educational qualification of the respondents (Table No. 4.15 under "Profile of the sample") reveals that 15.43 per cent of the sample are illiterates, 4.24 per cent are lower primary, 4.7 per cent are upper primary and 17.35 per cent are secondary educated. Of them, the proportion of respondents who want girls to be educated beyond the secondary school level is 23.15, 27.77, 50.00 and 79.62 per cent respectively. Thus, with successive levels of education, there is an increase in the percentage of those who favour college education for girls.

It is surprising to note that there are women who want girls to be educated for lower levels than the ones upto which they were educated. Their percentage is highest among those with professional education. Around 34.00 per cent of the professional educated prefer collegiate education for girls, i.e., both basic and post-graduate degrees. Among those with vocational education, 11.35 per cent of the respondents prefer secondary education for girls. Even among the intermediates and graduates, 7.5 and 3.39 per cent of the respondents favour secondary education for girls.

Thus, the pattern that emerges from the data is that respondents with no education and below high school education favour secondary education ; those with secondary and pre-university education favour collegiate and professional education and those with collegiate education prefer professional/technical education. Further, it is seen that nearly one out of every six illiterate employed women vote for college education (general) to girls and there are a few (6.4 per cent) who are in favour of professional education also. On the other hand, one out of every three professional/technically educated and employed women are not in favour of such education for girls. In general, three out of every four women favour post-school education for girls which may be either collegiate or professional/technical education.

The attitude of women towards co-education indicates that majority of the respondents, irrespective of their level of education, are of the view that girls should be encouraged to attend co-educational institutions. Even among the illiterates and primary educated respondents, the percentage of those who favour girls attending co-educational institutions is as high as 48.28 per cent and 60.19 per cent respectively Among those with intermediate education and above, around 90.0 per cent of the respondents prefer co-education.

As sensitivity to co-education gathers significance only at a particular stage of education, the women were asked their view about the level upto which co-education should be encouraged. It is observed that among the illiterates and those with primary education, a lesser percentage prefer co-education at the secondary level than at the primary and collegiate levels. Even among those with secondary education and above who do not prefer co-education at all the levels, a higher proportion of respondents prefer co-education at the collegiate rather than the primary and secondary levels.

Thus, bulk of the respondents indicate that among all levels of education except at the illiterate and primary level, respondents favour co-education at all levels. Among those who disagree with co-education at all levels, quite a few are not opposed to it at the collegiate level.

Among respondents who send their daughters to co-educational institutions, majority of the respondents with no education and primary education send their daughters to schools meant for girls only. Among those with secondary education and above, majority of them send their daughters to co-educational institutions.

A comparison of their attitude with behaviour reveals that among levels of education a higher proportion of respondents prefer sending their daughters to co-educational institutions than they really do.

Attitude towards girls being taught by female teachers only and the level of education at which female teachers are favoured indicates that while majority of the illiterates and primary educated respondents favour the view that girls should be taught by female teachers only, majority of those with secondary education and above do not agree with the view. Among respondents who favour only female teachers for girls, those with upper primary education and below favour it at the secondary school level while those with secondary education and above, for all levels of education. A higher proportion of respondents with above secondary education favour female teachers at the primary school level than those with secondary education and below.

With the advocacy of equal opportunities for women in education, it was considered important to find out the attitude of women towards girls taking up a male-dominated course like engineering. Majority of the illiterate, primary and secondary educated respondents favour the view that girls should not be encouraged to take up courses in engineering. This may be due to the persistance of the traditional attitude that such courses are exclusively meant for men.

Among those with vocational education and above, majority of the respondents favour girls taking up courses in engineering. The reason for the favourable attitude may be that with higher education, women are more aware of the value and new outlets in engineering and consequently they no longer accept the belief that engineering should be the sole monopoly of males. However, as per an estimate, there are over 8,000 engineers in Bangalore City out of whom nearly 6,000 are working in establishments. But there are in all hardly 60 women engineers.[1]

Thus, with successive levels of education, there is a decrease in the percentage of respondents who agree that girls should not take up engineering, indicating an inverse relationship between the attitude and education of the respondents.

The attitude of women towards girls staying in hostels and going out of their home-towns to receive education reveals that as high as 67.49 per cent of the illiterates agree that girls should not be allowed to stay in hostels. Among all other educational groups, majority of the respondents favour girls staying in hostels. However, the percentage of secondary, vocational and intermediate respondents who agree that girls should not be encouraged to stay in hostels is higher than that of the primary educated respondents.

As regards going out of their home-towns to receive education, it is observed that nearly 78.0 per cent of the illiterates disagree with the view. The percentage falls as the level of education increases. While majority of the upper and lower primary educated respondents agree that girls should not leave their home-towns, majority of them with secondary education and above disagree with the view.

It is further observed that the proportion of the illiterate and primary educated respondents who agree that the girls should not be encouraged to go out of their home-towns to receive education is higher than those who agree that girls should not be allowed to stay in hostels. Among the secondary, vocational and intermediate-educated respondents, a higher percentage favour girls going out of their home-towns than staying in hostels. An almost equal proportion of college educated respondents favour girls staying in hostels and going out of their home-towns to receive education.

1. A.S. Seetharamu : "Women in Organised Movements", Ambika Publications, New Delhi, 1981, p. 75.

Attitude of respondents towards parents taking decision about the education of their daughters shows that the proportion who favour parents decision decreases with successive levels of education. But, surprisingly, a higher rate of professional educated respondents favour parents decision than the graduates and post-graduates.

As there is an inverse relation between the education of the respondents and their attitude towards parents taking decision, one would expect that in actual practice also, the respondents with higher education would allow their daughters to decide the level upto which they should be educated. Hence, to find out the extent to which the respondents attitude and behaviour are related, responses of married women having daughters were analysed.

The proportion of respondents who allow their daughters to decide about the level upto which they should have education increases as the level of education of the respondents increases. At all levels of education, the proportion of husbands of the respondents deciding is less than the proportion of respondents deciding themselves for their daughters. Among those who decide in consultation with one another, the percentage is highest for the vocational educated, followed by the graduates and post-graduates. Further, at all levels of education except at the illiterate and professional levels, the per centage of respondents who allow their daughters to decide by themselves about their education is less than those who agree with the view that daughters should take the decision.

Attitude of respondents towards education of girls under economic constraints reveals that 91.13 per cent of the illiterates favour education of sons than daughters under conditions of economic constraints. There is a sharp decline in the proportion of respondents favouring, under economic pressure, boys education to girls among those having post-secondary and collegiate education. Lowest percentage of agreement has come from the post-graduates (21.15 per cent).

Thus, in general, respondents who have received more than secondary education are more inclined to agree that there should be no differentiation between girls and boys in receiving education under conditions of economic stress, while those with secondary and below are less inclined to agree that boys education should get preference over that of girls under economic constraints.

## II. Attitudes and Behaviour of Women towards Employments

The culturally accepted role of women is that of house keeping and child bearing. Restriction on women to enter the labour market vary widely and involve considerations of family status, fear of neglect of the home and children and the fear of being economically independent and hence unconventional. In spite of these objections, the uumber of working women in the labour force has been increasing considerably. However, the reasons for the increased participation of women in labour also vary widely. Since the present sample of employed women have been exposed to various experiences outside the home, it is anticipated that their attitudes and behaviour pattern would be in favour of employment of women. It is also assumed that education will have an influence on their attitudes and behaviour towards 'employment'.

As the sample constituted of only employed women, as expected a vast majority of the respondents disagree with the view that the husband should be the sole bread winner of the family. However, what is surprising is that there are women who irrespective of their education agree with the view. Perhaps, they comprise of those women who are compelled to work.

While majority of the respondents favour women to continue to work inspite of having children within the school-going age, the proportion of those who do not favour this view is higher among respondents with college education than those with school education. Thus, women with higher levels of education agree in greater proportion that women should not work and that they should take care of the children who are within school-going age.

An analysis of the persons who look/looked after the non-school going children of the respondents indicate that basically the respondents leave their children with their parents or parents-in-law. Majority of the working women, thus, depend upon non-working members in the family to take care of their children. However, among the illiterates and primary educated respondents, quite a significant percentage of the children are left without adult care. As these women can ill-afford to employ servants and moreover creches are not provided by the establishments they work for, a case is being made to open creches especially for women belonging to the lower socio-economic order. Even where creches are provided, which is quite significant, they are sparingly used among the respondents irrespective of their education. Therefore, it is suggested that an attempt should be made by the establishments to provide or improve the existing creches and popularise them among the employed women having non-school going children.

Respondents, irrespective of their educational qualifications, agree that a woman should work in order to supplement the family income. In practice also, a high percentage of respondents indicate that they have taken up employment for economic reasons, i.e., mainly to support or supplement the income of the family.

In general, when respondents are categorised on the basis of education into three groups as ; (1) Illiterate, lower and primary educated, (2) Secondary, vocational and intermediate educated and (3) Graduate and above educated, it is observed that 95.13, 72.64 and 46.37 per cent respectively work to meet their basic needs.* Thus, the proportion of respondents who

* Reasons : "No alternative", "To support the family" and "To supplement income", are combined to arrive at figures for "basic needs".

work to meet their basic needs decreases with successive stages of education.

In a social structure where man enjoys a superior position to woman, her achievement, especially in terms of higher income, may pose a threat to his status. Because of the women's higher earnings, he might develop an inferiority complex due to which, conflicts between the partners may arise.

Though the general view among the respondents is that conflicts will be less where husband earns more than the wife, the proportion who agree with this view is higher among the illiterates and primary educated respondents.

More than 80.0 per cent of the respondents at all levels of education earn less than their husbands. Though the proportion of respondents who earn more than their husbands is quite low, they were questioned as to whether there were conflicts in the family exclusively due to their higher earnings. Though no generalisation about the pattern of behaviour can be drawn, the trend that exists is that the illiterates and lower primary educated respondents reported the highest percentage of conflicts in the family exclusively due to their higher earnings, than those with secondary education and above. This may be due to the better understanding between the spouses among the educated than the un-educated and less educated respondents.

Regarding the view of respondents towards the discrimination of women in recruitment to jobs, there is no definite pattern in the relationship between education and their attitude. However, it is to be noted that irrespective of the level of education, at least three out of every seven working women feel that a woman is discriminated against recruitment to jobs.

As nearly 44.0 per cent of the total respondents are of the view that women are discriminated in their recruitment to jobs, their responses as to how they secured their present jobs were analysed. The data indicate whether in actual practice they have been discriminated.

Though nearly 44.0 per cent of of the respondents agree that women are discriminated, since majority of the respondents with secondary education and above have secured jobs on the basis of their qualification and through the Employment Exchange and also through recommendations, discrimination does not seem to be prominent. Perhaps they must have kept in view their waiting period for employment and felt discriminated against. But, from a mere perspective of waiting period in general, it may be observed that there is nothing un-usual about the women under study.

Attitude towards work load and wages for women reveals that more than 50.0 per cent of the respondents at all levels of education disagree that a women can do all the jobs a man can do. It is surprising to note that even among the educated, this attitude prevails Thus, education does not seem to be a differentiating factor influencing the proportion of respondents at various levels of education in regard to their attitude towards women doing all the jobs that a man can do.

Regarding work-load for women, except for the lower primary and vocational levels, there is no difference in the percentage of respondents who favour less work-load for women, below the intermediate level. However, when the respondents are categorised into two groups as : those with intermediate education and below, and those with graduation and above, the proportion of the former group who favour the view is by and large twice as much as that of the latter group. At graduate and higher levels of education, a high proportion of women agree that women should take on as much work-load as men do.

Coming to the operational part of payment for jobs, the respondents were asked to give their view on men and women getting equal wages for a similar job. More than 90.0 per cent of the respondents, irrespective of their education, agree that men and women should get equal wages for a similar job. Surprisingly, there are still some women, at all levels of education, who feel that women should be paid lesser than men for similar jobs.

The attitude of respondents towards the view that employers tend to exploit women workers, reveals that a higher proportion of respondents in agreement among those with less than secondary education, is in conformity with the general observation that the less educated, unskilled/semi-skilled labourers and those working in the private sector would be more likely to be exploited by their employers.

The study of the attitudes of respondents towards work and wages indicates that women feel that they are discriminated against in so far as their recruitment, work-load, wages and exploitation are concerned. It would be interesting to discover whether in actual practice they are discriminated and if so, the conditions under which they are discriminated.

An analysis reveals that irrespective of the education of the respondents, a great majority of them have not been discriminated The percentages are notable only among the primary educated and illiterates, where discrimination is mostly with respect to working conditions, facilities and wages.

Attitude towards reservation of seats for women in employment, in general indicates that as the level of education of the respondents increases, the percentage of those in favour of reservation of vacancies for women decreases. Thus, education is inversely related to the percentage of those who favour reservation of jobs for women. However, the observation drawn from the data is that irrespective of education, majority of the respondents are in favour of the view that a percentage of jobs should be reserved for women.

**Decision about Working**

The data regarding the decision making role of women with regard to their taking up a job shows that the parents, husband and the respondents themselves have been the major decision-makers. The proportion of parents taking decision that the respondents should work is highest for the illiterates. However, the percentage of parents who have taken decisions decreases considerably with successive levels of education. As regards the decision taken by the respondents themselves, it is seen that there is a direct relationship between education and the respondents as decision-makers. Thus, as the level of education increases, the proportion of respondents taking decision also increases. Another highlight of the data is that among the college educated, in a notable percentage of respondents, decisions had been made through mutual consultations.

The general trend that emerges is that as the level of education of the respondents increases :

1. The proportion of parents/husbands taking decision decreases.
2. The proportion of respondents taking decision by themselves increases, and
3. Consultation with other family members is also significant among women with higher levels of education.

**Control over Independent Earnings**

Here an analysis is made as the earnings of the respondents. Questions were asked as to whether the respondents keep their salaries to themselves or not ? If not, to whom did they give their salaries and whether they gave their whole salaries. To those who did not keep their salaries, a question whether they had a voice in the way their earnings are spent was asked ; if not, who decides the way it is spent. Finally, how they manage money for their personal expenses. The answers to these set of questions give us a fairly good idea of the person/s who are vested with authority in the family. It is assumed that with increasing levels of education, the respondents will have more control over their earnings and a voice as to how it is spent.

It is observed that a higher percentage of women keep their salaries with themselves only among the illiterates, lower primary and higher levels of (Post-graduate and Professional/Technical) educated women. Here, a distinction should be made between the lower and higher levels. While an illiterate and lower primary educated woman who keeps her salary with herself may have to spend it on her family or children as the husband may not be responsible, in the case of those who are post-graduate and professionally educated, may be to acquire comforts.

Among those who do not keep their salaries with themselves, it is seen that majority of them give their salaries either to their parents or husbands. While basically the unmarried respondents give their salaries to their parents, the married respondents give it to their husbands. Quite a significant percentage of illiterate and lower primary educated respondents give their salaries to their parents-in-law.

Of those who give their salaries, it is observed that they basically give their whole salaries. However, the proportion of respondents who give their whole salaries decreases with increase in education. Thus, while education does not seem to have an influence on the proportion of respondents who keep their salaries with themselves, the proportion of respondents who give their whole salaries decreases with education.

Responses to the question as to whether the respondents have a voice in the way their earnings are spent reveals that of those who give either part or whole of the salaries, a higher percentage of women among the lower and higher levels of education have a voice in the way their earnings are spent. While at the lower levels the respondents have a voice, may be in so far as the maintenance of the family concerned ; among those with higher levels of education, apart from running of the family, it might also include the buying of gadgets and luxury items.

Of those who do not have a voice in the way their earnings are spend, it is observed that the parents and husbands form the major decision makers in the family. While parents take the decision for majority of the un-married respondents, husbands take the decision for the married women. Only among the illiterates and upper primary educated respondents, the decision about the way the earnings of the respondents are spent is exclusively taken by the parents-in-law. Among the post-graduates and those with professional education, a significant percentage of respondents take decisions on a consultative basis.

Educatlon does not appear to have an influence on the proportion of respondents who have a voice in the way their earnings are spent.

**Financial Security of the Respondents**

Here an analysis of the savings behaviour of the respondents is made in terms of whether they save, and of those who save, whether their savings are in their own name or jointly with someone else. The responses to the latter part of the question will indicate whether the respondents have easy access to their savings.

It is observed that while the illiterates do not save at all, a negligible percentage of the primary educated respondents save. This may be due to their inability to save. There is a significant increase in the proportion of respondents who save beyond the secondary level.

Among those who save, a great majority of the respondents have an account in their own name. More than 90.0 per cent of the respondents with secondary education and above have their own accounts. It is interesting to note that among the secondary and higher educated women, there are women who have joint accounts.

## III. Attitudes and Behaviour of Women Towards "Marriage and Family"

In this section, the attitudes and behaviour pattern of respondents regarding marriage and family in relation to education are analysed. Wherever comparisons are made between the attitudinal and behaviour items, it should be noted that responses to attitude refer to all the respondents while that on the behaviour refer only to the married respondents who form 68.05 per cent of the sample.

### Choice of Marriage Partner

With regard to the attitude of women towards the person who should decide about the choice of marriage partner, education turns out to be an important differentiating factor. It is observed that as the level of education increases, the proportion of respondents who agree that parents should take the decision decreases. Correspondingly, the percentage of those who take the view that the choice should be on the basis of mutual concent of the boy and the girl to be married increases with education. There is no definite pattern of responses among the respondents who favour parents to make the choice with the consent of the boy and girl. However, when they are clubbed on the basis of education into three major groups illiterates, school and post-school education, and collegiate education, it is observed that as the level of education rises, the percentage who favour parents making the choice with the consent of the boy and the girl also increases.

In general, the more educated the respondents are, the more likely it is that they would consider it important to :

1. Consult the boy or girl concerned regarding his or her marriage, and

2. Obtain mutual consent of the boy and girl to be married.

An analysis of the actual practice followed by the families in the marriage of the respondents reveals that the proportion of respondents who have married the person their parents selected decreases as the level of education increases. Correspondingly, it is observed that the proportion of parents who selected the marriage partner for their daughters on their own with the consent of the respondents increases considerably as the level of education increases. There is not a single illiterate and lower primary educated respondent in the sample who has married the spouse of her choice with the consent of her parents or on her own. The proportion of respondents who reported that they have selected their own partners irrespective of their parents' consent is very low. Only among those with secondary and professional education, a relatively higher percentage of respondents have selected their own marriage partners.

A comparison of the attitudes and behaviour pattern of the respondents reveals that a higher percentage of respondents have in actual practice married the person of their parents' choice than those who favour the view that parents alone should choose the marriage partner. Correspondingly, the proportion of respondents who have been married with their consent is less than those who consider it necessary to obtain the consent of the person to be married. Even among those who consider that mutual consent of the boy and girl to be married is necessary, there is a higher percentage of respondents who favour such marriages than those who have undergone them.

The inconsistency in the attitudes and behaviour of the respondents may be to a certain extent due to the reflection of the behaviour pattern of the parents of the respondents than the respondents themselves. However, it is found that with increased education, the proportion in favour of parents selecting the marriage partner and those who have married the spouse of their parents' choice decreases. Highest consistency is observed between illiterate and secondary educated in their belief that parents should choose the spouse for their children and in actually allowing them to do so.

**Caste and Inter-caste Marriages**

Attitude towards caste and inter-caste marriage reveals that the percentage of respondents who object to inter-caste marriage is highest among the illiterates (90.64 per cent). This percentage decreases with the successive levels of education. The data reveals that though the trend that emerges is in favour of inter-caste marriages, with the acquiring of more education, a comparatively larger proportion of respondents at all levels of education are in favour of marriages within the caste.

Whether in actual practice the women have married within their caste or outside the caste, shows that irrespective of their education, they have married within their caste. However, when the respondents are classified on the basis of their education into illiterates, school and post-school educated ; and college educated, it is observed that as the educational level rises, the percentage of inter-caste marriage also increases.

A comparison of their attitude and behaviour reveals that while a larger proportion of respondents among all levels of education seem to have a favourable attitude towards inter-caste marriages, they are still uncommon even among the educated.

**Attitude and Behaviour Pattern of Women towards Register Marriages**

A direct relationship is observed between education of respondents and the percentage of those who agree that register marriages should be encouraged as they reduce the financial burden of the parents However, in actual practice, more than 90 0 per cent of the respondents, irrespective of their educational attainment, have undergone Social/religious marriages.

The percentage of respondents who underwent registered marriage is insignificant.

Thus, higher the education, higher the proportion of respondents who have a favourable attitude towards the encouragement of register marriages. However, such a generalisation egarding their behaviour cannot be drawn due to the negligible number of respondents who in actual practice underwent such a marriage. As may be expected, the behavioural change is beyond their control and is subject to several interesting forces in their social environment.

**Dowry**

The general trend regarding the attitude of respondents towards dowry reveals that most of them disfavour the practice of dowry. While quite a high percentage of respondents (around 70.0 per cent) disagree that by giving dowry, parents can get a good husband for their daughter, a lesser percentage (65.0 per cent) disagree that giving dowry enhances the sense of security and status of the woman in her husband's house. And, finally, as high as 70.0 per cent of the collegiate educated women are of the view that by educating the girls, dowry can be avoided.

To analyse the behaviour pattern of the women with regard to dowry, questions were asked as to whether the respondents paid dowry ; whether they objected to paying dowry ; and the reasons for paying or not paying dowry. Further, questions were asked about who met the dowry requirements, in what form it was given and who used the dowry.

It is observed that more than 90.0 per cent of the married respondents have not paid dowry. Among those who paid dowry, the percentage is highest for those with professional education followed by those with vocational and secondary education. While the illiterate and primary educated respondents did not object to pay dowry, those with secondary and above objected to pay dowry. Among those who did object, for every two matriculates, vocational educated and undergraduates, three graduates, post-graduates and professional educated have objected. Thus, higher the education, the proportion of respondents who objected to pay dowry is higher. The generalisation made in respect to those who objected to pay dowry has a limitatiom in so far as it refers to a very small proportion of respondents who have paid dowry.

A comparison of the attitude and behaviour reveals that a lesser percentage of respondents with primary and no education have paid dowry than those who agree that the system of dowry should continue. Among those who have secondary education and above, a higher percentage of respondents have paid dowry than those who agree with the view that dowry should continue.

It may be recalled here that hardly 13.87 per cent of women in the sample have paid dowry. They are mostly secondary, vocational and professional/technical educated. However, an analysis of the reasons offered by the respondents who paid dowry reveals that the main reason for paying dowry was that they were compelled to pay. Another significant reason forwarded for paying dowry is that it is a prestige symbol. One more reason for giving dowry is that it gives status and security to the women in her husband's house. Surprisingly, professional educated respondents have also paid dowry because it gives status to the women.

Among those who did not pay dowry, there is no definite pattern in the relationship between education and reasons for not paying dowry. However, an analysis of the reasons indicate that a higher proportion of illiterate respondents and those with primary education did not pay dowry as it was not demanded, while among the secondary and higher educated respondents dowry was not paid as they are employed or because they underwent love-marriages. It is interesting to note that except for the post-graduates, a very negligible percentage did not pay dowry because they are educated,

Thus, education of the respondents does not appear to be an important criteria for not paying dowry. It is their employment status that has played a greater role.

The way the dowry requirements were met reveals that with higher education, the possibility of meeting the dowry requirements through their own earnings is high. One of the strong reasons for women to work may be to earn money for their marriage and dowry expenses, thereby they may be able to bring a greater relief to their parents.

The person/s who used the dowry reveals that irrespective of the education of the respondents, the money given as dowry was either used by the parents-in-law or husbands. Only among the post-graduates and professional educated respondents some degree of control of the money was exercised by the respondents in so far as they had joint accounts with their husbands. Even otherwise, in only 10 10 per cent of the cases the dowry amount was kept as savings.

**Family Composition**

From a comparative picture of the attitude and behaviour of respondents towards family composition, it is observed that the percentage of respondents who live in nuclear families but consider a joint family as advantageous is highest among the primary educated respondents followed by the illiterates. The proportion falls considerably at the secondary level. At the post-graduate level a higher percentage of respondents live in nuclear families than those who consider it advantageous to live in joint families.

Correspondingly, the proportion of respondents living in nuclear families and who consider it comfortable is quite low among all levels of education. While at the post-graduate and lower primary levels an almost equal proportion of respondents live in nuclear families as those who consider it comfortable, at the professional level a lesser percentage live in nuclear families than those who consider it comfortable.

In general, a higher percentage of respondents live in nuclear families than those who favour it. However, as the level of education rises, the difference in the percentage who favour and who actually live in nuclear families decreases.

**Attitude and Behaviour of Women towards Household Work**

It is assumed that there may be a relation between education and the attitude and behaviour of women towards the role of women in household management. As such, statements relating to this aspect were analysed.

Attitude towards female members doing household work reveals that around 80.0 per cent of the illiterates agree that women should do all the household work entirely by themselves. This percentage falls as the level of education increases. Also it is observed that the proportion of respondents who agree that men alone should plan the monthly budget of the family is highest among the illiterates. The percentage decreases successively from lower to higher levels of education.

An interesting observation is that while majority of the respondents with secondary education and above would expect men to join hands in household work, majority with lower primary education and above want to join men in planning the monthly budget.

Questions were asked to ascertain whether in actual practice the household work in the family is distributed or done exclusively by the female members. The questions were asked in relation to the following specific household tasks and responsibilities :

(1) Cooking ;

(2) Washing dishes ;

(3) Washing clothes ;

(4) Dusting ;

(5) Shopping ;

(6) Up-bringing children ;

(7) Education of children ; and

(8) Disciplining children.

A review on the sharing of work in the household reveals that cooking food is a task done exclusively by the female members irrespective of their education. There are certain other tasks like cleaning the utensils, washing clothes and dusting which are also mainly performed by the female members under all categories of education. However, among those who have secondary education and beyond, quite a significant percentage of women employ servants to do the tasks.

The percentage of males doing shopping is higher than that of females only where the purchase of provisions are concerned. Proportion of women purchasing of vegetables and clothes is higher than those of their husbands. It is observed that with increasing education those who do shopping in cooperation with their husbands increases.

Up-bringing children is basically a women's task among those without education and primary education. Among those with secondary education and beyond, it is mainly a shared responsibility.

Taking care of the education of the children is also mainly a shared task, the proportion increasing with an increase in the level of education of the respondents, while at the lower levels of education (i.e., among illiterates and primary respondents) the male members take the responsibility, among all other levels of education, it is mainly a task performed by the female members.

Disciplining children is mainly a shared responsibility as the level of education of the respondents increases. It is observed, in general, that the percentage of respondents who discipline their children is higher than that of their husbands.

**Decision making in the Family**

This section refers to the part played by women in decision-making on different issues in the family. The questions asked were related to the following specific situations :

1. Education of children,
2. Occupation of children, and
3. Marriage of children.

Answers to this set of questions will indicate the extent to which authority is attributed to a single person and the extent to which it is considered to be shared. The expectation is that in most families, the eldest male or the husband will be the main decision maker. However, it is hypothesized that with increased education women will also play a part in the decision-making and that decisions will be taken more so on a consultative basis. It is also assumed that among respondents with higher education, children will be allowed to take decisions for themselves.

In actual practice also, it is observed that decisions regarding the education, occupation and marriage of children are essentially taken on a consultative basis. The proportion of families of the respondents who take such decisions in consultation with one another increases as the level of education rises. Also with higher education, the proportion of families where children are allowed to take decisions for themselves is also high.

**Attitude and Behaviour of Women towards Family Planning**

It is hypothesized that with increased education, there will be increase in the proportion of respondents who :

1. Have favourable attitude towards family planning.
2. Desire less number of children.

3. Will not resist family planning on religious grounds.

4. Favour sterilisation, and

5. Use family planning methods.

It is observed from the attitude of respondents towards the number of children in the family that more than 75.0 per cent of the illiterates and nearly 85.00 per cent among the educated favour the view that a family should have two to three children only. While a higher percentage of illiterates and primary educated respondents favour three children, among all the other levels of education, they favour the idea of two children only. Among the percentage of respondents who support the view that a family should have as many children as they are capable of looking after, that of the illiterates is the most.

Attitude of respondents towards family planning methods being used against the sanctions religion indicates that majority of the respondents, irrespective of their education, disagree with the view that family planning methods should not be practised if they do not have religious sanctions. The percentage of respondents who disagree slightly increases as the level of education rises. While 75.86 per cent of the illiterates disagree, the percentage increases gradually to 83.33 per cent among the professional educated respondents.

Thus, among all the levels of educated, majority of the respondents favour family planning methods irrespective of religious sanction. However, it is surprising to find that even college educated women want religious sanctions to practice family planning methods even though their proportion may be small, i,e., one out of five or six respondents.

The percentage of respondents who agree that sterilisation should be encouraged increases from 43.38 per cent among the illiterates to 69.85 per cent among the professional educated. Around 38.0 per cent of the college educated respondents also disagree with sterilisation being encouraged, This may be due to the perceived side-effects of sterilisation on health and working ability. In general, with education, a slightly higher proportion of respondents favour the view that sterilisation should be encouraged.

The attitude of respondents towards the item that sterilisation affects the working efficiency of a women reveals that as high as 58.62 per cent of the illiterates agree that it does. This percentage falls gradually as the level of education rises. Thus, the corresponding percentage of post-graduate and professional educated respondents who are in agreement with the view that the working efficiency of a women is affected because of sterilisation, is about 25.0 per cent only.

In general, it is observed that with education, the percentage of respondents who agree that sterilisation affects the working efficiency of a women decreases.

As regards tubectomy, an almost equal percentage of respondents among illiterates and primary educated on the one hand and among the secondary and higher educated on the other, agree that tubectomy is a sound family planning technique, 44.41 and 53.87 per cent respectively. While respondents have a favourable attitude towards family planning, they do not favour sterilisation because they feel that it affects the health of the working women and to some extent working efficiency also.

The following is an analysis of the responses of married women to the questions : whether in actual practice the married respondents have accepted family planning techniques ; if yes, the time of adoption and the method adopted and in case of those who do not use family planning methods, the reasons for not adopting.

The proportion of married respondents who have accepted family planning techniques increases as the level of education rises. Thus, the percentage of respondents who have accepted family planning techniques is least among the illiterates and highest among the professional educated respondents.

It is observed that only respondents with college education have accepted family planning techniques soon after marriage (i.e., graduation and above), the percentage being highest for the post-graduates. While there are no respondents in the illiterate and lower primary groups who have used family planning techniques after the birth of the first child, the percentage increases steadily with successive levels of education.

Among those who have accepted family planning techniques after the second child, the proportion increases from 27.27 per cent among the illiterates to 50.0 per cent among the vocational educated and again falls with successive levels of education. More than 20.0 per cent of the respondents with vocational education and below use family planning methods after the birth of the third child, the percentage being the highest among the lower primary educated respondents, 34.44 per cent. While the overall percentage of those who use family planning methods for the purpose of spacing the children is less, it is a little popular among those with intermediate education and above

Though the proportion of respondents who have used family planning techniques is quite low, especially at the lower levels of education, the trend that emerges is that there is a relation between education of the respondents and the time of adoption of family planning techniques. Thus, education is directly related to the percentage of those who use family planning techniques soon after the marriage, after the birth of the first child and for spacing of children. Higher the education, greater the chances of using family planning techniques immediately after marriage or after the first child.

**Family Planning Technique Accepted**

Regarding the technique of family planning adopted by the respondents, it is assumed that while the self restraint techniques of family planning (that is natural methods of abstinence and rhythm and withdrawl) will be prominent among the educated, sterilisation will be more prominent among the illiterates and less educated respondents (i.e., the artificial method).

The proportion of respondents who practice abstinence is highest among the graduates and professional educated respondents. Among those who use the rhythm and withdrawl technique, the percentages are highest among respondents with vocational, post-graduates and professional educated. Though there is no definite relationship between those who use contraceptives and education, the proportion is the least among illiterates and lower primary educated respondents. The proportion of respondents who underwent sterilisation decreases as the level of education rises.

Thus, education appears to be related to the method of family planning accepted. While around two out of three illiterate and lower primary educated respondents are sterilised, one out of two respondents with vocational education and above use the abstinence and rhythm and withdrawl technique. A higher proportion of vocational educated, graduates and professional educated women use natural methods in preference to contraceptives. A higher proportion of the husbands of the respondents without any formal education and school education have undergone sterilisation than those with college education.

An analysis of the reasons for not adopting family planning methods reveals the following information :

The main reasons offered are that either they have no children or they want more children. The percentage of those who have not accepted family planning methods because they do not have children, increases as the level of education rises. One explanation for the higher percentage of secondary educated and beyond who have no children is due to the increased age of marriage among them. The percentage of respondents who want more children and hence have not accepted family planning techniques is highest among the matriculates.

The next important reason for non-acceptance of family planning techniques is that it is injurious to health, the percentage is highest among the upper primary educated and least among the graduates and professional educated.

73.39 per cent of the illiterates do not practice family planning techniques because children are given by God and hence, their birth should not be prevented. Surprisingly, around 12.0 per cent of the graduates and professional educated respondents also give the same reason. As high as 20.0 per cent of the post-graduates do not use family planning methods because it is against the sanctions of religion. Among those who have given the reason that a big family offers protection and security in old age, the percentages are negligible at all levels of education.

Education does not seem to have any bearing on the reasons given by the respondents for not accepting family planning techniques.

The following analysis is confined to only those respondents who have children. It presents information regarding the health care measures taken by the respondents for their children.

It is observed that majority of the respondents with secondary education and above have taken all the three health measures for their children ; vaccination, polio and triple immunisation. Majority of the respondents without education and with lower primary education have not taken the above health measures for their children. A higher percentage of upper primary educated respondents have not taken the health measures than the lower primary respondents.

Thus, in general, while those with upper primary education and below have not taken the preventive health care measures, those with secondary education and beyond have taken these measures for their children.

### Attitude towards Abortion

Abortion was legalised by the Medical Termination of Pregnancy Act of 1971. It was passed in order to reduce the incidence of criminal abortion which posed grave risks to pregnant women. The act allows termination of pregnancy on : (1) Therapeutic ; (2) Eugenic ; (3) Humanitarian ; and (4) Social grounds. However, opposition to abortion has arisen due to two beliefs. The first is that it affects the health of the aborted person and the second is it encourages immorality. The following analysis gives the attitude of respondents towards the item : 'abortion should have not been legalised and it affects the health of the aborted woman'.

Irrespective of the education of the respondents, majority agree with the view that abortion should not have been ligalised. The proportion of the respondents who agree with this view is highest among the illiterates, 83 25 per cent. There is a decline in the percentage of those who agree with the statement, as the level of education rises, thus reaching a minimum of 53.85 per cent among the professional educated respondents.

### Attitude towards Widows

Here responses to the following two attitudinal items relating to widows are analysed :

1. Should an employed widow look after herself ; and
2. Should a childless widow be encouraged to adopt a child.

Responses relating to the behaviour of the widows are not analysed as they constitute only 9.74 per cent of the sample (i.e., 142 respondents). Further, when they are categorised on the basis of their education, they form a very small proportion on which no valid generalisations about the relationship between education and their behaviour could be drawn.

It is observed that the percentage of respondents who agree that an employed widow should look after herself increases with successive levels of education. The proportion is highest among the post-graduates, 94.23 per cent. One of the explanations for disagreement to this among quite a significant proportion of vocational and school educated or illiterate respondents may be that a widow will feel insecure when she is to look after herself.

While more than 50.0 per cent of the illiterates and lower primary educated respondents do not favour the view, majority of the respondents with upper primary education and above agree that a childless widow should be encouraged to adopt a child. 57.41 per cent of those with upper primary education favour the view. The percentage among those with secondary education and beyond is almost evenly distributed, 70.0 per cent.

While education is directly related to the percentage of respondents who agree that a childless widow should be encouraged to adopt a child, education does not appear to be a differentiating factor beyond the secondary level.

### Attitude towards Divorce

Due to the sacramental nature of marriage, religious sentiments are against the dissolution of marriage. Hence, even to-day, though legislation has provided for divorce, it is not a socially accepted norm among many sections.

The respondents were asked their views on the following two items :

1. An woman should not be free to initiate a divorce ; and
2. A divorced woman should not expect financial support from her former husband.

As there are no divorcees in the sample, an analysis of their behaviour is not made. Further, the proportion of separatees is also insignificant to warrant an indepth analysis of their behaviour, i.e., 0.96 per cent or 15 respondents only.

Among those who agree with the view that women should not initiate a divorce, the percentage is highest among the illiterates and primary educated respondents (around 70.0 per cent). This percentage declines with successive levels of education. Thus, as high as 75.0 per cent of those with professional education feel that women should be free to initiate a divorce.

The percentage of those who agree that a divorced woman should expect financial support from her former husband is highest among the illiterates and primary educated respondents (this may be due to their insecurity due to their lower economic status). The percentage who favour support from former husbands decreases as the level of education rises. Every alternate woman agrees with the view among those with secondary education and above.

Thus, with increase in the levels of education, there is an increase in the percentage of respondents who agree that a divorced woman should not expect financial support from her former husband.

## IV. Attitudes and Behaviour of Women towards "Politics"

In this section, the political attitudes and behaviour of women are analysed. The items elicit the attitudes of respondents towards participation of women in political activities, political campaigns, elections and membership in political parties, their views on the educational requirement of those who exercise franchise, and reservation of seats for women in legislative bodies. The questions on behaviour elicit responses relating to the political behaviour of respondents in terms of their membership and activities in political parties, reading of political literature, canvassing in elections, attending political campaigns and voting.

The proportion of respondents who agree that women should not take part in politics is highest among the illiterates, 64.54 per cent. This percentage falls considerably for women with education and successively to those with higher levels of education, reaching a minimum of 14.78 per cent among the professional educated. Thus, majority of the respondents with lower primary education and above favour women's participation in politics.

Respondents who agree that women with family responsibilities should not take part in politics also decreases as the level of education increases. It is observed that among all levels of education, a higher percentage of respondents disagree with the statement that women with family responsibilities should take part in politics, than women in general. Thus, as against 90.0 per cent of the illiterates who favour the non-participation of women with family responsibilities, 64.54 per cent favour non-participation of women in general. Even among the college educated respondents, the percentage who agree with the view that family women should not take part in politics is twice that of those who agree with the view that women in general should not take part in politics.

Thus, education is seen as an important factor associated with the attitude of respondents towards women taking to politics and also women with family responsibilities taking part in politics.

Barring the illiterates, majority of the respondents agree that women should read political literature. While around 41.0 per cent of the illiterates favour the view that women should read political literature, the proportion increases to about 61.0 per cent among the lower primary educated respondents. Further, this percentage increases steadily with successive levels of education and reaches a maximum of 87.74 per cent among those with professional education. Still, one out of eight professional/technical educated women and one out of seven post-graduate women are those who do not approve of women reading political literature. Education appears to be directly related to the percentage of respondents who favour women reading literature pertaining to politics.

However, in actual practice, it is seen that majority of the respondents do not read political literature. Only respondents with secondary education and above read political literature. The proportion of respondents who read political literature rises from 4.93 per cent among the matriculates to 18.92 per cent among the post-graduates. One out of every six college educated women on an average read political literature. Education does not seem to have a significant relation with the habit of reading political literature among women.

Since majority of the respondents do not read political literature, information was elicited regarding their habit of reading newspapers.

Majority of the respondents read newspapers among those with secondary education and above. A relatively lesser percentage of primary educated respondents read news-papers. It is seen that the percentage of those who read news-papers increases as the level of education rises. What is surprising to note is that even among the educated women, there are some women who do not read the news-papers. Education appears to be directly related to the proportion of those who read the newspapers.

Of those who read news-papers, barring those with primary education, majority of the respondents with secondary education and above, read all types of information given in the newspapers. Among those who read political information, about 11.0 per cent are primary enducated and about 22.0 per cent are secondary educated and above.

The proportion of those who read exclusively about entertainment is highest among those with primary education (47.01

per cent). Around 17.0 per cent of those with secondary education and above read information regarding entertainment only. The percentage is least among the professional educated respondents. A negligible percentage of respondents read about the economic situation or sports. Even among the educated at the higher levels, there are respondents who read only about entertainment or economic or sports information in the newspapers. There is an observed difference between the primary and secondary educated in their news-paper reading interests. Differences are not much between and among the secondary and higher educated respondents.

**Attitudes and Behaviour Towards Participation of Women in Political Campaigns**

The proportion of respondents who agree that women should not take part in political campaigns declines with successive levels of education. Higher the education of respondents, higher is the proportion who favour women participating in political campaigns. For every two out of four secondary/vocational educated women who do find anything wrong in the participation of women in political campaigns, there are three such among the college educated.

Regarding the participation of repondents in political campaigns during the 1977 General Elections, majority of them have not attended. Of those who have attended, the percentage is highest among the graduates, 30.83 per cent. The second highest proportion is that of those with intermediate education, 21.74 per cent. A highest percentage of the lower primary educated respondents than the upper primary, secondary and vocational educated respondents have attended political campaigns.

Education does not seem to be definitely related to attendance at political campaigns. It may, at best have a marginal influence on the college educated respondents (general education upto graduation).

**Attitudes and Behaviour Towards Women becoming Members of Political Parties**

It is observed that the proportion of respondents who agree that women should not become members of political parties decreases as the level of education increases. As high as 71.02 per cent of the illiterates agree with this view, while among those with professional education only 17.92 per cent agree that women should not become members of political parties. If every alternate woman among the upper primary, secondary and vocational educated agree with the view, one out of four women among college educated (general) and one out of six among professional educated women agrees with it.

Higher the education of the respondents, the proportion of those who favour women becoming members of political parties also increases.

In reality, a great majority of the respondents at all levels of education are not members of any political group. While none of the respondents in the illiterate, lower primary and upper primary groups are members, a negligible percentage of respondents among other levels of education are members. The highest percentage of respondents who are members of a political group, are those who are professionally educated, 4.59 per cent.

Education does not appear to be an important factor influencing the membership of respondents in political groups. However, beyond the primary level of education, there is participation* in political parties among women though such participation is very low and negligible.

Among all levels of education, more than 25.0 per cent of the respondents have not participated in the activities of any political party. Of the negligible percentage who have participated, around 40.0 per cent are respondents from the secondary

* Participation is defined in terms of primary membership at least.

and intermediate levels. Education does not seem to influence the participation of respondents in the activities of a political party.

A vast majority of the respondents have not canvassed at the time of elections. Among those who have canvassed, the percentage is highest among those with graduation and above (about 50.0 per cent). The percentage is negligible among all other levels of education. The percentage of participation is very low to infer any relation between education and canvassing during elections.

It is seen that the percentage of respondents who agree that women should not contest elections decreases as the levels of education rises. While majority of the respondents who are illiterates and lower primary educated agree with the view that women should not contest elections, those with upper primary education and above favour women contesting elections. Education is inversely related to the percentage of respondents who agree that women should not contest elections.

**Attitudes Towards Voting**

The respondents were asked to express their views on the eligibility for voting, i.e., whether the right of voting should be :

1. Restricted to those with primary education and above ;
2. Restricted to those who are matriculates and above, and
3. Voting should not be restricted at all (adult franchise).

It is observed that the proportion of respondents who favour adult franchise is highest among the illiterates and primary educated respondents, 92.44 per cent. This percentage declines considerably as the level of education rises. Correspondingly, the percentage of respondents who agree that voting should be restricted to those with primary education and above increases as the level of education rises. The proportion of respondents who agree that the right of voting should be restricted to those with secondary education and beyond also increases as the level of education increases. It is surprising to note that 4.44 per cent and 2.93 per cent of the illiterates agree that voting should be restricted to those with primary education and above, and matriculation and above respectively. Majority of college educated women, intermediate (one out of two), graduates (four out of seven), post-graduates and professional educated (three out of four) (do not favour adult franchise). They want some education whether primary or secondary as essential requirement for entitlement to voting rights.

Education is inversely related to those who favour adult franchise and directly related to those who favour that voting should be restricted to those who are primary and secondary educated and above.

The voting behaviour of respondents during the 1977 General Elections for the Parliament reveals that among all levels of education, majority of the respondents have voted. At the upper primary stage, a comparatively lesser percentage of respondents have voted than the lower primary educated and illiterates. It is observed that even at the intermediate and graduate levels, surprisingly, a lower percentage of respondents have voted than those with secondary education and below. Education does not appear to be a decisive factor influencing the voting behaviour of the respondents as illiterates also participate in voting in significant numbers.

The analysis of the responses to the question as to how were they guided in casting their votes, reveals education as an important factor influencing the choice of a candidate. While majority of those with secondary education and above voted because they considered the candidate fit to win, those with less than secondary education have done so because ;

1. They identify themselves with the party of the candidate ;
2. Their husbands/parents asked them to do so ; and
3. The candidate belonged to their caste/religion.

However, it is interesting to note that even among the educated there are women (though in negligible numbers) who have voted for these reasons.

The non-voters at all educational levels, form a minority group. One of the main reasons offered for not voting is that the respondents are not interested in politics. The proportion of respondents who gave this reason is highest among the illiterates. While a high proportion of primary (50.0 per cent) and secondary (38.0 per cent) educated women did not vote because they were not eligible, among those with vocational education and above, almost one of every three respondents did not do so because they were not enrolled.

The post-graduates form the single largest educated group of women who did not vote because they have no faith in elections. Only among the illiterates nearly 18.0 per cent of them gave family commitments as a reason for not voting. Among post-graduates, 12.5 per cent did not vote because the polling booth was too far, which is quite strange.

While the reason that they were not eligible for voting is beyond the control of the respondents, they doing so because their names were not enrolled needs comment. It is seen that among those who are eligible, the educated appear not to bother to get their names enrolled, whereas the lower educated respondents are enrolled in larger proportions. Thus, the major reasons that stand out for the respondents are that their names were not enrolled and that they are not interested in politics. Reasons which do not appear to weigh much with the respondents are :

(1) They had family commitments which did not permit

them to vote ; (2) they did not like any of the candidates ; (3) polling booth was too far ; and (4) their belief in non-party politics.

Barring the illiterates, majority of the respondents discuss politics. And among those who discuss, they are mainly held with their family members and friends.

Regarding reservation of seats for women in the State Legislature, it is seen that, in general, the proportion of respondents who favour the view increases with increase in education.

Membership in trade union is negligible among respondents irrespective of their education. Only among matriculates, as high as 69.0 per cent are members. Industrial trade unionism has been popular for quite some time and secondary educated industrial women-workers, perhaps, move with this current. It may not have any thing to do with their level of education. Education, thus, does not appear to be a significant factor influencing the membership of women in trade-unions.

**V. Religious Attitudes and Behaviour Pattern of Women**

In this section, the religious attitudes and behaviour of respondents are analysed. The statements on attitudes elicit responses regarding their belief in the existence of God ; worship ; visiting places of worship ; going on a pilgrimage ; observance of religious rituals ; celebration of festivals and participation of woman in festivals during menstruation. The questions on religious behaviour elicit responses relating to the ritualistic behaviour of the respondents ; participation in festivals during menstruation ; participation of widows in religious ceremonies and the performance of religious initiation for boys and girls.

A vast majority of the respondents among all levels of education favour the view that women should believe in the existence of God. Their attitude towards worship reveals that majority of the respondents agree that worship of God liberates a woman. As the level of education rises, the percentage of respondents who agree with the view decreases gradually upto the vocational level and then falls considerably at the collegiate level. Thus, more than 80.0 per cent of the respondents among the school and vocational educated agree as against less than 58.0 per cent among those who are college educated. Thus, education seems to be an important factor differentiating the attitude of respondents towards worship when they are classified dichotomously on the basis of their education into those with school and vocational education and those with college education.

Attitude towards prayer reveals that more than 90.0 per cent of the illiterates agree that a woman can secure happiness and long-life for her husband through prayer. This percentage falls steadily as the level of education rises. Surprisingly, around 50.0 per cent of the respondents even among the highly educated are of the view that happiness and long-life for the 'husband' can be sought through prayer.

The respondents' attitude towards the frequency of visiting the place of worship indicates that majority of the illiterate and primary educated women believe in the value of daily visits. This percentage decreases considerably with increase in education. Around 43.0 per cent of the school and post-school educated respondents favour visiting the place of worship regularly as against 20.0 per cent of the college educated. Also with education, the percentage who agree that women should visit the place of worship only on festivals increases. Correspondingly, the percentage of respondents who do not want women to visit the place of worship increases steadily with successive levels of education. While there is an apparent difference between illiterates and educated, there is also a difference between the school and post-school educated on the one hand and college educated on the other.

Attitude towards religious rituals reveals that there is a decrease with increase in education in the proportion of respondents who favour observance of religious rituals daily. If four out of five illiterate and primary educated women approve of daily observance of rituals, every alternate secondary/vocational educated women, one out of three intermediate and graduate educated and one out of four professional/technical and post-graduate educated women approve of it. Among those who favour the regular observance of rituals, the percentage increases from around 12.0 per cent among the illiterates to 30.0 per cent among the intermediates and then falls beyond this level. Of those who favour rituals only on festivals/functions, a higher percentage of vocational and college educated (15.44 per cent) favour observance than those with school education (6.39 per cent). Of those totally disagreeing with the practice of rituals, the percentage increases as the level of education rises.

The tendency among the lower levels of educated is to approve of the daily observance of rituals, while among the higher educated, it is to disapprove of such observances.

The religious behaviour of the respondents, however, indicates that irrespective of their education, more than 90.0 per cent observe religious rituals. Therefore, education does not seem to restrain respondents from observing religious rituals.

Regarding the periodicity of observing the various rituals, majority of the respondents among all levels of education offer prayer daily. Surprisingly, a lower proportion of illiterates than the educated do so daily. Among those who offer prayer regularly, the proportion is highest for the illiterates and decreases with inerease in education. The professional educated and post-graduate respondents form the largest group who offer prayers only on festivals. The proportion of respondents who never offer prayer is negligible at all levels of education,

Education does not appear to refrain women from offering prayer.

Fasting until prayer is offered as a common practice. The observance of such fasting either daily, regularly or on festivals and functions is highest among the illiterates (84.5 per cent). This proportion falls with successive levels of education. Barring the illiterates, majority of the women are those who fast either on festivals/functions only or not at all.

Regarding the periodicity of visit to the place of worship, it is seen that it has no definite relationship with education. As the frequency of visit to the place of worship is associated religion, the responses are analysed separately, religion and education wise. Among the Hindus, irrespective of the level of education, majority of the respondents visit the temples, 93 38 per cent. Of them, majority do so regularly, the percentage being highest for the illiterates, 58.38 per cent. At the secondary, graduate, post-graduate and professional levels, a higher percentage of respondents visit temples on festivals and functions rather than regularly or daily. Only at the upper primary level the percentage of respondents who visit the temple daily is higher than those who visit on festivals and functions. The proportion of respondents who never go to temples is very low among all levels of education. If 43.76 per cent of employed Hindu women visit temples regularly, around 36.32 per cent visit temples on occasions.

Irrespective of the level of education, majority of the respondents who are Christians visit the Church regularly (83.24 per cent). Of those who visit daily, surprisingly, the percentage is highest for the graduates and post-graduates. The proportion of respondents who visit the Church only on festivals and functions is very low for all levels of education. It is only among the lower primary educated respondents that a negligible 10.0 per cent never visit the Church. All other Christian women visit the Church.

Among the Muslims, it is seen that among all other levels of education except the graduate and professional levels, none of the respondents go the mosque. Of those who go, 33.33 per cent and 20.0 per cent of the graduate and professional educated respondents respectively do so only on festivals and functions*. In general, religion has a stronger influence than education on the respondents' behaviour.

Attitude of respondents towards going on a pilgrimage for purification reveals that those in agreement is highest among the illiterates, 84.73 per cent. This percentage falls considerably with successive levels of education. Thus, among professional educated only 13.65 per cent favour the view. As the level of education rises, the percentage of respondents who agree with the view decreases.

In practice, it is observed that irrespective of the level of education of the respondents, majority of them have gone on a pilgrimage. There is no relationship between education and the proportion of respondents who have been on a pilgrimage to holy places.

Among those who have been on a pilgrimage, as high as 91.84 per cent and 81.56 per cent of the illiterates and lower primary educated respondents respectively, have been to pilgrim centres of their religion only. Among all other levels of education, more than 50.0 per cent of the respondents have gone to pilgrim centres of their religion and those of others also. In general, while those with less education mainly visit pilgrim centres of their religion only, respondents with increased education visit both their own religious places and those of others.

* Note : While the Muslim women are debarred from visiting the mosque, they are barred from using the main prayer hall due to the observance of purdah. There are partioned enclosures wherein women could pray. These are mainly utilised by women belonging to the higher socio-economic status on festivals and functions.

The percentage of respondents who have visited because they believe in other religions, is highest among the illiterates and lower primary educated respondents, around 61.0 per cent. This percentage falls considerably as the level of education rises. The other important reasons offered are that they visited the place of worship of other religions due to curiosity and because their friends belong to other religions. It is seen that among all levels of education, except at the illiterate level, a higher percentage of respondents have visited due to curiosity than because of their friends' persuation.

In general, while majority of the illiterate and lower primary educated respondents have visited because of their belief in other religions, those with upper primary education and above have visited out of curiosity and because of their friends who belong to other religions.

The attitude and behaviour of the respondents towards women celebrating all the religious festivals or only the important ones of their community reveals that with education, the proportion of respondents who favour celebration of all the festival of their community decreases. Thus, while majority of the illiterates and those with school and vocational education favour celebration of all festivals, majority of the respondents with collegiate education favour the view that women should be selective. None of the respondents favour boycott of festivals. In general, with successive levels of education, there is a decrease in the percentage of respondents who favour the celebration of all festivals of their community.

Whether the respondents in actual practice celebrate all the festivals of their community or only those which they consider important, shows that, irrespective of education, majority of them celebrate all the festivals of their community. While the proportion of respondents who celebrate all the festivals is least for the illiterates, it is almost evenly distributed among other levels of education. There were none who did not celebrate festivals at all.

A comparison of their attitude and behaviour indicates that except for the illiterates, a higher percentage of respondents belonging to all educational levels celebrate all the festivals than those who favour such celebration. This may be due to the low economic status of the illiterates. Further, a significantly higher proportion of the college educated than the school and vocational educated celebrate all festivals than they favour. The difference in their attitude and behaviour is of the order of about 6.0 per cent for the school and vocational educated, 28.0 per cent for the college educated (general) and 42.0 per cent for the professional/technical educated.

The respondents' attitude and behaviour towards participation of women in festivals of other religions reveal that the illiterates and the primary educated from the highest proportion who disagree with the view (73.4 per cent and 69.9 per cent respectively). However, majority of the respondents with secondary education and above favour the participation of women in such festivals, (85.0 per cent). In general, as the level of education rises, there is a decrease in the percentage of respondents who agree with the non-participation of women in the festivals of other religions.

Regarding actual participation, it is seen, that at all levels of education, majority of the respondents have not participated in the festivals of other religions. Of those who have participated, the proportion is highest among the secondary and vocational educated (48.0 per cent) and least among the illiterates (13.0 per cent). The percentage is almost evenly distributed among those with intermediate education and beyond.

A comparison reveals that for all levels of education, a lower percentage of respondents have participated than those who agree that women should participate in festivals of other religions. The difference in the percentages between the attitude and behaviour of respondents increases with education, thus, indicating inconsistency to a greater extent among those with higher education.

Attitude and behaviour towards the participation of women in religious festivals during menstruation reveals that the percentage of respondents in agreement increases as the level of education decreases. Thus, around 7.0 per cent of the illiterates favour the participation of women in festivals/ceremonies during menstruation, against 64.0 per cent of the post-graduates.

But, whether in actual practice, the respondents participate in religious festivals during menstruation reveals that irrespective of education received, majority of them do not participate in such activities. Of those who participate, it is seen that higher the education, higher is the percentage of participation in religious activities during the period of menstruation.

An analysis of the extent to which the respondents have freedom during the period of menstruation, such as in cooling food, in moving freely in the house, in entering the prayer room, and in visiting temples/churches/mosques was made. These activities are restricted by religion : The Hindus are restricted to a greater extent than the Muslims and the Christians ; and the Muslims more than the Christians. The Hindus are restricted on all the four activities mentioned, the Muslims on the last two activities and the Christians have no restrictions at all. In this context, the religion and education-wise analysis of restricted/free behaviour of respondents was made.

Among Hindus, the proportion who cook food during menstruation is least for the illiterates (36.36 per cent). This percentage increases with education. Of those who move freely in the house, the percentage increases from 37.5 per cent among the illiterates, with successive levels of education to 73.69 per cent among the professional educated. Irrespective of education, majority of the respondents do not enter the prayer room. When classified into those with intermediate education and below and those with higher education, while only 4.7 per cent of the former group enter the prayer room, as high as 27.10 per cent of the latter do so. A great majority of the respondents at all levels of education do not visit temples during menstruation. Of those who visit, the percentages are negligible for all levels excepting the post-graduate and professional levels where around 30.0 per cent visit the temples.

In general, a higher percentage of respondents move freely in the house than those who cook food and a lesser percentage visit temples than those who enter the prayer room. While education is directly related to the percentage of those who cook food and move freely in the house, only among those with higher education a higher percentage of respondents enter the prayer room and visit temples during menstruation than those with school education.

Among Christians, more than 90.0 per cent of the respondents cook food and move freely in the house. Also, majority of them, irrespective of their education, enter the prayer room and visit churches. However, at all levels of education, nearly 20.0 per cent do not enter the prayer room and the church. Beyond the primary level, it is observed that the percentage of those who do not visit the church during menstruation is higher than that of those who do not enter the prayer room. Though the Christians are not restricted by religion to carry out these activities, a small percentage do restrict themselves. Education does not appear to be related to the behaviour of respondents who do not enter the prayer room and churches during menstruation.

Among Muslims, it is observed that, irrespective of education almost all respondents cook food and move freely in the house, while none of them enter the prayer room or visit the mosque during menstruation.

Thus, there is no influence of education on these activities. They are basically governed by religion.

An influence of education is possible only where there are restrictions. As mentioned earlier, there are more restrictions on Hindus than on Muslims and Christians; on Muslims than on Christians—A comparison reveals that while education has an influence on the behaviour of Hindus, it has no influence on that of the Christians and Muslims with respect to non-observation of religious restriction. It appears that religion continues to have a strong influence on the behaviour of the Muslims and Christian respondents.

**Participation of Widows in Religious Ceremonies**

Widowhood being considered inauspicious, widows are debarred from participating in religious ceremonies. It is hypothesized that with increased education, the respondents would allow the widows to participate in religious ceremonies. Majority of the respondents had atleast one widow in their families (92.80 per cent).

The participation of widows is least for the illiterate group, 75.94 per cent. As the level of education rises, the percentage of respondents who allow them to participate increases. A higher percentage of vocational educated respondents (66.29 per cent) permit the widows to participate than those with higher education (55.36 per cent).

**Religious Initiation**

Regarding religious initiation for boys and girls, it is observed that majority of the illiterates (89.31 per cent) and lower primary educated (61.69 per cent) respondents have no initiation for either boys or girls. This may be because most of them are scheduled castes and lower caste Hindus. Those respondents who have religious initiation for both the sexes are basically the Christians, the Muslims and the Lingayats. The proportion of respondents who have initiation only for boys is among those who are upper caste Hindus. There is no religious initiation only for girls among all levels of education/religions. Thus, education perhaps has no influence on the percentage of those who have religious initiation only for boys, girls, for both or neither of the sexes. Religion and caste, perhaps, stand out as the most prominent factors influencing the initiation for boys and girls.

## VI. Special Attitudes and Behaviour Pattern of Women

In this section, an analysis of the social attitudes and behaviour pattern of the respondents are made. The items on social attitudes elicit responses regarding the extent to which the respondents favour inter-caste and inter-class social relations of women. Social relation may be taken to mean : receiving home people of other castes and classes, visiting them, going out with them to cinemas/picnics, dining with them and having marriage alliances. Further, there are items on the 'attitudes of respondents towards girls learning dance, music and taking part in public performances and attending mixed parties. The questions on social behaviour elicit responses on the extent to which respondents and their daughters mix with people of other castes and classes, their and their daughters participation in cultural activities and the participation of their daughters in mixed parties.

### Attitude Towards Mixing of Women with other Castes

In Hindu society, caste hierarchies may be observed both in actual social interactions and in sanctions for the same. The individual's position in the caste structure is determined by birth which carries with it a socially recognised advantage or handicap in status and privilage. Thus, the caste is superior or inferior to another and individuals within it are consequently aided or hampered in their personal struggle for position, wealth and social recognition. Castes in any one of the linguistic divisions of India can be arranged in an hierarchical order, and each person knows the relative position of his caste. Although certain positions may be in doubt at any one time, with a few castes claiming greater recognition and others accepting degradation, no caste is so low that it cannot refer to another below it in the hierarchy. This is vividly brought out by the following observations : "As the society now stands ..... the place due to each community is not easily distinguishable, nor is any common principle of precedence recognised by the people themselves by which to grade the castes. Excepting the Brahmin at one end and the admittedly degraded castes like the Holeyas at the other, the members of a large proportion of the intermediate castes think or prefer to think that their caste is better than their neighbours' and should be ranked accordingly."* Thus, in a caste society which is hierarchical, enforced restrictions on feeding, social intercourse and marriage are a common feature. In such a context, it would be interesting to study the impact of the level of education on the rigidity/relaxation of such restrictions.

The following is an analysis of the influence of education on the attitude and behaviour of women towards the extent of their mixing with people of higher/lower castes.**

Regarding the attitude of respondents towards the extent to which women can mix with people of higher castes, it is seen that though majority of them favour visiting and receiving home people of higher castes, the percentage is higher for those with college education than those with school and vocational education. As regards going out to cinemas/picnics etc., and dining with them, the proportion of illiterates and lower primary educated respondents who favour these activities is considerably less when compared to those with upper primary education and beyond. Disapproval of marriage alliances with higher caste families is quite high among illiterates and primary educated, and considerably high among all other levels except among the post-graduates. It is further observed that among all levels of education, the proportion of respondents who favour receiving and visiting people of higher

*Mysore Census, 1901, Census of India, 1901, Mysore Report, p. 400.

**'Higher/Lower Castes' means castes which the respondents consider higher/lower than their own caste.

castes is considerably higher than those who favour going out, dining and having marriage alliances with them.

In practice, it is observed, that majority of the respondents, irrespective of their educational qualification, have received and visited people of higher castes. The proportion of respondents who have received and visited them is least for the illiterates, 72.84 per cent and 79.63 per cent respectively. At least eight out of nine respondents at all levels of education have visited and received people of higher castes. Among illiterates, it is around seven out of nine. Education does not appear to differentiate the respondents in these social behaviours.

The intermediates and the graduates from the highest groups who have gone with them, around 82 0 per cent. Among the illiterates only 49.38 per cent have gone out to cinemas/picnics, etc., with upper caste people. Barring the illiterate and the upper primary educated respondents, more than 70.0 per cent of the respondents belonging to all other educational levels, have dined with upper caste people. A vast majority of the respondents among all levels of education have not had marriage alliances with them. Of those who have gone out and dined with them, the percentage is least for the illiterates. Education does not appear to influence marriage alliances with people of higher castes.

A comparison of the attitudes and behaviour pattern of the respondents towards mixing with people of higher castes reveals that a higher percentage of respondents at all levels of education have received and visited upper caste people than those who favour the view. As regards going out, the percentage of respondents who have favoured it and those who have gone out are almost the same. With regard to marriage alliances, it is observed that while a higher percentage of illiterate and lower primary educated have had marriage alliances than they favour, it is the other way round for all the other levels of education.

The extent to which the respondents have allowed their daughters to mix with children of higher castes reveals that majority of the respondents allow their daughters to play with children of higher castes. However, the percentage of respondents who allow them to play is relatively less among the illiterates and primary educated respondents than those who are secondary educated and above.

While more than 70.0 per cent of the respondents among all levels of education allow their daughters to dine with upper caste children, education does not appear to have any influence on the percentage of respondents who allow them to dine. Majority of the respondents allow their daughters to receive and visit the children of upper castes. However, a slightly higher percentage of respondents among all levels of education except at the upper primary level, receive than visit them.

In general, while there is no relationship between education of respondents and their practice of allowing their daughters to mix with children of upper castes, a relationship arises when the respondents are classified under illiterates and educated. By and large, a lesser percentage of illiterates allow their daughters to play, dine, receive and visit children of higher castes than the educated.

On comparison, it is observed that a higher percentage of respondents allow their daughters to receive and dine with upper castes than themselves. However, a higher percentage of respondents visit them than their daughters.

The attitude of respondents towards the extent to which women can mix with people of lower castes reveals that those with upper primary education and beyond favour the view that women should receive, visit and go out with people of lower castes to a greater extent than the illiterate and lower primary educated respondents. The percentage of respondents who favour dining with lower caste people increases with successive levels of education. While majority of the respondents disapprove marriage alliances with the lower castes, this disagreement is stronger at the illiterate and primary levels than at the secondary level and beyond.

In actual practice, with successive levels of education, a higher proportion of respondents have received, gone out and dined with lower caste people. In respect of visits, a higher percentage of respondents with secondary education and above, have visited lower caste homes than those with less than secondary education. Education does not appear to be related to the percentage of respondents who have marriage alliances with lower caste people. It is further observed that at all levels of education, a higher percentage of respondents favour and mix with people of higher castes than with those of lower castes.

A further analysis of the data regarding the extent to which the respondents allow their daughters to mix with children of lower castes indicates that majority of them allow their daughters to play with lower caste children. However, the percentage of respondents who allow their daughters to play with them increases with successive levels of education. There is no consistent pattern between education and the percentage of those who allow their daughters to dine with children of lower castes.

As regards receiving home and visiting the homes of children belonging to the lower castes, a great majority of the respondents allow their daughters to do so. However, the percentage of respondents who permit their daughters to visit is less than those who allow their daughters to receive them. While education appears to have a direct relationship with the percentage of those who receive them home, their is no definite pattern for those who visit them.

It is seen on comparison that the respondents allow their daughters to mix with higher caste children to a greater extent than with lower caste children. Further, the respondents permit their daughters to mix with both the higher and lower castes to a greater extent than they mix themselves.

**Attitudes and Behaviour of Respondents Towards Mixing of Women with other Classes**

The division of society into distinct classes is one of the most striking manifestations of inequality in the modern world. Sharply contrasted with the caste system, the open class system can be placed at the opposite end of a continum. A social class consists of a number of individuals who share similar status often associated at birth but capable of being altered. Class, therefore, does not consist of organised, closed groups defined by law or religion as does caste, nor are the various strata in the system as rigid and easily identifiable. There are no firm lines dividing one category from another. Social class can be acquired and changed according to one's achievements and efforts, hence, there is much scope for mobility. The factors that ascribe status to the individuals are prescribed by society. The presence of the factors contribute to one's prestige and high status which may vary from society to society. Thus, while in some societies occupation, income, wealth and education may be considered, in some other societies ownership of landed property, ancestry and power of influence may be considered. In the present study, class is taken to mean the socio-economic status of the individuals. It comprises the factors—education, occupation, income and wealth. As no restrictions on social interaction between the various groups are enforced, the attempt is made to gain an insight into the attitude and behaviour of women towards their mixing with people of other classes.

The following data present the influence of education on the attitude and behaviour of women towards their mixing with people of higher/lower socio-economic status* and the extent to which they mix with them.

* "Higher/lower socio-economic status" means status which respondents consider higher/lower than their own.

Regarding the attitude of respondents towards the extent to which women can mix with people of higher classes reveals that illiterates and those with primary education favour to a lesser extent the mixing of women with people of higher socio-economic status than those with secondary education and above. Further, among all levels of education, the percentage of respondents who favour visiting and receiving them is highest. The percentages decrease gradually when preferences are given with reference to going out, dining and having marriage alliances with them. Thus, mixing with people of higher class is favoured in the order of visiting, receiving, going out, dining and marrying.

In actual practice, it is observed that a lesser percentage of respondents who are illiterates and primary educated have received, visited, gone out, dined and had marriage alliances than those who are matriculates and above. Further, among all levels of education, a lower proportion of respondents have had marriage alliances with higher class people than those who have dined, gone out with them, visited and received them home. Mixing with people of higher socio-economic status is in the order of visiting, receiving, dining, going out and marrying.

A comparison of the attitudes and behaviour pattern reveals that the proportion of respondents who have mixed with people of higher class in terms of receiving, visiting, going out and dining is higher than the proportion of respondents who favour such mixing. However, with respect to marriage alliances, the proportion of those who favour is by and large higher than those who have made such alliances. This is specially true of college educated respondents.

Perhaps, this may be due to a great majority of respondents with college education themselves belonging to the higher socio-economic status. Surprisingly, however, among all levels of education, respondents in actual practice mix with higher class people to a greater extent than they approve of.

The extent to which respondents have allowed their daughters to mix with children of higher socio-economic status reveals that irrespective of the education of the respondents, majority of them have allowed their daughters to play, dine, receive and visit such children. A lesser proportion of illiterates and primary educated respondents have allowed their daughters to participate in such situations than those who are matriculates and above. A higher percentage of daughters of respondents at all levels play with, receive home and dine with children of upper class than those who visit them.

Further, a comparison reveals that the proportion of respondents who allow their daughters to mix with children of higher socio-economic status is higher than the proportion of respondents themselves who approve of or mix with people of such class.

Regarding the attitude of respondents towards the extent of mixing with people of lower socio-economic status reveals that a great majority favour receiving and visiting. A slightly lower percentage at all levels favour going out than receiving and visiting. Though a majority of the respondents favour dining, their percentages are lower than those who favour receiving, visiting and going out. Majority of the illiterates, lower primary and vocational educated do not favour marriage alliances. In every respect, a lesser per cent of vocational educated favour social relations with lower class people than those with secondary education and below.

Though education does not appear to be a significant factor influencing the attitude of women towards the extent of mixing with people of lower class, it is seen that a higher proportion of the primary and secondary educated approve of receiving, visiting, going out and dining than those with vocational and collegiate education.

In practice, education does not appear to a factor differentiating the percentages between the various levels of education and their behaviour with regard to their mixing with lower class people. However, if the respondents are categorised on the basis of their education into illiterate and educated groups, it is observed that a lesser percentage of illiterates mix with them than the educated. Also, it is seen that among all levels of education, they mix with lower calss people to a greater extent in so far as receiving and visiting them is concerned. This proportion falls in regard to going out, dining and having marriage alliances with them.

A comparison reveals that a higher proportion of respondents favour the mixing of women with people of lower class than those who mix with them in actual practice. Further, while respondents among all levels of education mix with higher class people to a greater extent than they favour, they favour mixing with lower class people to a greater extent than they in actual practice mix with.

The extent to which respondents have allowed their daughters to mix with children belonging to lower classes reveals that a higher percentage of respondents with upper primary education and above have allowed their daughters to play and dine with them than the illiterates and lower primary educated. No such pattern arises among respondents who have allowed their daughters to either receive or visit them. Social relations are maintained in the order of playing with, receiving home, dining with and visiting them.

On comparison, it is revealed that the respondents mix with people of lower class status to a lesser extent than they allow their daughters to mix with. A further analysis reveals that a higher proportion of illiterate, primary and secondary educated respondents have allowed their daughters to mix with children of lower than higher socio-economic status. Barring the post-graduates, among all other levels of education, a higher percentage of respondents have allowed their daughters to mix with children of higher rather than lower classes.

**Attitudes and Behaviour of Respondents Towards Fine Arts**

Attitude of respondents towards dance education for girls reveals that the proportion of those who agree that girls should learn dancing increases with education. As regards giving public performances, among all educational categories a lesser percentage favour it than those who favour dance education for girls. Of those who favour girls giving public performances, it is observed that the percentage increases with education.

Regarding the behaviour of the respondents, majority of them have not learnt dancing. The percentage of respondents who have learnt dancing increases from nil for the illiterates to 12.11 per cent for the professional educated respondents. Of those who have learnt dancing, the percentage of respondents who have learnt and not given public performances is higher than those who have performed.

A comparison reveals that a lesser percentage of respondents have learnt dancing than that of those who favour girls learning dance. Hence, among all categories of education, there is no consistency between the attitude and behaviour of the respondents.

Data regarding dance education and performance by the daughters of the respondents reveals that majority of them have not had dance education. It is seen that as the level of education rises, the percentage of respondents whose daughters have learnt dancing increases except at the secondary level, where it is higher than those at the vocational, intermediate and graduate levels Of those who have given dance education to their daughters, quite a high percentage have not allowed them to give public performances.

It is seen that among all levels of education, a higher percentage of the daughters of the respondents have learnt and given public performances in dancing than the percentage of respondents who have learnt dancing and given performances themselves.

Regarding the attitude of respondents towards music education and giving public performances in music, it is observed that the proportion of respondents in agreement increases with successive levels of education. However, the differences in the percentages between the various levels of education is less for those in favour of the view that girls should learn music than girls should give public performances in music.

A higher percentage of respondents at all levels of education favour music education for girls than dance education. The differential attitude towards music and dance education is slightly lower among college educated respondents as compared to school educated and illiterate respondents. Again, there is a differential attitude at all levels of education towards public performances by girls in music and dance in favour of the former. However, in contrast to the difference between school and college educated with regard to differential attitudes towards music and dance education, a higher proportion of higher educated respondents are not in favour of public performances by girls in dancing than those with regard so music.

In actual practice, while majority of the respondents have not learnt music, the percentage decreases with successive levels of education. Correspondingly, the proportion of respondents who have learnt music increases from 5.6 per cent for the illiterates to around 40.0 per cent for the professional education. Of those who have learnt music, majority of them have not given public performances.

It is seen that a higher proportion of respondents have a favourable attitude towards girls learning music and giving public performances than those who have actually learnt and given performances in music.

The behaviour pattern regarding the respondents' daughters reveals that with an increase in the levels of education, there is an increase in the percentage of those having learnt and given public performances in music. Further, barring the professional level, for all the other educational categories, a higher percentage of the daughters have learnt and given public performances in music than the respondents themselves. For the professional category, while a higher proportion of the respondents than their daughters have learnt music, the proportion of those who have given performances is, however, higher among the daughters than the respondents themselves.

Regarding the attitude and behaviour of respondents towards girls participating in mixed parties, more than 75.0 per cent of the illiterates and primary educated respondents disagree with the view. Majority of the respondents with secondary education and above do not object to the participation of girls in such parties. It is observed that with successive levels of education, there is a decline in the percentage of those who disapprove of girls participating in mixed parties.

In practice, majority of the respondents with intermediate education and below have not allowed their daughters to participate in mixed parties, more than 80.0 per cent, while around 55.0 per cent of the college educated have done so. While the tendency among illiterates and primary educated is not to favour and not to send their daughters to mixed parties, there is a greater tendency among secondary and higher levels of educated to favour but not send their daughters to such parties.

Among the reasons given by the respondents for not sending their daughters to participate in mixed parties, barring the post-graduates and professional educated, the main reason is that their daughters will earn a bad name.

The most significant reason, especially among school educated, is that attending mixed parties is socially forbidden. Majority of the post-graduates and professional educated respondents have not allowed their daughters to participate as they are too young.

Education does not appear to have any consistent relationship with the reasons given for not sending their daughters to mixed parties. However, while majority of those with graduate education and below do so because their daughters will get a bad name and because it is socially forbidden, majority of those with post-graduate and professional education do so because their daughters are too young.

**Leisure Time Activities**

It is observed that the most favoured leisure-time activity among the illiterates is cinema-going, 71.20 per cent. This percentage falls as the level of education increases. Correspondingly, it is seen that the percentage of respondents who read is least among the lower primary educated respondents. Among all other levels of education, the percentage who read is almost equal i.e., around 33.0 per cent.

While tailoring and knitting are more prominent activities among the upper primary, secondary and vocational educated, fine arts like music, dance and drama are prominent among those beyond the post-school stage.

It is further observed that the educated women are involved in more than one leisure-time activity, while the illiterate women indulge mainly in cinema-going.

**Conclusion**

The study on the non-economic returns from education in terms of attitudes and behaviour of women towards the institutions of education, employment, marriage and family, politics, religion and social life reveals that education is a differentiating factor with respect to both attitudes and behaviour. Further, the researcher has attempted to find out the degree of cognitive consonance or dissonance between the attitudes and behaviour of women with different levels of education. For this, items on attitudes and behaviour were analysed by drawing two-way frequency tables. An analysis of the data reveals that cognitive dissonance (inconsistency) is higher for women with higher levels of education than for those with lower levels of education and no education. This was found to be specially true in the attitudes and behaviour of women in the areas of 'marriage and family', 'politics', 'religion' and to a certain extent 'employment'.

## II. C. RETURNS FROM INVESTMENT IN EDUCATION

Human reasources improvement has been recognised as an objective and instrument of economic development. For this, the need to invest in human capital has been increasingly emphasized. Of the many forms of investment, education has been found to be the most profitable, both in terms of monetary and non-monetary benefits that accrue to individuals. Chapters IIA and B have analysed in detail the economic and non-economic returns to women with varying levels of education in relation to the expenditure they have incurred in receiving that particular level of education.

This section, consolidates the private returns, both economic and non-economic, that accrue to women from investing in education. In interpreting economic returns, the study first explains the lifetime earnings of women with different levels of education on the basis of certain demographic and socio-economic characteristics. It then evaluates the viability of education as a form of investment for the individual by computing the present values and internal rates of return to increments in education (Refer Chapter IIA). Data on the non-economic benefits being of a qualitative nature, were analysed using the descriptive technique. Here, an attempt is made to link the economic and non-economic returns to investment made, with regard to the various levels of education.

Private economic returns evaluated by the internal rate of return method reveals that expenditure on education is viable from lower primary education to vocational education levels. The highest return is for secondary level followed by upper primary, lower primary and vocational levels. Professional

TABLE

**Economic and Non-Economic Returns from Education**

| Levels of Education | Economic Returns Internal rate of return | Non-Economic Returns: Education | | Employment | | Marriage & Family | | Politics | | Religion | | Social Life | | Total | |
|---|---|---|---|---|---|---|---|---|---|---|---|---|---|---|---|
| | | A* | B* | A | B | A | B | A | B | A | B | A | B | A | B |
| Illiterates | — | 22.8 | 26.1 | 21.7 | 17.9 | 18.6 | 7.6 | 33.9 | 2.7 | 22.3 | 22.5 | 42.6 | 29.5 | 27.0 | 17.7 |
| Lower Primary | 15.5 | 34.7 | 23.3 | 27.8 | 23.3 | 29.2 | 9.4 | 47.2 | 4.4 | 27.2 | 26.3 | 48.1 | 30.0 | 35.7 | 19.5 |
| Upper Primary | 23.3 | 38.4 | 32.0 | 32.3 | 29.8 | 33.0 | 12.4 | 55.1 | 2.2 | 32.4 | 26.0 | 52 1 | 34.6 | 40.6 | 22.8 |
| Secondary | 24 4 | 53.9 | 63.5 | 45.1 | 35.8 | 48.0 | 25.4 | 58.0 | 6.0 | 45.2 | 39.3 | 65.4 | 40.6 | 52.6 | 35.1 |
| Vocational | 18.0 | 64.3 | 62.7 | 44.5 | 38.6 | 38.0 | 26.2 | 60.7 | 6.4 | 48.9 | 48.6 | 64.9 | 41.7 | 53.6 | 37.4 |
| P.U.C./ Inter. | 31.6 | 67.5 | 70.9 | 51.3 | 39.4 | 58.5 | 26.0 | 73.7 | 6.0 | 57.1 | 38.7 | 72.0 | 44.9 | 63.4 | 37.7 |

| | | | | | | | | | | | | | | | |
|---|---|---|---|---|---|---|---|---|---|---|---|---|---|---|---|
| Graduate | 5.3 | 77.5 | 73.5 | 55.5 | 42.1 | 67.1 | 32.1 | 76.4 | 15.8 | 72.0 | 39.6 | 72.6 | 50.1 | 70.2 | 42.2 |
| Post-Graduate | 6.3 | 80.8 | 85.7 | 61.5 | 46.9 | 71.0 | 36.9 | 78.9 | 10.6 | 77.9 | 33.8 | 75.4 | 50.2 | 74.3 | 44.0 |
| Professional | 7.4 | 75.2 | 77.9 | 54.6 | 48.4 | 70.2 | 37.5 | 82.2 | 10.7 | 75.4 | 34.8 | 74.9 | 50 8 | 72.1 | 43.4 |
| Total | | 57.23 | 57.29 | 43.81 | 35.8 | 48.18 | 23.72 | 62.9 | 7.2 | 50.93 | 34.4 | 63.11 | 41.38 | 54.4 | 33.3 |

*A. Attitude.

*B. Behaviour.

education is found to be more profitable than graduate and post-graduate education. However, intermediate and post-graduate education are not considered as profitable investments as they yield negative returns.

Private non-economic returns from investment in varying levels of education in terms of attitudes and behaviour towards the institutions of education, employment marriage and family, politics, religion and social life have been analysed qualitatively. Irrespective of the level of education, there is unanimity on some items of attitude like men are no longer considered the sole bread-winners in the family, discontinuation of the practice of dowry, small family size, belief in the existence of God, prayer or scriptures, mixing with people of other castes and classes, etc. The consonance in attitude might not necessarily be the outcome of education but be the result of the influence of other factors like urbanisation, industrialisation and acculturation. However, there are items where education is a differentiating factor. Behavioural items are predominantly the function of education. Some of the key items of attitude and behaviour have been identified and accounting for the direction of the responses, the non-economic returns from education in relation to the economic returns have been evaluated. The trends in the responses have been made use of to decide whether the attitudes and behaviour of respondents are desired/favourable. Desirability is in the context of the changing social situation in the country. The table below gives a consolidation of the economic and non-economic returns to the different levels of education.

It is observed from the table that monetarily, private investment for women is profitable at the primary and secondary levels. For those wanting to receive education beyond the matric level, vocational and professional education is found to be more beneficial to general education. Intermediate and Post-graduate education are not viable investments.

However, figures relating to non-economic returns reveal that with increasing education, there exists a more desirable attitude and behaviour among the respondents. This indicates that education has played a vital role in bringing about necessary changes in the mental making and behaviour of women with regard to all the institutions in the desired direction. But, when behaviour is considered against the attitudes of the respondents, it is observed, that barring the institution of education, in all others behavioural returns is less when compared to attitudinal returns. Further, the distance or inconsistency between attitudes and behaviour is higher among the women with higher education than those with school education. The limited behavioural change might be due to the influence of the previous generation (mothers particularly of the respondents) on that of the respondents whose attitude and behaviour are unfavourable. It is anticipated that behavioural changes will not be restrained in the respondents' children who will constitute the next generation. Thus, while education has been able to bring about desirable changes in the attitudes of women, it has not been able to adequately develop the essential commitment for the desired changes.

From the above it is clear that though monetarily it is not profitable for women to invest in higher levels of education, in non-monetary terms, the benefits are high. These returns, especially for women, will help create a better society. To affirm in the words of Vaizey, "expenditure on education pays", by virtue of the fact, "that indirect benefits of education are so great that its direct benefits are not necessarily the most important".

CHAPTER 6

# Summary and Conclusions

The study report on Returns to Women's Education has been presented in the following way. In the introdutory chapter, the conceptual aspects of 'human capital theory' and the role of education in the development of human capital has been discussed. The need for the present study in the context of the role of education in human capital formation follows the conceptual discussion. The objectives set for the study are presented. An attempt has been made in the second chapter to clarify the conceptual, terminological, methodological and analytical aspects of the study through a review of related literature in India and abroad. The review was useful in providing insights for the design of the present study. In the third chapter, a detailed discussion of the methodology employed for the study in terms of operational definitions, universe and sample, questionnaire, statistical analysis and scope and limitations has been made. The fourth chapter is devoted to the description of the sample, with regard to the general characteristics of the respondents, their socio-economic background, education, employment, etc. Analysis of data and the interpretations therein are presented in the fifth chapter. There are two sections to this chapter. Herein the private costs of education are discussed in Section I while returns from education are discussed in Section II. Again, Section II comprises of Sub-sections A and B. Sub-section A deals with economic returns from education while Sub-section B deals with the non-economic returns defined in terms of attitudes and behaviours of women towards the social institutions of education, employment, marriage and family, politics, religion and social life. In this chapter is presented a summary of the work done, the major findings of the study and the conclusions emerging therein.

**The Problem**

During the last two decades, education has been looked upon as a viable investment, explaining a major portion of both the national and individual incomes. As such, in the less-developed countries, there has been a rapid growth of institutions of learning, resulting in the so-called "education-explosion". This has led individuals to also look upon education as a profitable personal investment yielding both monetary and non-monetary benefits. These personal benefits that secure to the individuals in turn determine the pressures on the entire educational system.

While individuals appear to exercise choices in the pursuit of various levels and types of education in terms of perceived returns, the available evidence on returns to education indicate the fallacies in the reliability of such choices. A possible explanation for the high under-employment and unemployment rates in developing countries could be due to inappropriate investment decisions in education. However, evidence regarding the level or type of education from which maximum profit can be derived is far from clear and such exclusive information for women is totally lacking. This may be attributed to the lack of appreciation of the role of women in national development efforts. Management of the home and upbringing children is still considered to be the primary responsibility of a woman and a woman's contribution to development efforts is under-rated. However, of late, policies have been framed to integrate women with the mainstream of the development process, both because natural justice compels it and the principle of optimum utilisation of human resource potential demands it. Education of women assumes importance in this context and it would be advantageous to examine the types and levels of education that are most profitable to women.

In a developing country like India, there is not only a large domain of unexploited women-power resources but also an enormous wastage of these resources in the form of underemployed womenpower. The low participation of women in the work-force may be due to their ignorance of the economic returns that will accrue to them through employment or because of their indiscriminate investment in education which retains them as either unemployed or leads to their underemployment. Apart from the economic returns that accrue to individuals by investing in education, there are also the non-economic returns from education which cannot be ignored. These non-economic returns may be in the form of worthwhile use of leisure, good citizenship and acceptable attitudes and behaviour, etc. Those who do not invest properly in education may do so out of ignorance of these accruing benefits.

The present study has been undertaken so as to provide insights about economic and non-economic returns from education to women. Further, the study is set in Bangalore City. Hence, the study is titled as "A Study of the Returns from Education to Employed Women in Bangalore City".

**Objectives of the Study**

The study has set for itself the following objectives :

1. To evaluate and compare the private costs of different levels of education to women.
2. To compare the lifetime earnings associated with the various levels of education.

3. To evaluate the net present value of lifetime earnings of women with various levels of education in relation to the cost of acquiring that education.
4. To compare the rates of return from investment in the various levels of education.
5. To examine and compare the attitudinal and behavioural returns from education towards the institutions of education, employment, marriage and family, religion, politics and social life.
6. To highlight the levels of education that are most viable for women from the investment point of view.

**Universe and Sample of the Study**

As the focus of the present study is the returns from education to employed women, employed women form the universe of study. In Karnataka, Bangalore City holds the highest percentage of educated and employed women. As such, Bangalore City has been chosen for the purposes of this research.

The study is confined to women working in the organised sector, both public and private sectors in Bangalore City. Multistaged stratified random sampling technique was used to draw the sample for the study. In all 75 establishments were visited ; 35 in the public sector and 40 in the private sector. Information was collected from 858 women employees in the public sector and 607 in the private sector. The total sample for the study consisted of 1465 women employees.

The tool used for collecting information regarding the economic and non-economic returns from education was a structured questionnaire. Both the questionnaire and interview techniques were used. Further sources of data were the gay-scale(s), allowances, tax payment, etc., obtained from the establishments.

Costs and lifetime earnings associated with each of the various levels of education were estimated at the 1960-61 Rupee Value. Adjustments were incorporated in the costs and earnings estimation. Costs were adjusted for foregone earnings. In estimating the lifetime earnings, adjustments in terms of increments, bonus, taxes and unemployment were made.

The techniques used for the analysis of data were as follows :

1. To compare the costs incurred by respondents with various levels of education, both annual and level-wise estimates at 1960-61 Rupee Value were derived.

2. Lifetime earnings were estimated taking into consideration increments, bonus, and additional earnings other than regular salaries. Further adjustments were also made for taxes and unemployment.

3. Correlation matrix involving the independent variables inclusive of the various levels of education and lifetime earnings of the respondents was developed so as to identify those independent variables other than education which may influence earnings.

4. Multivariate regression analysis was made use of to find out the extent of influence of the independent variables on lifetime earnings and to estimate the lifetime earnings of respondents, standardising for the influence of other earner characteristics.

5. To evaluate the economic return from education, both net present values at various discount rates and the internal rates of return methods were used.

6. To evaluate the non-economic returns from education with regard to attitudes and behaviour of women towards education, employment, marriage and family, religion, politics and social life, the descriptive method was used.

**Summary of Findings**

**I. Private Costs of Education**

(i) An estimate of the annual net tuition cost of education by levels indicates that the tuition costs of education increases with successive levels of education. However, the total net tuition costs of graduate education is higher than that of the post-graduates. This is because the duration of graduate courses is longer than that of post-graduate courses, they being three and two years respectively.

(ii) Annual net tuition costs of education by levels and type of management reveals that at all levels of education the cost of acquiring education in private institutions is higher than in the Government institutions. At the lower primary stage, the tuition cost in private institutions is five times that in government institutions, thrice at the upper primary stage, two and a half times at the secondary stage, twice at the graduate and professional levels and one and a half times at the vocational, intermediate and post-graduate levels.

(iii) The estimated annual non-tuition costs of education increases with successive levels of education, except at the vocational level which is less than that of the secondary level.

(iv) The annual non-tuition cost is higher for those who attended private rather than Government institution at all levels of education, except the post-graduate level. Thus, at the lower primary stage, the non-tuition cost is nearly four times more in private than that in Government institutions ; 2.3 times at the upper primary stage ; 1.77 times at the secondary level ; nearly 1.5 times at the intermediate, graduate and professional levels and is almost equal at the vocational and post-graduate levels.

(v) Foregone earnings were estimated before and after adjusting for unemployment. An adjustment for unemployment brings down the total foregone earnings at all levels of education by more than 50 per cent.

(vi) The estimated total annual private cost of education increases with successive levels of education. Foregone earning is seen to be a major component of cost at all levels of education even after adjusting for unemployment. In general, it contributes anywhere between 56.06 per cent (professional education) to 80.84 per cent (vocational education) of the total private costs.

## II. Return from Education

### A. Economic Returns from Education

(i) Returns evaluated by the net present value method show that while professional education, even after deducting costs, is most profitable at the zero per cent discount rate, it is secondary education which is most profitable at the five and six per cent discount rates. Vocational education is observed to be profitable at the zero per cent discount rate but not so at the five and six per cent levels. Intermediate and post-graduate education represents a loss at all the three discount rates.

(ii) Returns evaluated by the internal rate of return method reveals that private expenditure on education is a viable investment from lower primary education to vocational levels. However, the highest returns is to the secondary level followed by upper primary, lower pimary and vocational levels. Professional education yields a higher return than graduate or even post-graduate education. Intermediate and post-graduate education yield negative results and hence are not considered to be profitable investments for women.

## B. Non-Economic Returns from Education

### 1. Attitudes and Behaviour of Employed Women Towards 'Education'

The attitude of the respondents reveals that women prefer a higher level of education for their daughters than that achieved by them. With higher levels of education, the proportion of women who favour co-education for girls also increases. While those with higher levels of education favour co-education for girls at all levels, those without education and primary education do not favour it at the secondary level. The behaviour pattern of women reveals that with increased education, a higher proportion of women send their daughters to co-educational institutions. Attitude of women towards girls being taught by female teachers 'only' shows that those without education and those with primary education favour this view to a greater extent than those with secondary education and above, and further, they prefer female teachers at the secondary level. Women with less education still feel that girls should not be encouraged to take up courses in engineering, that they neither should be allowed to stay in hostels nor should they be encouraged to go out of their home-towns to receive education. A higher proportion of women with less education favour the view that sons should get preference over daughters in receiving education, under conditions of economic constraint.

### 2. Attitudes and Behaviour of Women Towards 'Employment'

Irrespective of the level of education, while majority of the women disagree that the man should be the sole bread winner in the family, they agree with the view that women should work to supplement the family income. In consonance with the view, it was further observed that the main reasons given by the respondents for taking up employment was either to support the family or to supplement family income. Irrespective of the educational attainment of the women, nearly 44 per cent of them are of the view that women are discriminated in their recruitment to jobs. But the distribution of responses on the items of whether they have in reality been discriminated against and the areas of discrimination reveals that majority of the women have not been discriminated against. However, at the lower levels where there has been discrimination, it was mostly with respect to working conditions, facilities and wages.

**3. Attitudes and Behaviour of Respondents Towards Marriage and Family**

The attitude of respondents towards the choice of marriage partner reveals that with higher education, the respondents favour the view that either the boy or girl concerned should be consulted regarding his or her marriage or that mutual consent of the boy and girl to be married should be obtained. However, the behaviour of respondents with respect of selecting their marriage partner reveals that a higher percentage have in actual practice married the person of their parents' choice than those who favour the view that parents alone should choose the marriage partner. Correspondingly, the proportion of respondents who have been married with their consent is less than those who consider it necessary to obtain the consent of the person to be married. The highlight is that higher consistency is observed between illiterate and secondary educated in their belief that parents should choose the spouses for their children and in actually allowing parents to do so. With more education, the trend that emerges is in favour of intercaste and inter-religious marriages. However, in practice, both intercaste and inter-religious marriages are still uncommon even among the educated. Inconsistency in attitude and behaviour is greater among higher levels of educated. Even regarding register marriages, it is observed that with higher education, respondents favour register marriages, but in practice, majority of them have undergone social/religious marriages. Though there is consensus among all levels of educated that dowry should not be given, a slightly higher percentage of those with secondary education and above favour the view than those with primary education and illiterates. Surpisingly, among those who have paid dowry in actual practice, a higher proportion of the more educated have done so than the less educated and illiterates. As regards family composition, a higher percentage of respondents live in nuclear families than those who favour it. However, as the level of education rises, the difference in the percentages of those who favour and who actually live in nuclear families decreases. While with higher levels of education, respondents disagree with the view that household work should be done entirely by female members of the family, it is observed that household work is still the domain of the females even among those with higher education thus indicating cognitive dissonance among those with higher levels than lower levels of education. Decisions regarding education, occupation and marriage of children are essentially taken on a consultative basis, this proportion increasing with an increase in education. Attitude and behaviour of women towards family planning reveals that more than 75 per cent of the illiterates and nearly 85 per cent of the educated favour the view that a family should have two to three children only. However, a higher proportion of illiterates and primary educated favour three children. The behaviour of women reveals that the proportion of respondents who have accepted family planning techniques increases with education. It is also observed that with higher levels of education, the chances of the respondents using family planning techniques immediately after marriage or after the birth of the first child are greater. Education appears to be related to the method of family planning pursued in the sense that a higher proportion of those with higher levels of education use the natural methods (abstinence as well as rhythm and withdrawal) than artificial (contraceptives) methods and sterilisation.

**4. Attitude and Behaviour of Women Towards 'Politics'**

It is observed that with increased education, respondents favour the participation of women in politics. Though the same trend remains with regard to women with family responsibilities participating in politics, at all levels of education a higher proportion favour the participation of women in general than those with family responsibilities. While majority of the respondents favour reading of political literature, the percentage of those who favour the view increases with higher levels of education. However, their behavioural pattern reveals that the proportion of those who read political literature is low at all levels. As regards women participating in political campaigns, the proportion who favour the view increases with education, but among those who have attended such campaigns, the participation is very low. The lower primary, intermediate and graduate respondents have attended campaigns to a greater extent than those with other levels of education. Higher the education of the respondents, the proportion of those who favour women becoming members of political parties also increases, however, only a negligible proportion of respondents hold membership in a political group. Thus, cognitive dissonance is more among those with higher levels of education. Regarding the respondents views on the eligibility for voting, it is observed that with increase in education, a higher proportion favour the view that voting should be restricted to those with primary and secondary education and above. Correspondingly, those without education and primary education favour adult franchise. Barring the illiterates, majority of the respondents discuss politics. A higher percentage of primary educated hold political discussions than the secondary and vocational educated. Though the proportion of respondents who favour reservation of seats for women in the State Legislature increases as the level of education increases, a higher proportion of primary educated favour the view than the secondary and vocational educated.

**5. Attitude and Behaviour of Women Towards 'Religion'**

Irrespective of the level of education, majority of the respondents favour the view that women should believe in the existence of God. With increased education, a lesser percentage of respondents agree that worship of God liberates a woman, and a woman can secure happiness and longlife for her husband through prayer. Majority of the respondents favour belief in the Holy Scriptures. It is observed that those with higher education favour reading of religious texts, visiting the place of worship and observance of religious rituals daily to a lesser extent than the illiterates and school educated respondents. The religious behaviour of respondents reveals that majority of the respondents irrespective of the level of education observe religious rituals. A higher percentage of respondents with collegiate education favour the non-observance of rituals than those who do not observe rituals. While a higher percentage of the college educated never read the religious texts, a higher proportion of respondents at all levels of education favour than actually read the religious texts daily. As regards visiting the place of worship, it is observed that religion has a stronger influence on the respondents' behaviour than their education. While with increased education respondents disagree with the view that going on a pilgrimage will purify the pilgrim, it is observed that in reality they had been on a pilgrimage. Respondents with education upto the vocational level favour the celebration of all religious festivals of their community, while those with college education favour the celebration of selective festivals. The inconsistency between attitude and behaviour is greater among the educated in that a higher proportion of the educated celebrate all religious festivals than they favour. Majority of the respondents favour the non-participation of women in religious functions during menstruation. However, with successive levels of education, the proportion of those who agree that women should not participate in religious functions during monstruation decreases. As regards participation in actual practice, it is observed that majority of the respondents do not participate during menstruation. Even among the educated, a higher proportion of respondents do not participate during menstruation than they approve of. Thus, inconsistency in attitude and behaviour is more among the educated than the illiterates and less educated.

### 6. Attitude and Behaviour of Women Towards 'Social Life'

It is observed that irrespective of the level of education of the respondents, majority of them favour the view that women should mix with people of higher castes. A comparison of the attitude and behaviour of women towards the extent of mixing with people of higher castes reveals that a higher percentage of respondents at all levels of education have received and visited them than those who favour the view. As regards going out, the proportion of respondents who have favoured it and those who have gone out is almost the same. With regard to marriage alliances, while a higher percentage of illiterate and lower primary educated have had marriage alliances than they favour, it is the other way round for all the other levels of educated. Further, the analysis reveals that a higher percentage of respondents allow their daughters to receive and dine with upper castes then themselves.

As regards their attitude and behaviour towards mixing and the extent of mixing with people of lower castes, it is observed that majority of the women from all levels of education favour mixing with lower castes, though the proportion is slightly lesser than those who favour mixing with upper castes. While there is an increase in the percentage of respondents who favour and mix with people of lower castes, it is observed that as regards receiving, visiting, going out and dining, a higher proportion do so than they favour. With respect to marriage alliances, the inconsistency between attitude and behaviour is highest for the college educated. Further, it is observed that respondents allow their daughters to mix with lower caste children to a greater extent than they mix with lower caste people themselves, and also that they allow their daughters to mix with higher caste children to a greater extent than with those belonging to the lower caste.

The attitude and behaviour of respondents towards the extent of mixing with people of higher socio-economic status reveals that illiterates and primary educated favour and mix with them to a lesser extent than those with higher levels of education. Mixing in terms of both attitude and behaviour is in the order of visiting, receiving, dining, going out and having marriage alliances. It is also observed that the proportion of those who have received, visited, gone out and dined is higher than that of those who favour such mixing. Irrespective of the level of education, majority of the respondents allow their daughters to mix with children of upper socio-economic status to a greater extent than they approve of or mix with themselves.

As regards mixing with people of lower socio-economic status, education does not appear to be a differentiating factor in the attitude and behaviour of respondents. But a higher proportion of respondents favour mixing with people of lower socio-economic status than those who mix with them in actual practice. Again, it is observed that respondents among all levels of education mix with higher socio-economic status people to a greater extent than they favour, while they favour mixing with lower socio-economic status people to a greater extent than they in actual practice mix.

With respect to daughters being allowed to play and dine with children of lower socio-economic status, those beyond the upper primary level have done so to a greater extent than the illiterates und lower primary educated. Further, the data reveals that a higher proportion of illiterate, primary and secondary educated respondents have allowed their daughters to mix with children of lower than higher socio-economic status, while it is the other way round for those educated beyond the secondary level.

The attitude and behaviour of respondents towards the fine arts reveals that with increase in education, there is an increase in the proportion of respondents who favour and in actual practice learnt and participated. However, at all levels, there is a considerable fall in the proportion of those who favour and those who have learnt and given public performances. In general, there is no consistency between the attitude and behaviour of respondents in this respect.

**Conclusion**

The analysis of the unregressed and regressed data for various levels of education through both the net present value and the internal rate of return methods have shown that private investment on education is most profitable at the secondary level for women. Among the post-secondary levels and types of education, vocational education yields higher returns than all the other types and levels of education including professional education. However, professional education yields better returns than graduate and post-graduate levels. The demand for general higher education among women irrespective of its lower monetary returns as compared to secondary education may be explained thus :

It may be recalled that a major portion of the private educational costs comprises of foregone earnings. Those foregone earnings which also in turn boost up the rate of return for secondary education will have the potential for capital investment or earnings. It has been observed that much earnings are rather consumed than invested or saved. As such, women find it convenient to forego earnings in favour of higher eduation. An additional advantage in going for higher education is that it carries with it justifiably or not so, a higher social status value than secondary education. This may also play a decisive role in marriage alliances. As such, even though from the point of view of lifetime earnings and rates of return, secondary education is the most profitable level, women tend to go beyond this level.

The results from the analysis of data on non-economic returns indicate that higher education has not been able to develop adequately the commitment essential for desired social and economic changes, though its performance is better with respect to orientation of women towards the desired changes.

In other words, the inconsistency between the responses of women respondents in this study for the same items on attitude and behaviour is higher among the higher educated women than among the school educated women. For instance, though women with higher education favour associations with lower caste groups, still they have not displayed it in their behaviours. (Associations being defined in terms of visiting, receiving, going out, dining and having marriage alliances). This is not the case with school educated women. They neither highly favour such associations nor involve themselves in this regard. Hence, higher education appears to be better than school education in so far as development of a set of desired attitudes (desired in the context of the changing social situation in the country) while it has so far not succeeded in bringing out the concomitant behavioural change.

The overall conclusion emerging out of this study is that education is in general a profitable investment for the individual (woman) at the primary, secondary and vocational levels. At the post-matric levels, professional education is more profitable than general education. Furthermore, evidence in this study supports the contention that women aspiring for education beyond the matric level should profit more from vocational education rather than pre-university and college education. However, they profit from professional education in contrast to that from general higher education.

The results of the study bring into relief certain misconceptions in the field of education. One of them is that higher the level of education, higher will be the earning capacity of an individual. This study has shown that secondary education is the most profitable level of investment for women aspiring for employment. In this sense, a demand fore higher education appears to be irrational. It is only vocational education rather than higher education (with exception of professional education) which appears to be profitable beyond the post-matric level of education. The results of the study in this sense have profound implication for re-allocation of funds and re-organisation of education therein in the country in general and women's education in particular. It has also implications for private and social investment decisions in education. One may wonder as to why there should be a mad rush for general higher education even though it is less profitable than secondary education. One of the ways to discourage this mad rush or demand for higher education among women by the Government and the society at large would be to lower the present level of encouragement to women to acquire higher education by curring down on investments, subsidies and provision of facilities. The capital, thus, saved may be diverted towards secondary education for women. Women may be encouraged to participate in larger numbers at the secondary stage of education in the interests of private returns to women as well as national development afforts. However, women who want to persue education beyond the school-final stage may be encouraged to opt for vocational education in performance to general higher education. Facilities should be provided for extended vocational education and degrees may be awarded for the same which will also bring them the perceived social status. The generalisations arrived here though should be strictly limited to women's education, may also rise serious doubts about the value of general higher education for all.

APPENDIX A

# The Occupation Composition

The composition of the occupation groups used are as follows :

1. **Non-workers** : House-wives, Retired, Dependent, Unemployed.

2. **Professionals and related** : Physical Scientists, Physical Science Technicians, Architects, Engineers, Technologists and Surveyors, Engineering Technicians : Aircraft and Ship Officers, Life Scientists, Life Science Technicians, Physicians and Surgeons (including Dental and Veterinary Surgeons), Nursing and other Medical and Health Technicians, Scientific, Medical and Technical Persons, Mathematicians, Statisticians and related Workers ; Accountants, Auditors and related Workers ; Social Scientists and related Workers ; Jurists, Teachers, Poets, Authors, Journalists and related Workers ; Sculptors, Painters, Photographers and relative creative Artists, Composers and Performing Artists, Professional Workers, n.o.c.

3. **Administrative and related** : Elected and Legislative Officials ; Administrative and Executive Officials, Government and Local Bodies ; Working Proprietors, Directors and Managers, Whole-sole and Retail Trade ;

Directors and Managers, Financial Institutions ; Working proprietors, Directors and Managers, Mining, Construction, Manufacturing and related Concerns ; Working Proprietors, Directors, Managers and related Executives, Transport, Storage and Communication ; Working Proprietors, Directors and Managers, Other Services ; Administrative, Executive and Managerial Workers, n.o.c.

4. **Clerical and related :** Clerical and other Supervisors, Village Officials, Stenographers, Typists and Card and Tape Punching Operators, Book-keepers, Cashiers and related Workers ; Computing Machine Operators ; Clerical and related Workers ; Transport and Communication Supervisors, Transport Conductors and Guards; Main Distributors and related Workers ; Telephone and Telegraph Operators.

5. **Sales and related :** Merchants and Shop-keepers, Whole-sale and Retail Trade ; Manufacturers, Agents, Technical Salesmen and Commercial Travellers, Salesmen, Shop Assistants and related Workers ; Insurance, Real Estate, Securities and Business Service Salesmen and Auctioners ; Money Lenders and Pawn Brokers ; Sales Workers, n.o.c.

6. **Service and related :** Hotel and Restaurant Keepers ; House-keepers, Matern and Stewards (Domestic and Institutional), Cooks, Waiters, Bartenders and related Workers ; Maids and other House Keeping Service Workers, n.o.c.

7. **Farmers and related :** Farm Plantation, Dairy and other Managers and Supervisors, Cultivators, Farmers other than Cultivators ; Agricultural Labourers ; Plantation Labourers and related Workers ; Other Farm Workers ; Forestry Workers ; Tenant Cultivators.

8. **Productions and related :** Miners, Quarrymen, Well Drillers and related Workers ; Metal Processors, Wood Preparation Workers ; Chemical Processors and related

Workers ; Tanners, Fellmongers and polt Dressers ; Food and Beverage Processors ; Tobacco Preparers and Tobacco Product Makers ; Tailors, Dress Makers, Sewers, Upholsters and related Workers, Shoe-makers and Leather goods Makers, Carpenters, Cabinet and related Wood Workers ; Stone Cutters and Carvers ; Black-smiths : Tool Makers and Machine Tool Operators ; Machinery Fitters, Machine Assemblers and Precision Instrument Makers (except Electrical) ; Electrical Fitters and related Electrical and Electronic Workers ; Broadcasting Station and Sound Equipment Operators and Cinema Projectionists ; Plumbers, Welders, Sheet Metal and Structural Metal Preparers and Erectors ; Jewellery and Precious Metal Workers and Metal Engravers (except Printing) ; Glass Framers, Potters and related Workers ; Rubber and Plasters Product Makers, Printing and related Workers, Painters, Production and related Workers, n.o.c. ; Brick-layers and other Construction Workers, Stationery, Engines and related Equipment Operators, Oilors and Greasers ; Material Handling and related Equipment Operators, Transport Equipment Operators ; Labourers, n.o.c.

APPENDIX B

# Derivation of an Index of 'Social Class'

In developing an index of social class certain assumptions were made. Social class was defined in terms of family background. Education, occupation and income were considered to represent the essential and significant components of family background. Further, as more than 80.0 per cent of the mothers of the respondents were housewives and hence did not earn an income, they were not included in the development of the index. Only the father's education, occupation and income were taken to reflect family background.

It is appropriate to state the limitation of this index. The weightages given are by and far subjectivistic and need to be refined for further use. However, this exercise gave the researcher enough scope to understand (in however limited sense it may be) the type of families from which women enter labour force.

In developing the index, the following stages were formed.

**Stage 1**

It consists of giving weightages to the education, occupation and income categories. The number of years taken to complete the levels of education was taken as the weightage for education. Thus, the weightages for the various levels of education are as follows :—

| | | | |
|---|---|---|---|
| Illiterates | — 0 ; | Lower Primary | — 4 ; |
| Upper Primary | — 7 ; | [a]Secondary | — 11 ; |
| [b]Vocational | — 13 ; | [c]Inter/P.U.C. | — 13 ; |
| Graduates | — 16 ; | Post-Graduates | — 18 ; |
| Professional | — 20 ; | | |

For occupation, based on the nature of work, they were first classified into the following groups ;

Professional/Technical

Administrative, managerial and executive

Clerical Workers

Production, transport, etc.

Sales Workers

Service, labourers, farmers, etc.

Unemployed

They were given weightages on an occupational distance scale of 0 to 10. These weightages were applied to the Occupational categories used in this study, thus getting a weightage scheme of :—

| | |
|---|---|
| (1) Professional/Technical | 10 |
| (2) Administrative, Executive | 7 |
| (3) Clerical and related Workers | 5 |
| (4) Production, Maintenance, Transport, etc. | 4 |

a. It refers to the former scheme of 11 years secondary education with 4 years of elementary, 4 years of lower secondary and 3 years of secondary or matriculation examination.

b. It covers both 2 years certificate and 3 years diploma course.

c. It covers earlier intermediate course of 2 years after 11 years of secondary.

| | |
|---|---|
| (5) Sales Workers | 2 |
| (6) Service Workers | 1 |
| (7) Farmers | 1 |
| (8) Workers not classified | 1 |
| (9) Unemployed | 0 |
| (10) No responses | 0 |

For the income categories, the weightages were continuous and coinsided with the ranges on which income data were collected.

| | |
|---|---|
| Less than Rs. 150/- | 1 |
| Rs. 151/- to Rs. 300/- | 2 |
| Rs. 301/- to Rs. 500/- | 3 |
| Rs. 501/- to Rs. 750/- | 4 |
| Rs. 751/- to Rs. 1,000/- | 5 |
| Rs. 1001/- to Rs. 1,500/- | 6 |
| More than Rs. 1,500/- | 7 |

**Stage 2**

The proportion of the fathers of the respondents in the education, occupation and income categories (taken as percentage break-up or of every 100 in the categories) in the various employment sectors were multiplied with their respective weightage scores under each level or category. The individual weighted scores were summed up for each sector. This total for each sector was then divided by 100. The following table gives the derived total weighted score for the various sectors.

## TABLE No. 1

**Weighted Education, Occupation and Income Scores by Sector of Employment**

| Sector | Family Back-ground | | | |
|---|---|---|---|---|
| | Education | Occupation | Income | Total |
| Private | 7.88 | 3.34 | 2.93 | 14.15 |
| Central Govt. | 10.03 | 5.05 | 3.59 | 18.67 |
| Central Govt. Quasi | 7.68 | 3.41 | 3.22 | 14.31 |
| State Govt. | 9.34 | 4.48 | 3.00 | 16.82 |
| State Govt. Quasi | 10.19 | 4.87 | 2.97 | 18.03 |
| Corporation | 2.59 | 1.89 | 2.04 | 6.52 |

**Stage 3**

In the third stage, maximum weightages possible (either actual or mean) were distributed to the four categories representing family background. The categories are lower, lower middle, upper middle and upper class families. Table 2 presents the education, occupation and income groupings and weightages for the family background categories :

TABLE No. 2

| Family Background | CLASS | | | |
|---|---|---|---|---|
| | Lower | Lower middle | Upper middle | Upper |
| Education | Illiterates, L.P. & U.P. (7) | Secondary, Vocational P.U.C. (12) | Graduates (16) | Post-Graduates and Professional (19) |
| Occupation | Service Farmers etc. (1) | Sales (2) | Clerical Production (4.5) | Administrative Prof/ Tech. (8.5) |
| Income | Less than Rs. 300/- (2) | Rs. 301/- to 750/- (3.5) | Rs. 751/- to 1,000/- (5) | Rs. 1,001/- & above (6) |
| Total | 10 | 17.5 | 25.5 | 33.5 |

Thus the cut-off points arrived at are as follows :

**Social Class Index**

Less than 10 — Lower class

10.1 to 17.5 — Lower middle class

17.6 to 25.5 — Upper middle class

25.6 to 33.5 — Upper class

A close look at table No. 1, in the light of the foregoing social class index, reveals that there is no participation of women from upper class family background in the labour force. Only those working in the Corporation come from lower class families. While State Government, Central Government Quasi and Private Sector women employees belong to the lower middle class, those working in the Central Government and State Government Quasi Sectors belong to the upper middle class families.

# Bibliography


1. Aarrestad, Jostein—"Returns to Higher Education in Norway", *The Swedish Journal of Economics*, Vol. 74, No. 2, June 1972.

2. Abramovitz, Moses—"Resource and Output Trends in the United States Since 1870," *American Economic Review*, Vol. 46, No. 2, May 1956.

3. Admad, Karuna—"Recruitment and Relevance," *in* Amrik Singh and Philip G. Altbach (ed)—The Higher Learning in India, Delhi, Vikas, 1974.

4. Agarwala, A.N. and S.P. Singh (ed)—Accelerating Investment in Developing Countries, London, Oxford University Press, 1969.

5. Ahluwalia, M.S.—"Income Distribution and Development : Some Stylized Facts", *American Economic Review*, Vol. 66, No. 2, May 1976.

6. Anderson, C.A. and Bowman, M.J. (ed)—Education and Economic Development, Chicago, Aldine, 1965.

7. Argyle, Michael—Religious Behaviour, London, Routledge and Kegan Paul, 1961.

8. Arkoff, Abe—Explorations in Human Behaviour, New York, McGraw-Hill Book Co., 1971.

9. Arregger, C.E. (ed)—Graduate Women at Work, London, British Federation of University Women, 1966.

10. Baumol, W.J.—Economic Theory and Operations Analysis, 4th ed., New Delhi, Prentice-Hall, 1978.

11. Becker, Gary S.—Human Capital, New York, National Bureau of Economic Research, 1964.

12. ———————Human Capital, New York, Columbia University Press, 1964.

13. ———————"Under Investment in College Education", *American Economic Review*, Vol. 50, No. 2, May 1960.

14. Becker, G.S. and Chiswick, B.R.—"Education and the Distribution of Earning", *American Economic Review*, Vol. 56, No. 2, 1966.

15. Beller, H. Andrea—"The Effect of Economic Conditions on the Success of Equal Employment Opportunity Laws : An Application to the Sex Differential in Earnings," *Review of Economics and Statistics*, Vol. 62, No. 3, Aug. 1980.

16. Benson, Charles S.—The Economics of Public Education, 2nd ed., Boston, Houghton Mifflin, 1968.

17. Barnard, Jessie—The Future of Marriage, London, Souvenir Press, 1972.

18. Bhasin, K. (ed)—The Position of Women in India, Bombay, Shakuntala Publishing House, 1975.

19. Bhattacharya, Narendranath—Ancient Indian Rituals and their Social Contents, Jaipur, Manohar Book Service, 1975.

20. Blaug, M.—"The Rate of Return on Investment in Education in Thailand," *The Journal of Development Studies*, Vol. 12, No. 2, Jan. 1977.

21. ———————An Introduction to the Economics of Education, London, Allen Lane, The Penguin Press, 1972.

22. ———————"Approaches to Educational Planning" Economic Journal, Vol. 77, No. 306, 1967.

23. Blaug. M.—"The Rate of Return on Investment in Education in Great Britain", *The Manchester School of Economic and Social Studies*, Vol. 33, No. 3, Sept. 1965.

24. Blaug, M., Layard, P.R.G. and Woodhall, M.—The Causes of Graduate Unemployment in India, London, Allen Lane, The Penguin Press, 1969.

25. Blitz, Rudolph C.—"A Calculation of Income Foregone by Students : Supplement to Nations Educational Outlay", *in* Selma J. Mushkin (ed)—Economics of Higher Education, Washington, United States Dept. of Health, Education and Welfare, 1962.

26. Boserup, Ester—Woman's Role in Economic Development, New York, St. Martin's Press, 1970.

27. Boulding, Elise—"Familial Constraints of Women's Work Roles", *Signs Journal of Women in Culture and Society*, Vol. 1, No. 3, Part II, Spring 1976.

28. Bowles, S.—"Schooling and Inequality from Generation to Generation", *Journal of Political Economy* Part II, May/June 1972.

29. Bowman, M.J.—"The Contribution of 'Eds' to National Income Growth," *Journal of Political Economy* Vol. 12. No. 5. 1964.

30. Bridgman D.S.—"Problems in Estimating the Monetary Value of College Education," *Review of Economics and Statistics*, Vol. 42. Aug. 1960.

31. Carnoy, M.—"Rates of Return to Schooling in Latin America," *Journal of Human Resources*, Vol. 2, Summer 1967.

32. Cartier, Robert—"Non-Economic Factors in the Study of Economic Development", A.I.D. Microfiche, No. PN AAB-186, 1975.

33. Cohen, S. Percy—"Social Attitudes and Sociological Enquiry", *The British Journal of Sociology*, Vol. 17 No. 4, Dec. 1966.

34. Cooney, Rosemary S.—"Female Professional Work Opportunities : A Cross National Study" *Demography*, Vol. 12, No. 1, Feb. 1975.

35. Denison, E.F.—"Measuring the Contribution of Education to Economic Growth," *in* The Residual Factor and Economic Growth, Paris : Organisation for Economic Cooperation and Development, 1964.

36. ———"The Sources of Economic Growth in the United States and the Alternatives Before Us," Supplementary Paper No. 13, New York, Committee for Economic Development, 1962.

37. Dumont, Louis—"Dowry in Hindu Marriage : As a Social Scientist Sees it", *The Economic Weekly*, Vol. 2, No. 1959.

38. Duncan, Greg J. and Saul, Hoffman—"On-the-Job Training and Earnings Differences by Race and Sex" *Review of Economics and Statistics*, Vol. 61, No. 1, Feb. 1979.

39. Epstein, Cynthia F.—Women's Place : Options and Limits of Professional Careers, Berkely, University of California Press, 1970.

40. Fabricant, S.—Basic Facts on Productivity, New York, National Bureau of Economic Research, 1959.

41. Fields, Gary S.—"Private Returns to Investment in Higher Levels of Education in Kenya," Discussion Paper 19, University of Michigan, March 1972.

42. Fredrik, Barth – 'Political Leadership among Swat Pathans', The London School of Economics, Monograph No. 19, 1959.

43. Gendall, Murray—"The Influence of Family Building Activity on Women's Rate of Economic Activity" *in* World Population Conference 1965, New York, United Nations, Vol. 4, 1976.

44. Gerard, Adams F.—"The Size of Individual Incomes: Social Economic Variables and Chance Variation", *Review of Economics and Statistics* Vol. 40, No. 1, Nov. 1958.

45. Ginzberg, Eli and Associates—Life Stules of Educated Women, New York, Columbia University Press 1967.

46. Gittinger, Price J.—Economic Analysis of Agricultural Projects, Baltimore : London, The Johns Hopkins, University Press, 1972.

47. Glick, Paul and Herman, P. Miller—"Educational Level and Political Income", American Sociological Review, Vol. 21, No. 3, June 1956.

48. Goldstein, Rhoda, L.—Indian Women in Transition : A Bangalore Case Study, Metuchen, N.J., The Scare Crow Press, 1972.

49. ———"Tradition and Change in the Roles of Educated Indian Women", *in* Dhirendra Narin (ed), Explorations in the Family and other Essays, Bombay, Thacker and Co., 1975.

50. Gordon, Margaret S.—"Higher Education and the Labour Market" (ed). The Carnegie Commission on Higher Education, 1974.

51. Gounden, Nalla A.M.—"Investment in Education in India", *Journal of Human Resources*, Summer, 1967.

52. Goyal, R.P.—Shifts in Age at marriage in India and Different States during 1961-71, Delhi, Institute of Economic Growth, Demographic Research Centre, 1975.

53. Griliches, Z. and Mason, W.—"Education, Income and Ability", Discussion Paper No. 207, Cambridge : Massachusetts, Harvard University, Institute of Economic Research, 1971.

54. Gustman, Alan—"On Estimating the Rate of Return to Education", Applied Economics, Vol. 5, No. 2, 1973.

55. Hanoch, G.—"An Economic Analysis of Earnings and Schooling", *Journal of Human Resources*, Vol. 2, No. 3, 1967.

56. Hans, Heinrich and Martin Carnoy—"Cost-Benefit Analysis in Education : A Case Study of Kenya", International Bank for Reconstruction and Development, 1972.

57. Hansen, W.L.—"Total and Private Rates of Return to Investment in Schooling", *Journal of Political Economy* Vol. 71, No. 2, April 1963.

58. Harris, S. (ed) –Economic Aspects of Higher Education, Paris : Organisation for Economic Co-operation and Development, 1964.

59. Hause, J.—"Earnings Profile : Ability and Schooling", Journal of Political Economy, Vol. 70, No. 5, Part II, May/June, 1962.

60. Hines, F., Tweeten, L. and Redfern, M.—"Social and Private Rates of Return to Investment in Schooling by Race, Sex Groups and Regions", *Journal of Human Resources*, Vol. 5, No. 3, 1970.

61. Hauthakker, H.S.—"Education and Income", *Review of Economics and Statistics*, Vol. 41, No. 1, Feb. 1959.

62. Huber, Joan (ed)—Changing Women in Changing Society, Chicago, University of Chicago Press, 1973.

63. Hunt, A.—"A Survey of Women's Employment", London, H.M.S.O., 1968.

64. Hunt, Shane—"Income Determinants for College Graduates and Return to Educational Investment", *Yale Economic Essays*, Vol. 3, Fall 1963.

65. International Labour Office—"Women Workers in a Changing Society", (Employment of Women with Family Responsibilities), Geneva, 1964.

66. Jain, Devaki (ed) –Indian Women, New Delhi, Publications Division, Ministry of Information and Broadcasting, Govt. of India, Jan. 1975.

67. Jain, S.—Size Distribution of Income : A Compilation of Data, Washington DC, World Bank, 1975.

68. Juster, Thomas F. (ed) – Education, Income and Human Behaviour, A Report prepared for the Carnegie Commission on Higher Education and the National Bureau of Economic Research, 1975.

69. Kapur, Promilla—Marriage and the Working Women in India, Delhi, Vikas, 1972.

70. Karnataka, Economics and Statistics (Bureau of—), Women in Government Service in Karnataka, 1976.

71. Kelsall, R.K., Poole, A. and Kuhn, A.—The Graduates : The Sociology of an Elite, London, Mathuen and Co. Ltd., 1972.

72. Kirer, B.F.—"The Historical Roots of Concept of Human Capital", *Journal of Political Economy*, Vol. 74, No. 5, 1966.

73. Klein, V.—"The Demand for Professional Women Power", British Journal of Sociology, Vol. 17, No. 2, June 1966.

74. Kothari, V.N.—"Factor Cost of Education in India", Indian Economic Journal, Vol. 13, No. 5, June 1966.

75. Krauss, Wilma Rule—"Political Implications of Gender Roles : A Review of the Literature", *American Political Science Review*, Vol. 68, No. 4, Dec. 1974.

76. Lauwerys, J.A., Bereday, G.Z. and Blaug, M. (eds)—World Year Book of Education, 1967, Educational Planning, London, Evans Bros. and New York, Harcourt and Brace, 1967.

77. Lipman, Blumen Jean – "Role Differentiations as a system Response to Crisis : Occupational and Political Roles of Women", *Sociological Inquiry*, Vol. 43, 1972.

78. Long, E. James and Ethel, B. Jones—"Labour Force Entry and Exit by Married Women : A Longitudinal Analysis", Review of Economics and *Statistics*, Vol. 62, No. 1, Feb. 1980.

79. Lutz, F.A. and D.C. Hague (ed)—The Theory of Capital– Proceedings of a Conference held by the International Economic Association, London, MacMillan, 1965.

80. Magee, B. John—Religion and Modern Man—A Study of the Religious Meaning of Being Human, New York, Harper and Row, 1967.

81. Maglen, L and Layard, R.—"How Profitable is Engineering Education ?", *Higher Education Review* Vol. 2, No. 2, 1970.

82. Mambu, V.J.V.—Development of Human Resources through General Educational Needs, Vocational Training and Associated Technical Education, Geneva, International Institute for Labour Studies, 1972.

83. Mathur, Gautham—"Economic Principles of Long-term Educational Planning", Hyderabad, Osmania University, Department of Economics, Oct. 1965, (Cyclostyled).

84. McClelland, D.C.—"Does Education Accelerate Economic Growth", *Economic Development and Cultural Change*, Vol. 14, No. 3, 1966.

85. Michel, Andree (ed)—Family Issues of Employed Women in Europe and America, the Netherlands, E.J. Brill, 1971.

86. Miller, Herman P.—"Annual and Lifetime Income in Relation to Education, 1939-59", *American Economic Review*, Vol. 50, No. 5, 1960.

87. ————"Life-time Income and Economic Growth", *American Economic Review*, Vol. 55, No. 4, Sept. 1965.

88. Mincer, J.—"Personal Income Distribution", *Journal of Political Economy*, Vol. 66, No. 3, 1958.

89. ————"On-the-Job-Training : Costs, Returns and Some Implications", *Journal of Political Economy*, Vol. 70, No. 5, Part II (Supplement) 1962.

90. Mishan, E.J.—Elements of Cost-Benefit Analysis, London, George Allen and Unwin, 1976.

91. Misra, Lakshmi—Education of Women in India—1921-1966, Bomba,y MacMillan and Co., Ltd., 1966.

92. Mitra, Asok—"Employment of Women", *Manpower Journal*, Vol. 16, No. 1, April-June 1978.

93. Morgan, et. al.—Income and Welfare in the U.S.A., New York, McGraw-Hill, 1962.

94. Morgan, James and Martin, David—"Education and Income", *Quarterly Journal of Economics*, Vol. 77, No. 3, Aug. 1963.

95. Mushkin, S. (ed)—Economics of Higher Education, Washington, D.C., Govt. Printing Office, 1962.

96. Musgrave, Richard A.—Notes on Educational Investment in Developing Nations", *in* The Economics of Education, Paris, O.E.C.D., 1966.

97. Mustafa, Mohamed-El-Murtada—Manopower and Employment Problems in the Sudan, Geneva, International Institute for Labour Studies, 1972.

98. O.E.C.D.—"Targets for Education in Europe in 1970", Policy Conference on Economic Growth and Investment in Education, Vol. 2, Paris, O.E.C.D., 1962.

99. ———"Methods and Statistical Needs for Educational Planning", Paris, O.E.C.D., 1967.

100. Panchamukhi, P.R.—"Employment and Education Policy : The Indian Experience", *Manpower Journal*, Vol. 14, No. 1, April-June, 1978.

101. Pandit, H.N.—"Economic Approaches to Investment Decision-Making in Education", *Indian Educational Review*, Vol. 5, No. 1, Jan. 1970.

102. ———"Cost Analysis of Education in India—Private and Social Participation", *Indian Educalional Review*, Vol. 7, No. 2, July 1972.

103. Papanek, Hanna—"Men, Women and Work : Reflections on the Two Person Career", *American Journal of Sociology*, Vol. 78, No. 4, 1973.

104. ———"Purdha in Pakistan : Seclusion and Modern Occupations for Women", *Journal of Marriage and the Family*, Vol. 33, No. 3, 1971.

105. Pinera, Sebastian and Marcelo Selowsky—"The Opportunity Cost of Labour and the Returns to Education under unemployment and Labour Market Segmentation", *The Quarterly Journal of Economics*, Vol. 92, No. 3, Aug. 1978.

106 Pratima, Asthana—Women's Movement in India, Delhi, Vikas, 1974.

107. Prest, A.R.—Notes on Financing of Education in India, Monograph No. 7, Task Force on Educational Finance, Education Commission, New Delhi, 1965.

108. Psacharopoulos, G.—"Measuring the Marginal Contribution of Education to Economic Growth", *Economic Development and Cultural Change*, Vol. 20, No. 4, July 1972.

109. ——— and Marvin, A.—"Schooling and Income Distribution", *Review of Economics and Statistics*, Vol. 58, No. 3, Aug. 1976.

110. ——— and Hinchliffe, K.—Returns from Education : An International Comparison, Amsterdam, Elsevier Scientifie Publishing Co., 1973.

111. Rani, Kala—Role Conflict in Working Women, Bombay, Chetana Publications, 1976.

112. Rao, Kamala Gopal and Mullick, Saroj Studies in Family Planning—India, New Delhi, Abhinav Publications, 1974.

113. Robbins, Loid—The Theory of Economic Development in the History of Economic Thought, New York, MacMillan, 1968.

114. Rogers, Daniel C.—"Private Rates of Return to Education in the United States—A Case Study", *Yale Economic Essays*, Vol. 9, No. 1. Spring 1969.

115. Sabota, Gain S.—"Book Review of T.W. Schultz", *Economic Development and Cultural Change*, Vol. 23, No. 3. April, 1975.

116. ———"Theories of Personal Income Distribution : A Survey", *Journal of Economic Literature*, Vol. 16, No. 1, March 1978.

117. Sanyal, Bikas C. and Versluis, J.—"Higher Education, Human Capital and Labour Market Segmentation in the Sudan", (I.I.E.P. occasional paper No. 42), Paris, I.I.E.P., 1976.

118. Sarkar, B.N.—"Attitude to Induced Abortion in Calcutta (based on 1970 and 1974 Surveys)", Calcutta, Indian Statistical Institute, Demographic Research Centre, 1976.

119. Schultz, T.W.—"Returns to Education in Bogota, Columbia", The Rand Corporation Memorandum, RM-5645, RC/AID, Sept. 1968.

120. —— ——The Economic Value of Education, New York, Columbia University Press, 1963.

121. — ———"Capital Formation by Education", *Journal of Political Economy*, Vol. 68, No. 6, Dec. 1960.

122. Seetharamu, A.S.—"A Study of Responsiveness to Development Programmes from Educational Stimuli in Rural Areas", Bangalore, Institute for Social and Economic Change, 1977.

123. Selowsky, M.—"The Effect of Unemployment and Growth on the Rate of Return to Education : The Case of Columbia", Harvard University, 1968, (Mimeographed).

124. Sengupta, Padmini—The Story of Women in India, New Delhi, India Book Co., 1974.

125. Shaffer, H G.—"Investment in Human Capital : Comment", *American Economic Review*, Vol. 51, No. 5, Dec. 1961.

126. Shantha, N.—"A Study of the Profile of Employed Women in the Public Sector in Bangalore City", Pre-Ph.D. Project Report (un-published), Bangalore, Institute for Social and Economic Change, 1976.

127. Sharma, G D.—"Resource Allocation on Education-Research Studies : An Inter-Intra-Country and Inter-Temporal Pattern Analysis, Association of Indian Universities, 1978.

128. Sharma, R.C.—"Benefit-Cost Analysis of Educational Projects—A Review of Researches", *in* Pandit, H.N.—Measurement of Cost Productivity and Efficiency of Education, NCERT, 1969.

129. Singh, B. (ed)—Education as Investment, Meerut, India, Meenakshi Press, 1967.

130. Smith, Adam—The Wealth of Nations, New York, Modern Library, 1937.

131. Smith, J. and Bennette, N.—"Rates of Return on Investment in Education : A Tool for Short-term Education Planning I—Illustrated with Uganda Data, World Year Book of Education, London, Evans Bros. Ltd., 1968.

132. Solomon, Ezra (ed)—The Management of Corporate Capital, New York, Free Press, 1959.

133. Solow, Robert M.—"Technical Change and the Aggregate Production Function", *Review of Economics* and Statistics, Vol. 39, No. 3, Aug. 1957.

134. Srivastava, M.P.—Major Sources of Data on Employment and Unemployment, Poona, Gokhale Institute of Politics and Economics, 1973.

135. Strathern, Marilyn—Women in Between : Female Roles in a Male World, New York, Mount Hagen, 1972.

136. Streeten, Paul—"Economic Development and Education", Institute of Development Studies, University of Sussex, Stanmer, Brighton, Susses, Mimeo Series No. 10.

137. Sullepot, E.—Women, Society and Change, London, World University Library, 1971.

138. Szalal, Alexander—"The Situation of Women in the Light of Time-Budget Research", World Conference of the International Women's Year, New York, United Nations E/Con.66/BP/6, April 1975.

139. Taubman, Paul and Terence Wales—Higher Education and Earnings, New York, McGraw-Hill, 1974.

140. Thias, H.M. and Carney, M.—"Cost-Benefit Analysis in Education : A Case Study of Kenya", International Book for Reconstruction and Development, Report EC-173, Nov. 1969.

141. Thomas, P.—Hindu Women through the Ages, London, Asia Publishing House, 1964.

142. Triandis, Harry C.—Attitude and Attitude Change, Wiley Series in Social Psychology, New York, John Wiley and Sons, Inc., 1971.

143. United Nations Economic and Social Council—Consultative Committee for the World Conference of the International Women's Year, Draft International Plan of Action, New York, United Nations, E/CONF, 56/LD/2, Feb. 1975.

144. United Nations Industrial Development Organisation—"Guide to Practical Project Appraisal : Social Benefit-Cost Analysis in Developing Countries", New York, United Nations, 1978.

145. Vaizey, J.—Resources for Education, London, Allen and Unwin Ltd., 1968.

146. ——————The Economics of Education, London, Faber and Faber, 1962.

147. Warren, Neil and Marie Jahoda (ed)—Attitudes, Middlesex, Penguin Books Ltd., 1973.

148. Wasi, Muriel (ed)—The Educated Women in Indian Society today, New Delhi, Tata McGraw-Hill, 1971.

149. Weisbrod, Burton, A.—External Benefits of Public Education, New Jersey, Princeton Industrial Relations Centre, 1964.

150. ——————"The Valuation of Human Capital", *Journal of Political Economy*, Vol. 69, No. 4, 1961.

151. West, E.G.—"Private Versus Public Education - A Classical Economic Dispute", *Journal of Political Economy*, Vol. 72, No. 5, 1964.

152. Wilkinson, B.W.—"Present Values of Lifetime Earnings for Different Occupations", *Journal of Political Economy*, Vol. 74, No. 6, 1966.

153. Wine, Garden, C.R.—"Schooling and Income Distribution : Evidence from International Data", *Economica*, Vol. 4, No. 181, 1979.

154. Winston, Gordon C.—"Capital Utilisation, Physiological Costs and Preferences for Shift Work",

(Research Memorandum No. 42), Massachusetts, Williams College, Centre for Development Economics, 1971.

155. Wolfle, Dael and Smith, Joseph—"The Occupational Value of Education for Superior High School Graduates", *Journal of Higher Education*, Vol. 27. April 1956.

156. Youssef, Nadia—"Women and Work in Developing Societies", Population Monograph Series No. 15, Berkeley, University of California, 1974.

157. Zimbalist, Michelle R. and Louise Lamphere—Women, Culture and Society, California, Stanford University Press, 1974.

# Index

| | | |
|---|---|---|
| Roy, R.C., *IAS* | State Public Enterprise in India. | 200 00 |
| Varma, N.P. | Irrigation Change and Agricultural Development : An Impact Analysis. | 125.00 |
| Wishwakarama, P.K. | Urban and Regional Planning Policy in India. | 75.00 |

## EDUCATION

| | | |
|---|---|---|
| Bayti, Jamnalal | Problems of Education in the Third World. | 200.00 |
| Bayti, Jamnalal | Readings in Education. | 150.00 |
| Bhaskara, S. | The Effectiveness Instructional Materials on Verbal Creativity. | 225.00 |
| Dagar, B.S. | Culture, Education and Creativity | 150.00 |
| Mohan, N. Shantha | Returns from Education to Employed Women in India. | 225 00 |
| Paliwal, M.R. | Differential Effectiveness of Micro-learning. | 50.00 |
| Paliwal, M.R. | The Teacher Education on the Move : Today and Tomorrow. | 225.00 |
| Sachchidananda & Sihna, R.P. | Education and the Disadvantaged : A Study of Scheduled Castes and Tribes. | 275.00 |

## HISTORY

| | | |
|---|---|---|
| Anderson, G. & Subedar, M. | The Expansion of British India (1818-1858). | 150.00 |
| Barstow, A.E. | Handbook on Sikhs | 250 00 |
| Biswas, Atreyi | Political, Social and Cultural History of Ancient India (H). | 125.00 |
| Madan, J.C. | Indian Police. | 110.00 |
| May, L.S. | The Evolution of Indo-Muslim Thought from 1857 to Present. | 350.00 |
| Mohanta, Bijan | Administrative Development of Arunachal Pradesh 1875-1975. | 150.00 |
| Mohmood, Safdar & Javaid Zafar | Founders of Pakistan. | 225.00 |
| Qureshi, I. Hussian | The Struggle for Pakistan. | 250.00 |
| Rawlinson, H.G. | Indian Historical Studies. | 200.00 |
| Saeed, W.A. | Major Events of Medieval India. | 400.00 |
| Sikka, R.P. | The Civil Service in India. | 150.00 |
| Stobart, J.W.H. | Islam and its founder. | 225.00 |

## LAW

| | | |
|---|---|---|
| Ahangar, Mohd. Altaf Hussain | Customary Succession Among Muslims. | 175.00 |
| Chaudhari, R.L. | The Concept of Secularism in Indian Constitution. | 150.00 |
| Jagannadham, V. | Administration and Social Change. | 60.00 |
| Saksena, H.S. | Safeguards for Scheduled Castes and Tribes : Founding Father's View. | 200.00 |
| Sarkar, Amit | Naturalism, Humanism and Participative Jurisprudence. | 95.00 |
| Sarkar, Amit | Secularism and Constitutionality. | 95.00 |
| Singh, S S. | Administration of Natural Justice in India. | 250.00 |

## LIBRARY SCIENCE

| | | |
|---|---|---|
| Pandey, S K. Sharma | Dewey Decimal Classification for Indology. | 200.00 |
| Rajjan Lal and Kidwai, Nasira | Practical Cataloguing Procedure (Hindi) | 95.00 |

## POLITICAL SCIENCE

| | | |
|---|---|---|
| Baruah, A.K. | Systems Analysis in Political Science : A Marxit Critique of David Easton. | 125.00 |
| Chaudhari, R.L. | The Concept of Secularism in Indian Constitution. | 150.00 |
| Gabriel, Soloman | Foreign Policy of Canada | 95.00 |
| Ghosh, Partha S. | Sino-Soviet Relations : U.S. Perception and Policy Resp. | 100.00 |
| Kaushik, S.N. | Pakistan under Bhutto's Leadership. | 175.00 |
| Mahendra Singh | Indo-U.S. Relations : A Political Study. | 75.00 |
| Mahmood, Safdar & Javaid Zafar | Founders of Pakistan | 225.00 |
| Mishra, Upendra | Caste and Politics in India. | 225.00 |
| Misra, Sheela | Women Participation in Politics and Political Parties (Hindi) | 250.00 |

| | | |
|---|---|---|
| Mukarji, Nirmal and Ashis Banerjee | Democracy Federalism and the future of Indias' Unity. | 60.00 |
| Pai Panandiker, V.A. and Arun Sud. | Changing Political Representation in India. | 65.00 |
| Pal. J.J. | Jinnah and the Creation of Pakistan | 75.00 |
| Pandey, Jawaharlal | State Politics in India | 90.00 |
| Pillai, G. Narayana | Social Background of Political Leadership in India | 90 00 |
| Pirzada, Syed Sharifuddin | Evolution of Pakistan | 250.00 |
| Qureshi, I. Husain | The Struggle for Pakistan | 250.00 |
| Rao. V. Bhaskara, | General Elections in India. | 200.00 |
| Reddy, P. Ranjani | The Role of Dominant Caste in Indian Politics. | 125.00 |
| Seshadri, K. | Studies in Indian Polity. | 150.00 |
| Seshadri, K. | Studies in the Problems of the Third World. | 175.00 |
| Sharma, T.R. | New Challenges in Indian Politics. | 175.00 |
| Singh, L.P. *IAS* | Electoral Reform : Problems and Suggested Solutions. | 95.00 |
| Singh, L.P. | India's Foreign Policy. | 55.00 |
| Singh, S.P. | Perspectives in Indian Politics and Administration. | 60.00 |
| Verma, S.P. | Indian Parliamentarians : A Study of the Socio-Political Background. | 90.00 |
| Vijay Kumar | India and Srilanka-China Relations 1948-84. | 125.00 |

## PUBLIC ADMINISTRATION

| | | |
|---|---|---|
| Banerjee, Pramathanath | Public Administration in Ancient India. | 125.00 |
| Bava, Noorjahan | People's Participation Development Adm. in India. | 125.00 |
| Bhattacharjee, Debasish | Bureaucracy and Development in Meghalaya | 150.00 |
| Bhattacharya, Mohit | Bureaucracy and Development Administration. | 50.00 |
| Bhattacharya, Mohit | Management of Urban Government in India. | 50.00 |

| | | |
|---|---|---|
| Bhattacharya, Mohit | Management of Rural Development. | 90.00 |
| Bijan Mohanta | Administrative Development of Arunachal Pradesh, 1875-1975. | 150.00 |
| Chaturvedi, T.N. | Politics, Bureaucracy and Development : Some Issues. | 25.00 |
| Datta, P.K. | Public Administration and the State | 200 00 |
| Dey, Bata K. | Bureaucracy Development and Public Management in India. | 80.00 |
| Jagannadham, V. | Administration and Social Change. | 60.00 |
| Jain, R.B. and P.N. Chaudhuri | Bureaucratic Values in Development. | 120.00 |
| Jain, R.B. | Comparative Legislative Behaviour. | 50.00 |
| Padhi, A.P. | State Administration in India. (in 2 Vols.) | 500.00 |
| Panda, Basudev | Indian Bureaucracy : An Inside Story. | 60.00 |
| Pai Panandiker, V.A. | Bureucracy and Development Adm. | 75.00 |
| Partap Singh | Urban Government in India. | 45.00 |
| Pulparampil, John & John Hayes | Training Effectiveness : An Indian Case Study. | 150.00 |
| Rai, Haridwar and S.P. Singh | Current Ideas and Issues in Indian Administration. | 70.00 |
| Sharma, P.D. | Police and Criminal Justice Administration in India. | 125.00 |
| Sharma, P.D. | Police, Polity and People in India. | 125.00 |
| Sharma, P.D. | Police, Internal Security and Developmental Disorder in India. | 250.00 |
| Sikka, R.P. | The Civil Service in India. | 150.00 |
| Singh, L.P. *IAS* | Sardar Patel and Indian Administration. | 25.00 |
| Singh, S.S. | Administration of Natural Justice in India. | 250.00 |
| Sundeep Khanna, *IAS* | Civil Administration in India. | 60.00 |
| Trivedi, B.V. | Prison Administration in India: Model Prison Programme. | 120 00 |
| Wishwakarma, R.K. | Urban and Regional Planning Policy in India. | 75.00 |

## SOCIOLOGY

| Author | Title | Price |
|---|---|---|
| Ahangar, Mohd. Altaf Hussain | Customary Succession Among Muslims. | 175.00 |
| Amir Hussian, *IAS* | A Tribe in Turmoil : Socio-Economic Study of Jammu Gujars of Uttar Pradesh. | 150.00 |
| Brett-Crowther, M.R. | Brandt, Bread and the Bomb : Reflexions on the World Problematic. | 100.00 |
| Bava, Noor Jahan | People's Participation Development Administration in India. | 125.00 |
| Centre for Policy Research, N. Delhi | Population, Poverty and Hope. | 300.00 |
| Chaudhari, R.L. | The Concept of Secularism in Indian Constitution. | 150.00 |
| Durrany, KS.. | Religion in Society. | 200.00 |
| Ghosh, Shubhra | Female Criminals in India. | 125.00 |
| Jagannadham, V. | Adm. and Social Change. | 60 00 |
| Kamble, N.D. | Bonded Labour in India. | 60.00 |
| Kamble, N.D. | Migrants in Indian Metropolis. | 75.00 |
| Khan, Mumtaz Ali | Impact of Foreign Aid to Rural Artisans in India. | 125.00 |
| Khan, Mumtaz Ali | Muslims in the Process of Rural Development in India. | 150.00 |
| Khan, Mumtaz Ali | Scheduled Caste and their Status in India. | 75.00 |
| Khan, Mumtaz Ali | Status of Rural Women in India. | 75.00 |
| Khan, Mumtaz Ali | Social Legislation and the Rural Poor. | 50.00 |
| Krishnakumari, N.S. | Status of Single Women in India. | 125.00 |
| Mandal, B.B. | Tribals at the Polls. | 90.00 |
| Madan, J.C. | Indian Police. | 110.00 |
| Mandavdhare, S.M. | Caste and land Relations in India. | 310.00 |
| Menon, M. Indu | Status of Muslim Women in India. | 50.00 |
| Mishra, Upendra | Caste and Politics in India. | 225 00 |
| Nischal, Surendra | Effective Leadership : A Study of white Collar workers' Union Leaders. | 200.00 |
| Singh, D.R. | Social Inequality in Leadership | 125.00 |

| | | |
|---|---|---|
| Mishra, S.N. and Kushal Sharma | Problems and Prospects of Rural Development in India. | 80 00 |
| Mohan, N. Shantha | Status of Nurses in India. | 60.00 |
| Mohan, S. Shantha | Status of Banjara Women in India. | 125.00 |
| Omprakash, S. | Development of the Weaker Sections : Problems, Policies and Issues. | 150.00 |
| Paliwal, M.R. | Social Change and Education. | 175.00 |
| Pai Panandiker, V.A. and Ajay K. Mehra | People's Participation in Family Planning. | 160.00 |
| Pai Panandiker, V.A. R.N. Bishnoi and O.P. Sharma | Organisational Policy for Family Planning. | 125.00 |
| Pai Panandiker, V.A. and P.N. | Demographic Transition in Goa and its Policy Implications. | 40.00 |
| Pandey, K.K. | Rural Development in India : Continuity and Change | 125.00 |
| Pillai, G. Narayana | Social Background of Political Leadership in India. | 90.00 |
| Rajgopal, P.R. | Communal Violence in India. | 140.00 |
| Rajgopal, P.R. | Social Change and Violence : the Indian Experience. | 210.00 |
| Rajgopal, P.R. | Violence and Response : A Critique of the Indian Criminal Justice System. | 250.00 |
| Rastogi, P.N. | India 1981-86 : A forecaste on Economic, Political and Social Developments. | 50.00 |
| Ray, B. Datta | The Emergence and Role of Middle Class in North-East India. | 100.00 |
| Ray, B. Datta | The Pattern and Problems of Population in North-East India. | 250.00 |
| Rita Khanna | Agricultural Mechanisation and Social Change in India. | 125.00 |
| Rozario, M. Rita. | Trafficking in Women and Children in India. | 125.00 |
| Sachchidananda & Sihna, R.P. | Education and the Disadvantaged : A Study of Scheduled Castes and Tribes. | 275.00 |

| | | |
|---|---|---|
| Saksena, H.S. | Safeguards for Scheduled Caste and Tribes : Founding Father's View. | 200.00 |
| Seshadri, K. | Studies in Indian Polity. | 150.00 |
| Seshadri, K. | Studies in the Problems of the Third World. | 175.00 |
| Sharma, P.D. | Police, Internal Security and Developmental Disorder in India. | 250.00 |
| Sharma, P.D. | Police and Criminal Justice Administration in India. | 125.00 |
| Sharma, P.D. | Police, Polity and People in India. | 125.00 |
| Sharma, R.N. & Santosh Bakshi | Tribes and Tribal Development : Select Bibliography. | 250.00 |
| Sinha, R.P. | Social Dimensions of Trade Unionism in India. | 90.00 |
| Singh, K.P. | Tribal Development in India. | 325.00 |
| Singh, S.S. | Administration of Natural Justice in India. | 250.00 |
| Singh, S.S. and S. Sundram | Emerging Harijan Elite : A Study of their Identity. | 125.00 |
| Stobart, J.W.H. | Islam and its Founder | 225.00 |
| Trivedi, B.V. | Prison Administration in India. | 120.00 |
| Varma, B. *IPS* | Insurgency and Counter-Insurgency. | 225.00 |
| Wishwakarma, R.K. | Urban and Regional Planning Policy in India. | 75.00 |

## REFERENCE BOOKS

| | | |
|---|---|---|
| Ali, Ahmed | Selected Short Stories from Pakistan (translated from Urdu) | 150.00 |
| Desmukh, C.D. | Amarakosa : Gems from the Treasure House of Sanskrit Words. | 90.00 |
| Durrany, K.S. | Religions in Society | 200.00 |
| Pandey, S.K. Sharma | Dewey Decimal Classification for Indology | 200.00 |
| Sharma, R.N. and Santosh Bakshi | Tribes and Tribal Development ; Select Bibliography. | 250.00 |